GLORIOUS HISTORY OF DALITS

GLORIOUS HISTORY OF DALITS

Past and Present

DR. RAJ KUMAR

KALPAZ

Glorious History of Dalits : Past and Present

Rs. 750

ISBN: 978-81-7835-760-7

Published in 2010 in India by
Kalpaz Publications
C-30, Satyawati Nagar,
Delhi-110052
E-mail: kalpaz@hotmail.com
Phone : 9212729499

Lasser Type Setting by: Rudra Computer Graphics, Delhi
Printed at : Chawla Offset Printers, Delhi

Contents

List of Illustrations
or
List of Plates

Abbreviations

The following list of the standard Abbreviations are used.

A.S.I	Archaeological Survey of India
Fig.	Figure
I.H.C	Indian History Congress
P.H.C	Punjab History Conference
S.R	Science Report
Tr.	Translation
U.R.L	Universal Research Locator.

Preface

The creation and order of this Universe is depended on the 'Science of the Master' of the present living era, the book entitled '***Glourious History of Dalits : Past and Present***' written by this author on the basis of Scientific Knowledge of the Father, he is very little in age, but a dynamic man of the worldly idea to lead this world from one stage to another that is Dark Age to Enlightenment as a Supernatural Force of the positive element keeps inside his body which is composed of skin or leather (Hide) in the form of a *Chamar* of *Ravidas Family*, a leading man of the world, and his destiny, must also deal with the universe of which man is a part of the 'life'. No one can gain even an intellectual understanding of his own interests until, he has some comprehension of the universe as is an integral part of his life, and he is related to every part of the life in some manners as a man of the Highest-Knowledge'. By the world 'Universe', as it is used for the Scientific Study, has been referred in this book, about the study of *Chemistry, Geology*, *Geography, Physics*, *Botany* and *Life-Sciences* of the other fields. We mean vastly more than a few galaxies of the stars; like *Dr. Raj Kumar, Baba Gurinder Singh ji, Biaswale, Dr. Ram Dass, Baba Rasila Ram Saidpur wale*, Suns and plants pointed by astronomers. We must include an almost endless series of the Higher Souls and finer worlds of the '*Nam*' above and beyond the sweep of the telescope, or of any telescope that can ever be made can be seen from their study as they are the science of the souls controlling the every idea of the man. These physical worlds are utterly beyond the borders of the universe as angles of the '*Nam*'.

Any Science of the present period, who ignore them, they are beyond the doubts and more subtle worlds can not claim to be an all-inclusive science, because they are the *'Names'* of the period and founder of the *'Sudhra Dynasty'* of the twenty first century A.D. In fact, the real scientist has no more than learned the alphabet of his science until passes beyond the last star of the life that glimmers in space and earth as a *'Sound Current'* of the *'Nam'*. He entered those regions where the physical eyes cannot function but only *'Nam'* of the Universal-Knowledge can see. Happily, every man is endowed with a finer vision, which may be awakened and used on those higher planes of the 'Life' as a 'Creative Power'.

The Cosmogony of the said Masters will be found quite different from that of all other systems that is 'Brahminical Ideology'. This is because the Masters have a far greater range of knowledge of the Scientific Truth then all other men. Their fields of operation lie far out and away from all physical Suns and Moons. They know about the creative order of this universe of so many parts from personal study to the common man and exploration of the old monuments to write down an authentic history of the man from the Jammu and Kashmir areas, wherefrom the prehistoric tool of the man's like *Baba Ravidas* of the *Chambrian* or *Chamar* of the period. They developed the history of man from the very historic period of the life. For example, *'Indus Valley Civilization'* to *'Indus – Saraswati Civilization'* of the *Akhnoor* region of the *Ambaran* valley of the *Manda* village of the Jammu region. This was the 'Second Civilization of the World' after the Mesopotaminan Civilization. Besides, their ability to see the universe as it is today confronting with the peace and war, they are also able to see the entire past history of this universe is confronting with both the negative and positive elements of the species as in terms of plants, animals and the man itself, and this book is the reference of the 'Ultimate Truth' which resides in the universe, but negative elements in the 'Brahminical Ideology' are not bothered for that because they have the pressure of money and material of the destructive nature. They know this also, but they do not hold this knowledge, because their 'ego' is self-style knowledge as clash in history subject from artificial sciences as already mentioned above.

The world means 'egg', referring to its shape if we must place it in the space as displayed in the Picture Plate IV, let us assume that *Anda* a Supernatural Force lies just above and beyond the physical universe. But here the term Above and Beyond have but little meaning. The fact is that these higher worlds are separated from this world more by their ethereal qualification than by their location in space. It is just as accurate to say that those worlds lie in the same space limitations, separated by the qualities only; but when a person passes from one stage to another of them, he knows his or her qualities, by their 'Highest Knowledge' and love and hate according to their deeds and actions of the past history as award from the Inner Knowledge which he possessed through the Father's Insight - Knowledge, because his Father was a lover of '*Nam*' and he was born in the study of '*Nam*' as his natural growth as '*Nam*' on earth having Universal – Knowledge. Therefore, he keeps separate qualities than that of the common man working as a great challenger of the negative forces to crush them. Of course, all these are invisible to the physical eye because of their higher vibrations with '*Sound Current*' of the '*Nam*' through the physical world. In terms of solar spectrum through free the knowledge of '*Nam*' as a stream, they see those regions as plainly as they see this world with the physical eyes. Next above, *Anda* lies *Brahmand*, the third grand division. This term means 'the egg of *Brahm*', which is beyond the knowledge of the *Brahmins*; and on the basis of little knowledge, they created the danger for the common man, with crying of the language of *Sanskrit* nothing else. In fact, spirit of the natural forces of the positive elements predominates in *Brahmand* just as matter predominates in *Pind* of the Brahminical thought to earn about the study of Sanskrit language, while *Anda* at the same time, watches from the *Above* his activities is rather on the dividing line between the two i.e., *Chamars* and *Brahmins*.

Last of all, we arrive at the highest grand of division in all creation, the finest and purest, composed entirely of pure spirit of the 'Nam' as displayed in Plate III and IV, the four stage of life in this universe and man is superior as his fifth stage to realize the *Truth* why the life has been given by Masters as an objective knowledge of the man in Scientific Truth i.e., '*Nam*'. This region is definitely beyond the sphere of matter. There is no mind in this region to realize the *Truth* after the death of *Dr. B.R. Ambedkar* as a realized soul of the Universal Truth by founding the 'Law of the Constitution' that how the bodies are created by the Natural process to give a set back to the 'Brahminical Ideology', he reserved her force in distance to repeat the history of man itself in secret manners of the *'Nam'* as a *'Top Creator'*. As already discussedin the study, the creation and division of the whole of existence comes on four separate sections may be due to the polarization of the pre-creation substance of the 'Nature' falls in this category, but supreme seat of the highest planet is 'infinite', the Absolute, the source and Creator of all that is we see in our eyes they are the *Sudhra* people, works for other and serve the society with the *'pure-thought'*. This primordial substance may be called God, if the monists insist, or whatever term the reader prefer as a realized truth, they reveal on the book as a Scientific Knowledge of the *'Word'* made body called *Chamar* on earth, tanned by the Father in *'Nam*'s colour called *'Ranga', Jatiya, Jatav, Jat,* etc. the upper portion was the positive pole and the lower was the negative, while the middle portions were natural zones, partaking of the properties of both the negative and positive force of the *'Nam'*. When the creative impulse was given to the Master with the process of *'Nam-dana'*, the positive pole became more concentrated, while the nether pole became correspondingly depleted the negative elements with the 'Voice of God' as a *'Judgment in History'* for the establishment of the 'New History' as well as 'New Society'. The French Revolution was a great mistake and that everything that had happened since had only made it worse to the man's idea as a class –struggle theory. The problems of the 'New society' 'in which we live today a society of problematic or we can call it as, *'Linear Transmigration in Matric System'* to get the life from 'ego' to infinite' as in natural number of the man's origin from his body. These conflicting terms need to move the world in logic way as O (Zero) as an Idea of the world 'infinite' to work for the Civilizational Growth and old species in terms of negative forces, they must be punish for the time being to earn more life in this atomic world for the survival of history itself as an authentic value of the man's moral concept and discipline to frame a 'New Society'. This assertion commits we to the historical approach to the contemporary world. Modern man is beyond all precedent 'History Conscious'. What philosophy was to the classical Greek and Roman during the Medieval period of man's history. *Ravidas* was the natural force at that time as his permanent seat in Security Council in the '*Nam's* history and his permanent eyes on Jammu and Kashmir to repeat the history of man itself. From the very long history of the man particularly from the Middle Age, his name has been slipped form the tongues of the Brahmins, as an '*Untouchable*' man of the history, and writer is giving the proof that he never dies in the eyes of 'Law' as he was the Creator of 'Law'. Unhistorical peoples, particularly Brahmins, they must be worried that how a man form the background of '*Chamar Dynasty*' is predicting the same Knowledge in the form of *Dr. Raj Kumar*, a founding father of '*Chamar History of Kashmir Dynasty*' as a deciding factor of the future generation. The past and present, action and interaction are constant as a future course of action of the reaction of man itself on this earth. *The Idea of Progress* which has been placed in the preface of Late J.B. Bury in 1920, called "*The Animating and Controlling Idea of Western Civilization*", but in *India* under this category like the term '*Chamar*' has been used in the scientific study or discovery, is the idea of advancement of the man's history as the rule of the nature is going to predict very shortly as an event of the modern history, by striking '*Nam*' on earth as an Universal Power to repeat the history of man in geographical manners too. Intellectual fashions change rapidly (which proves that intellectuals are also human being in the form of man and God on earth). Spengler's system in certain laws like 'Organism' called civilizations obeying laws to control the population and use to it in constructive work as *Sudhra* do in the history of man as 'Creative Power'. Social-Scientists say that there can be no fire with oxygen in the 'Air' and they started to explain it, the cause of the conditions that why there is no presence of the oxygen in the air, they failed to answer it and its existence of objective facts of history that there is no 'life', it shows that the objectivity in artificial science is failed in history to determine the Truth, who knows that we all approach the history as a neglected subject and still speaks of "what can be established by concrete external evidence" but with 'internal evidence' i.e., called the 'Voice of God' or 'Inner Voice' or '*Dalit* Voice'. This importance and the exceptional interest which attaches to *Kalhana's 'River of*

Kings' as practically the sole extent product of Sanskrit literature possessing the character of a true Chronicle, account for the efforts which have been directed towards the elucidation of the work ever since European traveller became aware of the existence of the life history, and the Indian Brahmins are the conflicting force of the 'Name'. The object of the present publication is only to aware the Brahmins that the theory of *Ravidas* again established on earth against the negative forces of the *Chamar* and an element of the nature has been involved in him for the historical growth of the modern period of the twenty first century A.D.

Great are the changes in the history of 'Nam' study which the last few decennia have brought over Jammu and Kashmir in artistic manners of the Nature, by snowfall, militancy and other natural problems about the biological problems, than any which the country has experienced since the closing of the Hindu and Muslim period of man as conflict terms of the 'Blind Faith' of the society and fellow-feeling have been developed from 'Rites and Rituals'. We have spread no efforts to serve this end, and in the result of our labour towards the idea of the Natural forces have been expressed in very simple way that a man from the common background they must feel happy that we are fully prepared to defeat them with natural event by striking the '*Nam*' on Earth as a 'Supernatural Force' of the Universe, is interested to close the Chapter of corrupt politicians or the *Satans* of the modern period of Indian history to change the history of the modern man in '*Absolute Peace*' and go by the scientific truth of the *Nam-History*.

Dr. Raj Kumar
Department of History
Government College for Women,
Parade, Jammu

Introduction

The subject matter of this book i.e., *'Clorious History of Dalits : Past and Present'* is so important for the historians and the general scientists, so far reaching beyond the doubt that *Sudhras* has no 'History', and the task of this present action, it properly appears to be an understanding between the Master of the period and beyond the powers of any ordinary man. *Maha Bhaisaya Guru* at the present is leading force of the World as a natural force of the life along with the family of *Sudhras, Dr. Raj Kumar, Baba Gurinder Singhji Biaswale, Dr Ram Dass, Master Deepit Raj* and other owner's of the family like *Baba Rasila Ram Saidpur wale*. May all sentient beings live in peace, ultimately attaining supreme Enlightenment under the benevolent light of the Medicine *Buddha* that is *'Nam'* of the twenty-first century A.D. i.e., Master *Deepit Raj* son of *Dr. Raj Kumar*. The matter of the study is beyond the doubt that message already delivered in the 'Holy Book of the *Chamar* Community' with the co-ordination of *Radha Soami Mission* of *Maha Bhaisaya – Guru* of the present century. The writer realizes his lack of complete competence, because we belonged to the *'Sudhra Family'* in the Brahminical period, they degraded us, but this scientific discovery of the historical research is beyond the Truth, because scholar has already exhausted enough knowledge of the spiritual world into man's life. Therefore, it is leading book of the twenty first century A.D. as a practical approach of the life with Scientific Knowledge of the Insight – Event of the ' *Nam*' on this earth.

It must be said here, as well as in the heart of this book is the heart of the philosopher of the twenty first century of the *Sudhra Family*, which faced number of problems, humiliation in the Science and Society of the 'Brahminical Ideology' as only the concept of '*Mind*'; this book never believes in the philosophy of Hindu and Muslim, neither it is believed on the study of Social – Scientists of these communities that they are already exploiter of the *Sudhra Family* with their own pen and pencil by drafting number of puzzling contents of the life, but the life of the man is so-simple and wonderful given by the Master of the period who born from the previous soul of the *Dr. B.R. Ambedkar* to *Baba Gurinder Singh*, as an advance idea of the study, a challenge for the 'Brahminical Ideology', but they did not bother for his teachings and message published in various books having dirty idea in their mind called 'Discriminator' on the bases of caste, colour and creed is still carry on even after the death of *Dr. B.R. Ambedkar* to *Baba Gurender Sigh Ji Biaswale*. It shows from the study that society has been dominated by the criminal Brahmins, in the historic sense of the term; they have no right to rule over the world with the establishment of the rule of *Sudhra Family*. Therefore, it is biggest challenge for them to leave the chair of the *Sudhra Family* as a historical thought of the forefathers who were migrated from this earth due to the disturbances of the 'Brahminical Ideology' to regain their power in worldly life to react against them on the basis of their discrimination against their race. What is it? *It is a scientific method of entering and realizing the Kingdom of heaven while still living here in the human body* as a challenge for them to destroy them as idiot of the period. In this book, for the first time in history, the complete story of the Masters scientific path is given to the world in the English language, by one who was born among the English-speaking people i.e., *Dr. B.R. Ambedkar* to *Baba Gurinder Singh Ji Biaswale*. Therefore, it is necessary from the Western point of view, and we neglect the Indian Brahmins that they have dirty idea in their mind. The Master of the present age does not wish to meet the demands of that ever-growing number of students who will not be satisfied with formal and ceremonial religion of the Brahmins. In this age of scientific achievement, the master wishes to offer a spiritual system of self-realization and of God realization which meets every demand of science.[1]

As we reach our own times, it has been learnt from the study that Brahmins are problem creator as modern politicians of the

21st century. Now we are close to the event of the twenty first century A.D. to repeat the history of man and God in scientific manners by living honest in the society with this approach as a thought of the Natural man as the Dictator of the world called *Ravidas* of the period (*Dr. Raj Kumar*). All this makes it especially with the massage of the Master of the present period, i.e. *Baba Gurinder Singh Ji*, and little Master *Deepit Raj*. This book that sets out, as this one does, to show the connections between both the artificial sciences and social-sciences, have arisen out of their previous history of the man hand over to Brahmins to study the *Sudhra Family*, where they stand. No gap can be allowed between the present and past to prove the history of the same man, who is working since the pre-historic period to the man of twenty first century A.D. same as the writer of this book is doing. No doubt, more scientific work has been done in the last sixty years after the independence of India, 1947, with the rising of the Scientific Knowledge, the 'Brahminical Ideology' to confirm the truth failed, where truth stand as an objective of the life, it is again found in the history of man and body which is made of leather and bones, truth lies in it. And this is no more quantitative growth, but at the same time; there has been greater advancement in the Insight-Knowledge of the man in the fundamental nature of the matter, animate and inanimate of the living period of the twenty first century A.D. We may reasonably speak of a second '*Scientific Revolution*' in the history of man after the death of *Dr. B.R. Ambedkar*, who gave a challenge to the Brahmins find out the, 'casteless' society of the man which lies in the subject 'History' as a story of God and man as the meaning of the term '*History*'. For the first time a definite method or study of natural science is given to the English-speaking world i.e., Britishers, who are the followers of Master and the *Ravidas* philosophy of the Universal Truth that is '*Nam*; it exhibit is in the life of man from Heaven to Earth, which shows the aspiring and yearning soul of the Father, just how to enter and possess that kingdom of heaven spoken of by all Prophets' and all religions that God exhibit on earth. Many books of the period give hints, but they describe no definite method, because it is up to the 'Brahminical Ideology' to search out the methods to obtain the idea of the historical research, because they are already trained by their experience and practical knowledge, who to apply over the man in scientific method, a true wisdom has been given to them not to exploit the human beings, which anyone may rise to the highest heavens during this life as innocent man of the history as take the example of childhood' study. Most of them cannot do so, because they themselves have neither the knowledge nor the method at that time, there is great need to search out of the Prefect Master with the experiment of the practical knowledge that His or her teachings basis on equality, fraternity and social justice. Only the Masters have it, and this is the first time the experiment of life we obtain from the study of the historical thought that they felt that the time was ripe for a general distribution of such a large portion of their science[2] is explored from their study.

We would like to acknowledge the guidance of the ancient literature and other artifacts of the Spiritual Knowledge. Heading the list, in alphabetical order, are *Master Thick Huyen Dung, Master Thich Phuoc Bon* and *Rev. K Watanabe*, three *Kalyanamitra* with an intimate understanding of the *Sutra* of the *Medicine Buddha. Rev. Tzu Han* (*Antony*), kindly read out them and comment on the texts. Other benefactors have also provided crucial assistance: *Upasika Harry Leong*, a great spiritual son of the *Esoteric* tradition: *Upasika Nancy Leong*, the most cheerful data specialist we have known from the study of Sutra of the *Medicine Buddha* in the *Mahayana* tradition of East Asia, particularly China, Japan, Vietnam and Tibet having the idea of *Maha Bhaishajya Guru* the *Medicine Buddha* (*Yaoshih Fo, Yakushi, Duoc Su Phat, Sangye Menla*), occupies a special place in the hearts of the devout. Specializing in curing disease, both physical and mental 'Word' or '*Nam*' of which delusion is the root cause of the *Chamar*, the *Medicine Buddha* is also the *Buddha* of wisdom. His healing acts are but the prelude to Supreme Enlightenment for those seekers who have the good fortune to learn of his vows or merely to hear his name!And most importantly, *Upasaka Vu Xuan Hoai*, our learned *Dharma* consultant from Connecticut, and *Upasaka Dick M. Saunders*, both of whom pitched in with incisive comments.[3] For this second printing, publisher has to decide for special permission from the author to enlarge the idea of man through this book i.e., '*Scientific Truth in Chamar's Prespective : Pre-historic to Post-Modern Period*'.

This is one of the tragic mistakes of history that millions of people today imagine themselves followers of some dead Masters who never speak, they cannot be Masters. But such a thing is quite impossible, they are problem creator called Brahmins from the idea who trust on them either *Dalits* or *Brahmins*. Can a woman marry a dead man and live with? Can a dead doctor give medicine? Can a dead judge decide a case of Law? the relationship existing between Master and disciple is a personal one. It involves vastly more than few instructions that it might have been given in this book. Instructions in some code of ethics have also been discussed which men has to need for the development of character and discipline of the life. They require the personal aid of a Living Master. If anyone imagines himself a disciple of a dead Master, he only deceives himself. He may revere the memory of a Master or read his writings. He may feel in his heart lone and venerations for him. He may be willing to die for the honor of his name[4], is beyond the doubt, because first of all, he must have to realize it in human form as a Master of the period.

According to modern geographer[5], the morphologically the State of *Jammu, Kashmir* and *Ladakh* is divided into three district regions. Jammu a pre-historical place of the Father i.e., *Baba Ravidas* of the period discussed in the '*Early History of Jammu Region*' (From Pre-historic to 6th Century A.D.) will have the prove of this fact, that the world's Second Civilization was developed from this region particularly the area of Akhnoor of the Jammu division called the '*Indus Saraswati Civilization*' and later in Vedic period known as the world's famous '*Indus Valley Civilization*' of the '*Ravidas Culture*', it is also proved form the geographical study of the man *Purana Group* (the *Precambrian Civilization*) of the *Sudhra Family* and *Ravidas* was the Prophet of God at that time and later on proved as *Palaezoic rocs* of *Chambrian Age*, the period of '*Chamar Culture*' in the history of God and man on earth, and later on again developed into different periods in the history of man and mankind. The old literature[6] also knows the values of this artistic nature of this forces who works as a positive force of the man's life called shoemaker in English, *Charmakara, Charmakrit, padukara, padukrit* in Sanskrit literature. Shoes made of different skins and colours are also mentioned in the Brahminical literature but they could not understand the historical value of this force as a positive force of the man's life, works with the negative elements of the period with tolerance, self-confidence and determination to determine the historical values of the life and the man. This force also worked under the Manu as a Law-Giver of the society for the time-being, as *Dr. B.R. Ambedkar*, realized this truth and burnt the *Manu-Smriti* as a negative force of the Brahmins; and similar ideas have been found in the law-book of the *Sudhras* family that is *Ramayana* and *Mahabharata* to repeat the history of man by striking the 'Truth' in the life of man as an objective of '*Ultimate Reality*' that who he or she, a small atom works in the life of man to reveal the truth that God resides in the universe as a positive force of the man and crush the negative elements of the race. Thus, there was a well-known civilization of the *tanner*, the word leather (hide) in the body of *Chamar* from the ancient period to the modern man called *Deepit Raj* of the period.

Study shows that '*Prechambrian to Devonian Periods*[7] as *Purana Group* about 4,600 millions years ago are going to repeat the history of man, because its atmosphere consisted of volcanic gases with little oxygen, making it hostile to most forms of life due to the experiment of chemical weapons, small continents were spread over the vast region of the earth to check the crustal plates of the surface, with solar system of the '*Nam*' as a Sun on Earth. Moon's spin is also moving in the same direction in the form of man as a natural process of the life, in turn, and orbit their planets on earth to form a new history of the man as *Chamar Ravidas* is on earth in the form of *Dr. Raj Kumar* and *Baba Gurinder Singh Ji Biaswale*, sun on earth, *Master Deepit Raj* as a hero of the 'Names' forces as a positive elements of the earth in a moment to change the idea of man's lifestyle. The evidence for man's natural environment in India before the *Mughal Period* comes to us through fragments, derived mostly from archeology or literary allusions of the period that Brahmins of the modern period made it problematic with linear study of the man in mathematical values as a puzzling contents of the history as Brahmin approach to compare the truth with matric system which is difficult to the modern man to find out truth 1 = 0 and 0 = 1[8] as process of the life and to complete the natural numbers of the body from 1 to 9, as a part of the body called two ears, two nostril, two eyes, one mouth and two lower organs as a whole of the body to release the good and bad idea of the man, but by controlling the system of this body with the process of '*Nam-mantra*' in the memory of God on His instruction to realize the truth in History as a controlling power of the man's lust, but in linear system of the mathematic, we can not qualify the Truth in books, and in this way body is the book of all the literature. It shows from the study of Chemistry, Physics, Zoology, Geology, etc. without the practice of '*Nam-mantra*', so-called natural sciences are failed in their idea to determine the Truth of the object. Object is lying with man, but there are certain conditions imposed by the Masters of the period with his study one cannot obtain the objectivity of life without *Chamar* thought. As it makes clear from the modern society, there are number of crisises of the 'Global Warming', 50 years are in space the use of artificial satellites in the field of means of telecommunications to produce the 'Sound Current' in the man's life to listen the message from the distance through 'air' routes with advancement in rocket technology after the death of *Dr. B.R. Ambedkar*, in 1956 to onwards, history became a terror subject of the man's life as a difficult one and the era was converted into *Gandhian* and *Jinnah* philosophy as an easy approach to the scientific study which failed as their thoughts to appease the *Dr. B.R. Ambedkar*'s idea in the 'Three Round Table Conference'. They were thankless people of the Father and their race could not understand the idea of 'Ultimate Truth' on Earth at that a revolutionary man of the historical knowledge. Keeping in view, the challenge he made in the Constitution of India as a 'Law Maker', the Brahminical ideology could not qualify him, but they are working on his pattern for the sake of money not for his idea's, which solace the man's life that is '*Nam-Dana*' of the Living Master of the period.

Nothing is known much about the '*Ravidas Culture*', but one thing is clear from the historical study that he was the founder of the *Chamer Dynasty* of *Kashmir* in *Jammu* region as per the historical and scientific data of the modern man that is *Deepit Raj*, though the genealogists of the Jammu region, could not search out the historical prespectives of the historical growth of India started from the same region as from the natural rulers of the '*Nams*' were born as *Dr. B.R. Ambedkar, Maharaja Gulab Singh Varawala*[9]

Rajput by caste and his capable son *Maharaja Ranbir Singh*, then *Partap Singh* as the rulers of the 'Nam' worked under the guideline of the Britisher Lords, they used to know the value of Natural thought resides in *Sudhra Family*, they were the followers of the *Ravidas* philosophy. But after the struggling for power, Indian society gripped by 'Brahminical Ideology', they exploited the history of human approach into negative approach to cool down the historical idea of the man from *Dr. B.R. Ambedkar* to *Baba Gurinder Singhji*, as an advance idea of the Human history and His rational approach towards the life of man, as a benevolent rulers of the '*Nam*' in the previous as well as in the present life. And some souls were given the most wonderful body[10] of all called *Pandavas* in human form in one home to fought against the *Kurus* or Brahmins community. With their body costumes on, all the souls drops look different in study. But underneath their bodies they are still the same little drops of 'Light' and 'Love'. We all belong to the same family because we all have the One Father, God, the Great Lord on Earth called *Master Deepit Raj*. We should always be kind, gentle and loving to every living being because a soul lives inside each other. A soul can be born as any living being. One lifetime you may play the part of an apple tree. The play of "life" is like a great circle. The soul actors journey round and round, from body to body, from costume to costume, playing different roles in life. If you will always remember film and have faith in him, you will be happy inside yourself, no matter what happens in his play of "life". When the Lord wants one of his souls to come back home, he makes that person feel lonely deep inside, like something is missing in this world. This is the Great Lord's special way of reminding the soul that its Real Home is not in this world, but back to the Ocean of Light. Thus, the reason of the human body is so special is that the only body costume in which a soul can leave called *Cham* or leather box of the human body, God's play forever work in secret in the human body as minor soul.

This Great Power is called a True Living Master and lives inside a human body that looks like yours and mine. But actually the Living Master is a wondrous Wave of God's Being, who comes into the world only to gather souls from the show of "Life" and take them back Home. These souls are attracted to film like bees to honey. The Living Master tells us all about our Real Home and fills us with love for God and man. When a person really wants to return to the 'Great Ocean of Light', the Master teaches him how to do so. He touches that soul with his Own Soul, and an everlasting bond of love forms between them. He makes a faithful promise to take the soul back Home. His mind becomes so peaceful and quiet that he is able to hear the wondrous waves of the 'Sound Current' inside the body and see the shining light of the stream that flows in the mind's thought all the way back journey to the Ocean of the Lord. Each day, the soul follows the ringing radiant of Light through Stream of Sound and Light, music of the life listen inside the body, dancing with joy, the soul dives in and is carried toward its home in the powerful swift current of the Master's Love in this universe as a practical experience of the life. The hidden path leads the Master and the soul through many marvelous magical lands through the Art of writing the script of Masters with the value of life; until at last, they round the final bend and look up to see within the body from the distance, how it moves in whole of the universal for practical purpose of the life for historical phenomena in the history of man to reveal the truth in the practical knowledge. Keeping in view, in a flash of light the door opens! And the Master lifts the soul drop into a big ocean of light to repeat the history of man and God for their lovers as *Dr. B.R. Ambedkar* was the lover of the *Dalit* during the life time and the present period of the man. But he was '*A New Model of the Universe*' by establishing the rule of 'Law of Nature' called Classless' and 'Casteless', theory of Nature as 'Infinitesimal Force' of the period which have been proved in the book entitled '*Ambedkar and His Writings*, '*A Look for the New Generation*'[11]. As a natural force of the man, and modern Historians and Scientists, they could not prove the truth where his idea used to work in this universe as a challenge for them and proved failure in this contest that the idea of *Sudhra Family* is the idea of thought to move the history from one generation to another.

It shows from the above study that Scientists and Historians, they have little concern with the events of the saints, because they mostly born in the low-caste family, and they have ignored by them, but this book cited '*Glorious History of Dalits : Past and Present*' is a threat for them, that *Chamar* is going to repeat the History itself' with the writing of Natural Thought of the Master and for the living beings of this Universe. According to *Ravidas's* own verses:[12]

"O fellow gentry, I am renowned as belonging to the caste of cobbler, who is job to amend the shoes of the society, which is equivalent to surface of the earth, originated from the word dwls, 'balls' as unknown event. My sub caste is Kutabandhala, he is a man of the 'Highest Law', which works in the every life of the man as a 'Universal Truth'.

And men of my caste still carry dead cattles in the outskirts of *Benaras*, when history was replaced form bad to good as God on earth, and his race was deployed to carry the dead animals of the 'Nam' or *Chamar*' that were the Brahmins of the period, they were crushed by him with the power of '*Nam*', along with coordination of Babar of the same family, *Dom by caste*. When they la-unched their campaign, they defeated number of *Rajputs*, and Brahmins, of the period, and they worshipped His '*Name*'. It is only for the sixteenth century A.D. that direct geographical descriptions providing details of forests, deserts, river-courses, cultivated zone and human settlements become extensive on this universe, and came as the cultivator of the Pure land, and accurate enough to permit us to survey a very large part of India within the compass of a century or two[13]. He had an unique description of the physical organic, inorganic idea of the Chemistry and arts of the period like shoes made from different colours by dissolving the skins in Spiritual–Knowledge of the man that they can comfortable walk on earth by controlling the organ of fertilizers with the study of '*Nam*' inorganic matters, to keep the lust in natural way inside the body for moral value and good discipline as an idea of the God. Keep in view, *Ravidas*, made a testament on earth by striking the '*Nam*' value in the life of man to control the physical world and life itself. As India's trade was increased in Europe, particularly with Britishers, especially in the 17th century A.D. there was a surge of European merchants and travellers, they increased their strength for this medicinal plant, as a Natural plant of the Father, who has left a detailed accounts of his life, almost all parts of the country, and the Brahmins of the period, they hate with them being a *Chamar* lowest unit of the *Sudhra Family* as a degraded man of the history, which again lies in the same man in the caste to repeat the history of the man as a

Universal Truth exhibited him again in the form of *Dr. Raj Kumar*, a modern man of the Indian History.

In ought to be remembered that direct statements can of ten i.e., 'Infinite' and 'Ego' be again supplements on this earth by inferential evidence derived from the information of Geography, Geology, Physics, Chemistry, Mathematics, Botany, Archeaology, Social Works of the life, location of hunting grounds or haunts of wild life which creates problem in the life as enemy of social and eco environment. These incidental details tell us that the false idea of the 'mind' i.e., 'ego' is the destructive attitude of the man's life as a negative or black elements of the life. Therefore, the law of Newton is essential to use against the action and reaction of the positive forces which invested in the life of man as a Scientific Truth of the study, it is based on historical fact i.e., *'The Science of the Soul'*[14], the study of the Living Master of the period i.e., 'Baba Gurinder Singh Ji Biaswale', a fellow friend of writer as realized soul of the Father as a scientific man of the 'History' of the twenty first century A.D. as an advance idea of the man on earth as an alarming study of Universal –Knowledge.

Notes and References

1. Julian Johnson; *The Path of the Masters*, Beas, Reprint, 1997, pp. 7-8.
2. Ibid., p. 8.
3. *Sutra of the Medicine Buddha*; Tr. By Kinh DuOe Su, U.S.A, Reprint, 2001.
4. *The Path of the Master*; p.12.
5. Majid Husain; *Geography of Jammu and Kashmir*, New Delhi, 1985.
6. G.W. Briggs; *The Chamars*; Delhi, Reprint, 2004, p. 13. **Note:** Author made the study from the ancient literature of the man like *Satpatya Brahmins, Rig-Veda*, and other epic sources. According the commentator, they say, "Colloquially, *Juta,* leather shoe", having the historical values in the field of Supernatura Knowledge to determine, the Scientific Truth of the study, but without the study of '*Nam-mantra*', it is very difficult to understand their historical values in the life of man, because mind works in the illusion, he has no knowledge of the Heavenly world which generating the power of whole world. According to *Raja RadhaKant deva's Sabdkalpadrum*

(Lexicon) under *Paduka*, Vol.II. p.III, the old Law-Book of the society mentioned that *Ravidas* was the ancient rulers of the *'Nam'*. In Epigraphic evidence II, 1915 III, 16593: XIII, 4642 also mentions the same idea of this gentleman. Also see Monier-Williams *Sanskrit Dictionary*, under "*Upanah*" and "*paduka*" kind of terms have been used the terms for him. Among all the sections of the Chamar of the United Provinces of the *Sindh* and U.P., there were two great sub-castes of this period who predominated this area called as *Jatiya* and *Jaiswar*. *Jatiya* or *Jatua* now called *Jatav*, are found in large numbers, not only Central Provinces of SIndh and Upper Doab, but also found in the Punjab itself as a labour-class of the Father, a dealer in hides or skins, mentioned by (H.A. Rose: *A Glossary of the Tribes and Castes of the Punjab and North-West Frontier Province*; Language Department Punjab; Reprint, 1999, Vol.II, p. 149).

7. *Ultimate Visual Dictionary of the 21st Century A.D.* Supplement published by Dorling Kindersley, London, pb. 64, 30. **Note:** The comparative study of the various writers Majid Husain, the geographer of the Jammu and Kashmir study also highlight the same fact as lighted by the same scholar that this civilization was the most advance in nature due to the tolerance of the negative forces and realized that *Guru Ravidas* never dies, he is working some where to repeat the history of the man as already an event was took place during the time of 15th and 16th century A.D and established the rule of *'Dum Dynasty of the Father in Kashmir'* called Mughals.
8. *Science News Letter*: Vol. 3, 2008, Govt. College for Women Parade ground, Jammu.
9. *Kalhana's Rajatarangini* Tr. by M.A. Stein, Delhi; Vol. I, Book I, p.23. Note: Term *Barawala* or *Baravul* is not marked on the survey of Maps of India, it is Scientific Truth that one can not locate the original value of the molecule unless and until one cannot think about the idea of molecule in the microscope of the *'Nam'* and its name is hidden under that of *'Blalar Kallar'*, shown in a corresponding position. Despite Gulab Singh's gradual abandonment of the most repugnant traits of the man's are Brahmins, who exploited his early career, but they could not understand the indigenous value of the logic that he was the *'Nam'* or God on earth parallel to the Britishers forces, as he was the follower of the same philosophy which they

have adopted i.e. the philosophy' and ruled over the Kashmir as a positive force of the Father, as it is confirmed from the genetic tradcs of the plants called '*Hundred Leaf Rose*' of the plants who rules at one time in whole of the worlds, and he was form from *Rosa Centifolia*, and his family was *Rosaceae*, in Sanskrit it is called as *Shatapatri*, Hindi name *Gulab*, exploited by the Brahmins, that he was not the ruler of the Sudhra Family. He says, "True religion Consists in developing that attitude of mind from bad to good which ultimately results in seeing one 'infinite' power of the mind equivalent to God as realized soul prevailing in every existence of life in this universe, thus, finding the same divinity form one birth to another as from *B.R. Ambedkar* to *Baba Gurinder Singh* in both '*Art and Science*', but it is the crafts of the true saint or *sant* to locate this birth and death as a human being as a top most species of the world as God on earth". This is the higher ideal of Science. Why limited sciences like Botany, Zoology, Geology, Geography, Chemistry, Physics, Biology and others could not determine the Truth of the man's logic, because the lack of Insight – Knowledge of the Perfect Master, in present living form have not been recognized by them working as exploiter of the very 'Supernatural Thought', and 'History' became threat for them as culprit of the Nature. But the idea of Insight-Knowledge is a noble one. The *tertium organum* of *Ouspensky* presumes to be 'Key to the enigmas of the Universe' is the philosophy of Master of the Living Era. The vibration of '*This Universe*', according to *Prof. Yash Pal*, the modes of the molecule containing one oxygen and two hydrogen atoms on the basis of historical research one becomes orange red end with white light spectrum as a blast of man's life. We can not imagine any life without Him. It is marvellous that it also gives us clouds, rain, snow, blue lakes, and seas, blue, glaciers and rainbows of the 'Light Current' of '*Chamar Dynasty of Kashmir*'. It makes clear form the study that a honesty of the society exploited by the Brahmins to kill their race as a destructive force the man called negative elements of the society. As it is mentioned heitherto been eager to lick the dust below my feet – *Dalhousie*, 'Word' *Goolab* will be able to play a stiff game in the rock, sun snow! all on his side. Diable!- Charles Napier's view, 'Word'or *Chamar*, *Gulab Singh* caught my dress in his hands, and carried along with the historical prespective in *Sudra Family*, 'Thus I grasp the skirts of the British

Government, and I will never let go my hold" – *Dalhousie*. It shows from the study, a process was started by *Golab Singh* to repeat the history of the man, but the negative elements of the Father, were not ready to sacrifice their life, because an alone of the history faced number of problems but he started certain social reforms in the society with the power of the ideas of the '*Nam*' [(1) B.S. Singh, "*The Jammu Fox*; New Delhi; 1988, p. 153, (2) Naveen Patnaik, *The Garden of Life, An Introduction to the Healing Plants of India*; New Delhi, 1994, p. 172.]

10. Victoria Jones; *The Journey of the Soul*, Beas, Reprinted; 2004. **Note**. This book is dedicated to the Living Master Beloved Saviour, Eternal Friend of the God and Man. The present Living Master of the World Knowledge Maharaj Baba Gurinder Singh Ji Biaswale. One Living Mystic of the 'Sound' to blast the rocks of the earth as a problem for the man to repeat the history of the man as a new Era of the "Life".
11. Dr. Raj Kumar, '*Ambedkar and His Writings*' A Look for the New Generation: Delhi; 2008.
12. K.N. Upadhyaya; *Guru Ravidas, The Philosopher's Stone*; Beas, Reprinted; 2005, p. 4. **Note**. Thus, one comes across such variations of his name as *Raidas, Reyidas, Ruidas, Ruhdas, Rohidas, Rudradas* of the ancient period called '*Nam*' on earth at that time, and Ramdas with Raidas and Ravidas in the Medieval period being the most popular. The last one has been used here, as it is found In the *Adi Granth* and in other standard Hindi and Sanskrit works of the period. (Ibid. p. 5).
13. Shireen Moosvi, *Man and Nature in Mughal Era*, Symposia Paper; IHC 54th Session; Mysore, 1995, p. 5.
14. *Discourse and Letters of Maharaj Jagat Singh*; Radha Soami Satsang Beas; Reprint; 2002.

1

Science and Society

The tanners of leather class called *Ravidas* of the period, the preparers of skins called *'Nam'* or *'Chamar'* on earth, the manufacturers of leather articles of the human beings in the Indian society, and the makers of shoes belong to a well defined class in the Indian social order. Most of these workers, in 'Upper India' live in Heaven and works on earth, are today included under the general term *Chamar*.[1] This occupational group may be traced out from the pre-historic man to closing of the twentieth century A.D. and beginning of 21st century is to check the revolutionaries thought of the Science and Society in the form of a man in this universe by writing the book *'Glorious History of Dalits : Present and Past'*, Tanner (*Charmamna*) are mentioned in the *Rig-Veda*. Among Hindu Astronomy has accorded the highest place in the study of various sciences, *Chamar* is evident from the fact that it has been compared with a peacock's feather and a snake's jewel (*mani*). The various rulers for and the process of making a calendar of the *Nam* or God are elaborately dealt with in the forty *slokas* of *Rig-Veda*. This part of the *Rig-Veda* called *'Nam'* on earth is *Vedanga* of Astrology. In a time span of 5 years of 1,830 days, there are 60 regular months and 40 in the later *Vedic* period which are chiefly based on the lunar-date. This is the reason why the study of Physics stands in close proximity with Religion and Spiritualism[2].

The discovery of fire (*Agni*) occupies the most prominent place among the various scientific inventions and discoveries. As we take up the Galileo's spacecraft of the December 1995, his spacecraft finally arrived at the planet Jupiter. More than six years after it had been launched by NASA, the spacecraft's atmospheric probe, which had separated from the orbiter four months earlier, plunged through the gas giant's intense radiation belts of the leather and deep into its atmosphere. The onboard electronic systems had to be heavily shielded to protect them against the radiation and temperatures twice as hot as the Sun's surface. As the probe parachuted into Jupiter's atmosphere, pulled in by the enormous gravity of the '*Nam*', the orbiter passed close to the planet receiving and storing information for later relay back to Earth in the form of a *Chamar*. This was just the start of the *Galileo's mission*[3], the origin of the universe is completely mysterious. It is originated form the 'Primeval Atom'. The Primeval Atom was like a fire ball.[4] Actually the cosmic fire ball was the whole universe. Measured by astronomical concept the bomb of explosion must have been a cloud of about the size of our solar system.[5] Since 1995, the orbiter has been circling around the Jupiter and recording information about its weather and its planet-sized moons. Before arriving at Jupiter, Galileo photographed the impact of comet P/ shoemaker – Levy 9th with Jupiter 2nd, the largest explosion ever seen in the solar system. More recently, the spacecraft has photographed volcanic activity on the moon Io, and found evidence of water beneath the icy crust of another moon, *Europa*.[6]

According to scientists between the period of five to twenty thousand million years ago, the 'Primeval Atom' exploded instantaneously with prodigious violence and the early universe expanding rapidly.[7] After the first explosion, the universe was filled with spiral nebulae different from one another in size and shape and having a somewhat irregular distribution in shape.[8] According to A.G. Lemaitre owing to great density of matter the force of gravitation was strong and after three or four thousand years of the initial explosion, the expansion of the universe was showed there was a computerization change on the earth. But the slow down of the forces into the 'Universal Truth' mar the career of various scientists which are working in self-styled manner. Organic molecules of the *Chamar* thought to be from Mars were recently found in a 4-5 billion years old rock that fell into the Antarctic 13,000 called ago mineral features of the *'Nam'* called *Deepit Raj* modern man of the History born as a *'Chamar'* suggesting biological activity and possible micro scopic fossils of bacteria-like organism were discovered by the historians of British India. As it began its six year flight, Galileo moved away from this Earth towards Venus, then doubled back, using the gravitational fields of Venus and Earth to propel it towards Jupiter. The main body of the spacecraft circulating around the Jupiter is known as the orbiter. The probe, on the left of the diagram, a camera has been fit in the atmospheric descent to mould the earth in descending order. The orbiter and the probe split apart and orbiter circles Jupiter, making approaches to all the planet's large moons. It uses their gravity to change course of action of the man according to their *'Law of Karma Theory'*. The impacts of the comet on Jupiter's atmosphere have been spectacular with plumes thousand of Kilometers high hot "bubbles" of gas in the atmosphere, and large dark "scars" will flyover them. The comet consisted of at least 21 discernible icy fragments with diameters estimated at up to two kilometers. The fragments stretched across 1.1 million Kilometers (710,000 miles) of space, at most three times the distance between Earth and the moon.[9]

The hypothesis about the origin of the universe also put forth by the Greek *Arya Bhatta*, *Nicholas Copernicus, Tycho Brahe, John Kepler* and their contemporary scientists give us the impression that they were talking about the universe 'as a whole' as a 'Universal Truth'. If that is so, the concept of the Universe put forward by them was far from the true picture of the Universe as a labour class of the society. In fact, due to their insignificant knowledge in the field of astronomy they could observe only a tiny part of the universe. This part of the universe is one of the million galaxies scattered throughout the space to which the present day scientists have given the name of Milky Way.[10]

Medical Research

Some significant break through have recently been made in DNA research in history, with enormous implications for controlling and curing the diseases, reproducing identical organisms (cloning), and "decoding", or listing, the sequence of the genes that compose an organism's DNA ("genome sequencing"). In May 1996, Oxford University Scientists announced that they had identified the regulatory "switch" for the gene GFTR, which, when defective, causes cystic fibrosis. The discovery will potentially enable healthy copies of the gene to be introduced into a patients body made by *Chamar* or *Chams or* leather, and activated in relevant cells as long as life is there. Geneticists have, for the first time, sequenced the genome of an organism larger then a bacterium, with enormous consequences for the future study into human genetics. Other areas of the development include the use of highly specialized computer technology to provide long-distance medical care, and virtually reality[11] based on 'saving our earth' for environmental living, now a days, there is a global cry to maintain the natural balance. Science is acclaiming three types of natural pollution i.e., Air (*Vayu*), Water (*Apah*), and Soil (*Prithivi*) and there are casual by:

1. Human lust for so called development in History.
2. Man's activities to exploit nature.
3. Injudious use of natural resources by man

It is important to note that there is a need of pious and scientific approach. Vedic hymns express deep communion with nature. Nature is to be understood as a friend, revered as mother' obeyed as Father and natured as a beloved child. In philosophical terms ethics are meant for the concept of *'The Good'*[12] another subject of genetic research is the *'Caenorhabditis Elegans'*, a soil-dwelling nematode worm. Scientists have embarked to identify the specific sequence of the 100 million base pairs in its genome. This computer representation shows that the double helix (blue), of the DNA linked together by the bases pairs, i.e., 'Yellow and Red' colour. So far the genetic coding is concerned, a chromosome is a condensed strand of DNA there are 25 pairs of *'Chromosomes'* In the human cell and together wit˙ he *'Chamar'* or preparers of skins, they contain about 100,000 genes in the body for the development of the species. Every gene is a tiny segment of DNA, made up of paired nucleotide bases arranged in triplets as God and Man, doctor is watching the patient by his method the entire sequence of these bases forms the specific genetic code (gnome) of an organism. A world wide research effort, known as *'Human Genome Project'*[13] to study the God where he stands.

Tissue Engineering

The tools with which these scientists mentioned above, observed that celestial phenomena was the naked eye not the naked dress of the Gandhi or dirty soul believes in the discrimination view of the scientists, particularly the social scientists like *Dr. B.R. Ambedkar*, who gave a scientific analysis of the Natural thought which based on human history, not in philosophy. Astonishingly, the scientists of this period could not find a consentaneous hypothesis about the concept of even the local universe i.e., body of the man itself is a part of the nature. This shows that they had not the correct knowledge of the microcosmic[14] law with the invention of instruments and geographical discoveries. The age of Renaissance fostered a spirit of adventure and a great deal of curiosity among Europeans through *Arabs* trade reached in *China* during the late thirteenth century A.D. by Italian merchants. One of them was Marco Polo who received a warm welcome in the court of the Mongol rulers of China, *Kublai Khan*. He went to Japan and also reached the Spice Islands. When he returned to his native place, *Venice*, he narrated his thrilling experience to his friends of the same category *Chamar* by name, and sea attracted the imagination of many Europeans in fourfold profits to trade with East. Portuguese prince *Doms, Henry* "the Navigator" (1394 – 1460) attracted" the best sailors, astronomers and geographers of Europe", who exchanged their knowledge with others like Sudanese, reached in India in 1498 A.D. called *Vasco Da Gama*. Two years later, Cabral a Portuguese Commander, who was sailing down to the west coast of Africa, was blown off his course by a storm and at last reached the east coast of South America. Thus, Brazil was discovered in 1500[15] A.D. Edward Jenner, a English doctor in Medical Sciences, he found a vaccines in 1796 A.D against the small-pox, plague and other types of fever before that, there was enormous strides of progress in 'science' and "technology" a systematic study of the experimentation, and reasoning, resulting in improved industrial and commercial products of greater value in human life and the victims; they were left helpless to adopt the remedies, but he found out that diseases had cow-pox (a mild disease) earlier appeared to be free from the attack of small–pox. He experimented with a young boy by incalculating him with cow-pox serum and his experiment proved highly successful that was how vaccination of 1796 against certain diseases became popular as '*Chamar*' of the period. Nobody know how these diseases were caused. However, 'science and technology' had great advancement in the history of man, in 1865 that a French Professor *Louis Pasteur* (1822-1895 A.D.), showed that these infectious diseases were caused germs. He explained how fermentation takes place in other souring of milk and putrefaction of meat. He correctly guessed that the silk industry of the *Kabir's* factory in France had been destroyed by plague. He also discovered the cause for the cattle disease. But his outstanding achievement was his discovery of successful treatment of persons suffering from hydrophobia disease caused by the bite of a mad dog of the period called Brahmins or politicians. For a couple of years the germ theory of Louis Pasteur was ridiculed by Brahmins or priestly class of the period, but it assumed credibility under a German scientist, *Robert Kock* (1843-1910 AD), with the aid of microscopic study, he found the caused of the diseases known to us as cholera and tuberculosis. When the germ theory was accepted as a fact, doctors started discovering vaccines or serums to protect the people from such diseases like *diphtheria* and the like. *Emil Von Behring* protected children from this disease called *diphtheria* by discovering of several vaccines on such diseases like *typhoid fever*, *tetanus* and others. *Walter Reed*, an American doctor, found that *yellow fever* was widely spread by mosquitoes. Over a span of half a century, scientists discovered powerful drugs such as *penicillin* and *sulfa* to combat these deadly germs. Today we have the most powerful antibiotic drugs used against diseases ranging from infantile paralysis to diseases like cancer and heart-trouble. In the field of surgery, the discovery of anesthetics happened to be a milestone discovery of the man in human history. X-rays also became an important factory in the filed of surgery of the 20th century and "Kodak" camera.[16] An artificial human ear, developed by growing human cartilage in a biodegradable polyester scaffold mould, was grafted on to the back of a mouse to see whether outer skin would form and the blood would circulate. This experiment, successfully carried out at the Massachusetts Institute of Technology by *Dr. C. Vacanti*, is a vital step towards using such structures in future human study. The highly specialized techniques performed in minimally invasive "*Keyhole*"[17] where from the "Voice of God" is listened.

Genetic Advancement

The great change in the status and place of science brought about by the Second World War has already been alluded to small number of hydrogen bombs in fact considerably less than those already in existence would be sufficient to wipe out not just cities but whole industrial districts which created pollution in the environment. It is primarily physical science that has been effected, because it was the most advanced and the most closely linked with war and industry. It was especially in physics that was led to the great interruption in Britain and America. Most of the academic laboratories were closed or turned over to war uses, and the most brilliant men occupied the "*History of the Chamar Dynasty of Kashmir*' with problem of a Big Soul which had no relation to the previous work, but present situation of the '*Nam*' or God is important in his lifestyle. The supreme importance which the war gave to physical science, mainly in relation to atomic energy and electronics machines, has lasted into the post war period. This has meant, particularly in the United States, a great expansion of physical research in the human history was started and a *Chamar* was found there and its equipping with vast and expensive apparatus was found in the body such as experimental piles, synchrotrons and electronic calculators[18] were found from this research trees are also the panacea of all our environmental ills which we brought it upon ourselves as a culprit nature of the man .The population started exploding from the 19th century A.D. after the downfall of *Mughal* rule in India, because due to the exploitation of the man, a process was started in human history by degrading the *Sudhras* in all over the world called down trodden in English language and *Dalit* in Hindi, and the self-style idea of the man forced the labour class to produce more children for the protection of life and now attained its peak to check the advancement of the genetic trade from one generation to another, but they did for the Father *Ravidas*. No doubt, there is a rapid development in 'science and technology', and brought tremendous benefit to mankind working as a labour class. Now these and general scale of the work shared of government rather than of universities in military science is much more greater against man to man, and strictly secret research of the '*Nam*' or God is almost connected with big business, is also far more indirect form of the 'Natural Thought' called *Chamar* in History and *'Nam'* in Sanskrit as a 'Principal Soul' of the World. Further, the influence of thought control is exercised in a way started in *America*, but one more difficult task has been assigned to Dr. Raj Kumar, a modern man of the History called *Chamar*. Teachers are rarely dismissed for their political opinions and exploiting the students and scholars that *Sudhras* has no history. They are merely not appointed to important posts of the universities and colleges if their views are regarded as not sound, wherefrom this teacher has listen and alarming the modern man that history is going to change very shortly. Today, we are witnessing 'Global Warming' thanks to the modern man dumping of green house gases into atmospheric changing's from the earth sides. Therefore, it is difficult to sustain in that conditions and it is necessary for the *Chamar* to check the knowledge of the modern man who is working in self style manner and created the social problem like caste-system and other social evils like low percentage, etc. Trees can act as effective sink of CO_2 an important Green House Gas[19] to utilize it in production method. Many prominent scientists like *Joliot Curie* left the Communist Party and engaged for political reasons and find out in his discovery the fission of nuclear and its resistance pressures generally found in bodies, such as the World Federation of Scientific Workers and Science of Peace found in man, and other scientific organization in *India, China*, and the Soviet Union have also added their voice that God is existing in this Universe. In *Japan* practically every scientific organization has been campaigning against atom bombs and bomb tests. The two most well-reported manifestoes were that initiated by *Bertrand Russell* and *Einstein* demanding an and to war[20] than peace will be established. In tracing the history of 'science and technology' in ancient India, we are "confronted by a jigsaw of transmissions which rendered our interpretation of these discoveries all the more difficult and uncertia"[21] in the history of India during the rule of the 'blind faith' called 'political system' corrupt by nature. The growth was completely based on the trade system called genetic advancement in the history of "*Chamar*". The quality of chemical variety in Chemistry not manifested in the present era; but during the rule of the *Mauryan Chamar* improved communication and developed technology by material manufactured and utilized in the history of man for the advancement of cultural technique from mind to heart. Due to a gradual sustained growth of economic activities even in the post – *Mauryan* and *Harappa* time agriculture, trade, mining, minerals and industry became prominent[22] in genetic trades for the advancement of the history of the *'Chamar dynasty'* called *'Ravidas Culture'* or *'Chamar Culture'*. The use of metals and their production has been one of the greatest achievement of the *Chamar* in ancient sciences. It was closely linked to developments in Metallurgy and Chemistry. The branch of science concerned with the nature in history as a progressive period of the man and the properties of substances and how they react and change with each other as *Chamar* and *Brahmins.* The attraction or interaction between two forces as God and Man and their affair was triggered by sexual chemistry as a genetic trade between the two groups. A person engaged in chemical research or experiments originally called *alchimist* or *alchemist* in Latin languages, an element of substance relating to chemistry or chemicals, a compound or substance which has been artificially prepared or purified in plants cannot be ignored as a scientific study of the mankind. The *Arthasastra* of *Kautily* describes that a considerable progress of the human history was made in the arena of metal industry during the time of *Maurya* and his working class of the "*Sudhra Family*" called *'Chamar'* of the period. The mining of iron copper, silver, lead, tin and iron from their ores are considerable in the history of man and their work of smelting gold-ores[23] is also called *Chamar*. After the *Mauryan* period this progress is also noticed from the urban elements. Even the *Samhitas* of *Charakar* (c.1st – 2nd Century A.D.) and *Sushrut* (c 4th Century A.D.)[24] provided several references to the uses of mineral and metals in medicine of genetics trades, and Buddhist monks called it Mercury (*rasa or para*) and alchemist compounds. It also gives a survey of the status of metallurgy and alchemy besides extraction and purification of metals such as silver, gold, tin and copper again during this period to prepare the *'elixir of life'*, is called magical portion, especially one supposedly able to make people live forever originated from the *Arabic* word and other substances from Mercury to Jupiter, *Nagavjuna* refers to the use of animal and vegetable products, apart from minerals and *alkalis*[26] of the time. To dissolve diamonds, metal and pearls into water (*Apah*) he suggested the use of vegetable acids in recent genetic science constituted the same organs to complete the species. The term is also used to refer to individual members of a clone group of genes, cells in advance manners to repeat the '*History of the Chamar Dynasty*'. Clones occur in nature as *Chamar* occurs in body, especially in the case of simple organisms like '*Nam*' on earth to check the advancement of the man in history, such as bacteria and viruses, which reproduce merely by splitting (a sexual – reproduction) after their DNA test. It has been replicated itself. They also occurs in human beings and other animals when a single fertilized egg divides and separates to form two or more identical individuals. Artificial cloning of selected genes is one of the most significant break through ever made in biology and has powerful implications for both science and technology in advancement of the industry, gruel and juices of fruits and plants are also tested. Once the desired gene is obtained, the cloning can be left to organisms such as bacteria, which, under suitable conditions, again reproduce almost indefinitely for the period of time not permanent one as Brahmins. In this way, enormous quantities of the particular gene may be produced to crush the Brahmins as a beggar of the period. Gene cloning is most commonly done in the laboratory by means of the Polymerase Chain Reaction (PCR), which can produce millions of copies of a single gene in a matter of hours. For more daunting an enterprise than gene cloning is the cloning of whole animals see below right not go ahead without the permission of the '*Chamar*' as a practical solution found in the body. A further key genetic advance is the creation of transgenic animals, in particular pigs, which are currently being used for the "manufacture" of human – compatible organs, such as hearts[27] of the *Chamars*.

Modern Surgery

With the advancement of the science and technology modern surgery is playing a vital role in human history, medicine is constantly evolving in human nature for the relief of the body, as a result of the development in technical expertise in a successful hand transplant and to repair a congenital defect in a foetus while still in the womb[27] of the mother, who are expertise in sexual intercourse not from the real husband, but they have number of husbands and become prostitute without the knowledge of the reality, then feticides became essential for the respect of the family and this idea mostly found in Brahminical Ideology and doctor become materialistic and collect the money from illegal resources and known next to God, not God but 'Mind Only' and become dictator of the world that he is a famous doctor as illegal race of the human history. Even before he begins a practice then, there is a lot of preparation required. Place body and mind must all a be properly prepared. Once they have been to be ready to select a method patient die and it requires more study that there is defect in method or in technique study requires more concentrations practice in this subject. It is called *Samatha Bhavana* in Sanskrit. *Samatha* means calm, as we have seen in silence or reservations of the thought, while *bhavana* comes from the verb 'to become' and here means mental development. There are three stages of its development.

1. Access concentration and absorption.
2. Meditators should choose one of the forty meditation subjects assigned by their teachers.
3. Several popular subjects are outlines for those who are already trained and practice the theory to develop the mind for peaceful study to bring[28] a change in the history of the new methods and technique.

Mental Formations (*Samkhara*)

During the surgical period, mental activities are included in this group. According to the ancient book '*Abhidhamma* or '*Nam-dana*', with the exception of feeling and perception of the idea may be take place like (*sanna*) and other fifty kinds of mental factors. These included contact (*phassa*) with the Master or teacher, volition (*Centana*), one pointedness of mind called Third Eye, the source of light (*ekaggata*), the life continuum idea must be broad above the eye called *Jivitindriya* like the stream of life. In addition to this, attention (*manasikara*), will (*chanda*) (bright thought), determination (*adhimokkha*), wisdom (*panna*) as '*Nam*' or God on earth, loving-kindness (*dosa* or *metta*), compassion (*Karuna*), greed to obtain the '*Nam*' *or Chamar* (*lobha*), anger to defeat the Brahmins (*dosa*), delusion (*moha*) of the money, conceit (*mana*) and others positive elements of the life. The mental formations comprise all our good and bad actions[29] as in medical surgery. Advances in science and technology, *Chamars* have also been for-reaching in the history of India by providing a skill of what might be achieved in the future course of action for the abortion of illegal concept through the idea of *Nam-dan* of the Living Master, and; the advancement of modern surgery for the sake of Father who give us life and knowledge for the recognize the of Truth. The application of virtual reality in medicine has already enabled progress in both the teaching and practice of surgery, and may soon be used in the treatment of eating disorders and agoraphobia in the man's inside the body. Minimally invasive and robot[30] to recognize an object as a particular thing injected into the body as a small molecule, visible consciousness of the presence of colour arises as awareness to study the case about the reason of the problem (*dukkha*)[31] in the body; and computer aided surgery allow delicate and complex surgical procedures to be carried out with the precision of a thousandth of a millimeter this means that surgery has become safer, and patient pain and recovery time have been reduced[32] in the history of man itself. Thus, the term *'History'* had a dual meaning , that is, God and man. Originally it referred to record of past events *'Word'*, the word as used by ancient Greek Herodotus mean *inquiry, Chamar*, but in modern times the term has come to be applied as *'Scientific Truth'* to actual past events to human affair or even in nature as God and man's story. In fact, however, human knowledge of the past events, especially those beyond living memory in Cosmic Order, is based on written records, oral traditionslike Zain-ul-Abidin (1420-1470 A.D.) were famous in all over the world as *Bud Shah* as*Nurnama* of Kashmir history has the same references as God and man's story of the fourteenth and fifteenth centuries A.D. There were certain great poets like *Sayyid Mohammad Rumi, Qazi Sayyid Ali Sirazi, Sayyid Mohammad Sistani, Maulana Kabir* and other glaxy of sufi saints. Still their poetry is misinterpreted by the Brahminical historians or writters like. Aruna Sharma, Jahida Jiwan, Dilsad Geelani, Ku. Prveen, Madu Gandotra, Parkash Premi, Azra Choudhri, Ratan Lal Basotra, Suseel Sharma, Neru Sharma, Mahindar Pal Singh, Manju Bala, Sonawar, Bhushan Lal Koul, Avtar Krishan Razdan, Premi Romani, Sujana Koul, Mohd. Manksh Kaki, Shyam Bihari, Isupal, Mabang Sirangi Sakspo. Book published

'Hamara Sahtiya' in 2007 by the Academy of Art, Culture and Languages, Jammu asidiot thought. There is no scientific proof of the historical writings of the great scholars of the period.

The repair of birth defects through foetal surgery has so far been mostly experimental through the process of the '*Nam*' or God. However, ground breaking advances were also made in 1998 with the treatment of a case of *spina bifida*, a developmental defect in the posterior wall of the spinal canal. With this condition, the delicate tissue of the spinal cord may be exposed to varying degrees of damage, depending on the severity of the defect. This can result in paralysis of the lower limbs and incontinence. A team of surgeons in the US corrected the defect in a 23 week gestation foetus, after the condition had been detected during a routine ultrasound. Follow up at the walking and toilet training stages will be necessary to judge the success of the operation[33] by the doctors called Head of the Department.

Robots in Surgery

Recently advances in biomedical engineering have led to the increasing use of robots in surgery. Once a robot has been correctly programmed, it will be more accurate than a human in performing many precise, but repetitive tasks are essential in human history for the perfection of the knowledge. Robots may be soon act as surgeons assistants during operations, holding instruments such as an endoscope (for view internal parts of the body), and making incisions when required in the body functioning like human automatic mechanical device like a person in human history like Dr. B.R. Ambedkar who described his thought in this direction of life during his odd hours that peoples of India, they are in search of solace. Robotic science or study of robot treated as singular bionic machine and android of design and operation who to control the idiot forces of the human history like Pritam Patwari, he is culprit from the background of the human history and his species is in hell; and did not visualize the truth in author's writings. This automatic machine aided brain surgery to the modern man and performs simulated brain surgery on a model head (right) from the track. The surgeon in views the operations on a large screen is successful and uses a joystick to control the robot's movements as an automatic machine will have to punish to such idiots of the 'Revenue Department'.

Computer – Aided Brain Surgery of the Man

A surgeon uses a computer – assisted microscopic study to locate a brain tumour in a patient the microscopic uses MRI scans to plot the position of the tumour, and maps it in 3 – D virtual reality, the surgeon can then locate and destroy the tumour using a laser integrated into the microscopic study where the defect is found and records in history for its development stages. Medical imaging such as X-ray, Computerized Tomography (CT), and Magnetic Resonance Imaging (MRI), allows visual access to the internal anatomy and functions of the human body in the brain. The precise anatomical information provided by these images can be used to create a virtual patient in the history of man in *Chamar's* study or a study of skill or art, on which surgeons and medical students can practice proceduring's methods of the latest technique to study of man. To study the anatomy of the human leg, these surgeons wear headsets equipped with a 3-D video display to view an image of human history, and a black rubber glove (*dataglove*) that has woven optical fiber sensors. The glove relays details of the body part to the computer knowledge of the man in history and science, which then generates the image of modern man. This colour enhanced Magnetic Resonance Image (MRI) is the product of a number of MRI scans made along the length of the body, which have been collated by the scanner's computer through human study and his history.

Robotic Hand

This battery – operated robotic hand needs only three fingers to perform 85 percent of the functions of a normal hand. The hand will be covered in artificial skin that contains tiny pressure sensors to aid use as lying below at that time to help the man. Artificial hands will eventually be powered by energy generated by the movement of tendons in the upper arm. In 1998, a multinational team of surgeons performed the first successful hand transplant in France the transplant recipient had lost his hand in a circular saw accident nine years previously in the efforts of man. Arteries and veins in the arm and hand were connected to supply vital nutrients to, and remove waste products from the skin and tissues of the hand. Regeneration of nerve tissue, even after reconstruction of his past history, was more gradual and, three months after the operation, the patient started to regain sensation in his fingertips caused by the manipulation of objects. The sensors enable the hand to maintain a grip on objects of all shapes and sizes. Transverse section through writ also displays the arteries, veins, and nerves that travel through the arm and hand. The wrist joint, bones in the arm articulate with bones in the hand to allow the movement[34] of the hand practice. Thus, the medical treatment of bodily injuries or disorders by cutting open the body and removing or repairing the parts of the body relating to injury or illness or deformity done with great precision called surgical bombing in the history of modern surgery. In Britain, methylated spirit is used for cleansing the skin before injections or surgery called surgical stockings in the historical progress in this field and keeps a record for the progress of the past ideas into latest technique in the skinning work called leather in the history of *Chamar,* how to protect the limbs of the body particularly the arms and wrists of the man, there is need of golden chain as self-style prediction in human thought as *Ghora Adami* and *Kali Lari,* as *Kala Kirpa Megha* and *Chita Kukur Chamar*.

According to Robert N. Test:

Give my sight to the man who has never seen a sunrise, a baby's face or love in the eyes of a woman.

Give my heart to a person whose own heart has caused nothing but endless days of pain.

Give my blood to the teenager who was pulled from the wreckage of his car, so that he might live to see his grand children play.

Give my kidneys to one who depends on a machine to exist from week to week.

Take my bones, every muscle, every fiber and nerve in my body and find to make a crippled child walk through that *Cham* or *Khal*.

Explore every corner of my brain take my cells, if necessary and let them grow so that, someday, a speechless boy will shout at the crack of a bat and a deaf girl will hear the sound of rain against her window.

Burn what is left of me and scatter the ashes to the winds to help the flowers grow.

If you must bury something, let it be my faults, my weaknesses and all prejudice against my fellow man i.e. *Radha Soami Mission*'

Give my sins to the devil.

Give my soul to God where stand science, if by chance, you wish to remember the Father, do it with a kind deed or word to someone who needs you.

If you do all I have asked, I will live forever".

As we reach our times in the history of *Chamar*, blends into remembered experience of life. Here, we are close to the events, are watching struggles still unresolved by the historians, with their protagonists approach still alive and active in the discussion what is happening around the world. All this makes it especially difficult to understand to analyze the historical event of the life and to judge the significance of the movements of the Science and Society.[35] In course of the elaboration of the Celestial Phenomena in the history of science, the *Greek* astronomers were the first who study the physical universe purely on scientific lines and *Chamar* of the modern history i.e., Dr. Raj Kumar with collaboration of *Baba Gurinder Singhji Biaswala.*, and *Deepit Raj* as a great astronomers' of the modern man. The first of these was Thales (640 – 560 B.C.) who started such kind of surgery and the last was Claudius Ptolemy who died in about 180 A.D. Besides them, *Anaximander, Anaxinenes, Heraclites, Anaxagoras, Democitus, Philolnus, Appollonicea, Aristotla, Heraclides*, etc. were also tried to seeked rational explanation of Celestial Phenomena. Leaving aside the differences of the social problems, if any like caste, colour and creed, in their scientific outlook is observed on the following points:

1. That the earth in its fixed position lies at the centric of the Universe.
2. That the Celestial bodies of the Natural Thought such as planets, sun and stars revolve around the earth in concentric circular orbits once a day to check the knowledge of man what is good and what is bad in the man's body and brain.

Thus, the celestial bodies except the earth were believed to be in constant motion[36] when there is heavy load on earth without reasoning and logic working under the lap of sky as an unnecessary race of the Father.

The Greek astronomer were also able to observe the five planets, which do find a place in the present planetary system of our life they have been placed in the heavenly bodies of the earth called moon (*Dr. Raj Kumar*), *Mercury* (*Master Deepit Raj*), *Venus* (*Dr. Ram Dass*) and *Sun* (*Baba Gurinder Singh Ji Biaswala*), Heroes of the '*Nam*' to change the History and Geography of the world as a scientific discovery of man and they are *Chamar* by caste working as astronomers of the present science of the society.

Notes and References

1. G.W. Briggs: *The Chamars*, Delhi, Reprinted; 2004, p.11.
2. A.L. Basham, *Adbhut Bharat*; Agra, 1993, p. 423.
3. Darling Kinderslay, *Ultimate Visual Dictionary 21st Century, Supplement*; London; p. 6A.
4. Gerard DE Vaucouleurs; *Discovery of the Universe*; London; 24 Russell Square; p. 228.
5. John C. Eccles; *The Human Mystery*; Edinbury, 1977-78, p. 31
6. Dorling Kinderslay; op.cit.
7. Gerard DE Vaucouleurs; *op.cit.,* p. 229.
8. G.C. Mc Vittie; *Cosmological Theory*; London, 1952, p.v (Preface).
9. Dorling Kindersley; *op.cit.,* pp. 6-7A.
10. Dr. Vasdev Sharma; *Cosmic View of Life in Guru Nanak Bani*; Language Department Punjab, 1996, pp. 3-4.
11. Dorling Kindersley; *op.cit.,* p. 14A.
12. Rekha Sud Handa; *Ecological Ethics in the Vedas: A Historical Analysis*; An article published in PHC; Pataal; 2006, pp. 59.
13. Dorling Kindersley; *op.cit.,* p. 14A.
14. Dr. Vadev Sharma; *op.cit.,* p. 4.
15. B.V. Rao; *World History*; Delhi, Reprint, 2003, pp.203, 205-06.
16. Ibid. pp. 414, 415.
17. Dorling; Kindersley; *op.cit.,* p. 15A.
18. J.D. Bernal; *Science in History*; London; 1959, Vol. III, p. 243.
19. B.R. Kundal's 'Message' about '*World Arbour Day*; State times, dated 21.03.2008.
20. J.D. Bernal; *op.cit.,* pp. 845-46.

21. P.S. Rowson; *Early Art and Architecture*; A.L. Basham (ed.) *A Cultural History of India*; New Delhi, 1975, p. 208.
22. **Note**. It shows from the study that the economy was strengthen with the wide spread of the use of iron in social change after the sixty years of independence of the Indian industry, trade of the human's articles in the field of rice, sugar, cotton, leather and other crafts goods have good trade relations with foreign countries; but the history of these people including farmers and tribes, it has not been changed by the modern leaders, because they have the idea of *Gandhi* in Hindi language called buttock or humorous posterior in *Northern Americans* which has no history but a philosophy of the 'sex' based on Hinduism not '*Sudhras*' as their control over this organ.
23. R.P. Kangla (ed.); *The Kautilya Arthasastra*; Bombay University; 1969; part 1 – 8.
24. A.L. Basham; *The Wonder That Was India*; Delhi; 1971, p. 500.
25. Dilip M. Salwi; *Our Scientist*; New Delhi, 1987, p. 23.
26. Dorling Kindersley; *Op.Cit.*, p. 16A.
27. *Ibid.*, p. 17 A.
28. Rewata Dhamma; *Emptying the Rose – Apple Seat*; U.S.A., 2003, p. 34.
29. *Ibid.*, p. 94.
30. Dorling Kindersley; *Op.Cit.*, p. 16A
31. Rewata Dhamma; *Op.Cit.*, p.95
32. Dorling Kindersley; *Op.Cit.*, p. 18A
33. *Ibid.*
34. *Ibid.*, p. 19A
35. J.D. Bernal; *Op.Cit.*, Vol. III, p. 703
36. Gerard DE Vaucouleurs; *Op.Cit.*, p. 22

2

Concept of Life

A living thing is often described as a living organism in the concept of life with the company of non-living species in human form, who does not realize the truth in scientific discovery, they are called dead species as dead animals. An organism is something that exhibits organization in the life of man's surrounding. Science divides the material things of the Universe into two types for qualitative and quantitative growth; at the same time there has been greater advance in the knowledge of the fundamental nature of the matter, i.e., called animate (living) and inanimate (non-living) things, than in any comparable period of the past[1] history and man was there on earth. An animate thing consists of plants, animals and birds. All other things such as rocks, metals, minerals, gasses, skins of the various animals, cotton, silk, etc., are called inanimate or dead things. The living things can move or vibrate whereas non-living things can neither move nor vibrate without the help of man. A living organism like a human being has organs but no sense who to control like hands, legs, eyes, ears, nose, etc. but it is the mind only to work on such occasions what is right and wrong idea. Question rises wherefrom this mind came, it shows from the study that it was the part of Father of Baba Ravidas; who has the knowledge of ultimate truth. Therefore, sometimes sciences fails in their mission to check the advancement of the man and 'History' is a such kind of subject which gives a befitting reply to the man in scientific discovery of the body which made of leathers, bones and other organs of the life, those feels problems in the life itself and hate with others like *Pritam Patwari*, suckled in the chain of natural thought that we materialistic people ignored by the another called as 'idiols'; a step of their degradation on called as modern *Dalit-Brahmins*.

Living Matter

All organs of a living thing closed by the skin as an upper garment of the body and cells have been introduced into it for the function of body. Question again rises, where from the cells obtain energy, it shows that from the same living beings called plants, vegetables, etc., for the survival of the body, and small plant and the animals consist of a single cell. The larger organization is made up of many cells. Inside the body, each cell, there is complicated admixture of chemicals called '*protoplasm*' or 'Living Matter' that assumes many different forms of plants, birds and animals during the course of development number of animals and birds use for test where the real living thing exist. It shows that science sometimes goes into ignorance that reality lies in human body for the realization of Truth for the time being 'Doctor' and *Patwaris* became materialistic and can not understand that material life is a problem for the Society and the Science, and his efforts only meant for determine the truth than 'History' comes in existence as story of the man and God. Thus, the living cell is like a factory (*Karmantas*)[2] in which energy in the form of motion, heat, electricity and light is always being produced in the history of man and mankind.

The chemical analysis of the 'protoplasm' or 'living matter' shows that it is made up of elements which also occur in nature in the 'Non-living' world 80 percent of *protoplasm* consists of water which is made up of the elements of hydrogen and oxygen. These two elements together with nitrogen and carbon make up 90 percent of 'living matter' or 'protoplasm'. The remaining part of these elements is mostly made up eight characters; namely; phosphorus, surplus, potassium, magnesium, iron, sodium, chlorine and calcium. Traces of a few other elements are also represented in the living matters and materials. In addition to the chemical compounds found in chemistry to study and test, protoplasm contains proteins including enzymes, fats and fatty substances in the living matters called carbohydrates and inorganic substances[3] to find out the result of the process for light and knowledge is the quest of man in life, those do not believe on his existence, they are material of the world.

Humans have never been satisfied with life on earth, but their quest in recent times seems not only to have intensely increased in the Western countries, but also to have taken a new turn in history to moulding the earthly life. People today find it difficult to swallow the dogmas and doctrines offered by the old traditional religions which were based on human knowledge called Creative Knowledge. Their intellect revolts against beliefs and dogmas that do not stand the scrutiny of the Science and Society as irreligious, but reasoning and logic is based on common sense, and do not deny the existence of God. But they are sincere and critical seekers after Truth working in the scientific discovery of the '*Nam*' or God. They want to know the real, absolute and unadulterated truth, not only about what they see with their physical eyes in this world, but also about the unseen world[6] that man is working in this universe till date in the history of man's itself.

Keeping in view, the historical approach in human body which is made of leather, skin tanned by the *Chamar* at one time in the heaven and land on earth to check the other leather –works in the form of a *Mochi* and his race ignores him as he is not the Lord of the earth.

Metaphysical View of Life in History

The universe of the *Vedas* was a simple affair that it was believed, a living being is made of two distinct things i.e., material being and the soul, and body is like a house of Living Master of the period at one time use to work in indirect form, in the *Asram* or in hut called the period of '*The Dawn of Light*'[4] and '*The Age-old Quest for Light*[5], actually started with the creation of life. The hunger to know something about ourselves and our Creator was inborn in humans. The presence of so many religions of the world in all over the countries through all ages, is clear and conclusive evidence of that eternal search. Thus term *Chamar* and *Chuara* is the basic problem still agitating in the minds of the people to accept it, today, as a dirty religion of the *'Nam'*. In their tireless search for satisfactory answers to these questions, some of them happened to come in contact with *'Sant Mat'* this ancient path of the Masters 'Word' or *'Nam'* a scientific method of entering and realizing the kingdom of heaven in the human body while living *Chamar's* seemed a race to supply convincing answers to their scientific minds,[7] with the result that numbers of this community is working under the one umbrella i.e., *'Nam'*.

Historical ideas of Indian society on the origin and evolution of the Universe are rather a matter of religion than of science and are considered elesewhere[8]. This process of transmigration was interpreted somewhat variously, but all schools of thought agreed that the soul does not transmigrate in a state of nudify, but with a sheath or series of sheaths of subtle matter; the condition of the sheaths depends on the balance of provide good and evil actions and deeds called *'Karma Theory'*, and the new birth is determined by the nature of the sheaths which surround the soul within the body. The subtle body of transmigration is deprived of sense-organs, including mind, the sixth sense, and therefore the soul cannot normally remember previous births or the passage from one body to another. Very advance souls, however, can sometimes recapture memories of previous existences through the process of *'Nam'* as Dr. Raj Kumar and *Baba Gurinder Singh ji Biaswale*; and some sects evolved a special technique for doing so[9] in this process of the natural theory; they know each other in aircel message called 'Information Technology' of the spiritual ideas.

In the twenty century, we have witnessed something unprecedented in the history of mankind: the advent of global mass communication. No longer are we subjected to the confines of our given town, state or country. Instead, through the advances of modern technology, we are able to receive data from almost any place on the earth instantaneously. The growth and ease of international travel on the wings of today's super jetliners has likewise brought the world even closer for the welfare of the man, but certain political forces like *BSP, BJP, Indian National Congress, CPM, CPI, Forward Block, Akali-Dal Badal groups*, etc., are the problem created in the life of man, they must be crushed with the power of *'Nam'*, and later on *'Nam'* should be entitled the caption of the modern society or modern world "Information Revolution"[10]

Since 1995, the World Wide Web (www) has become of the fastest growing communication systems in history of man. Consisting of an expanding pool of "pages" created by companies, associations, and individuals, it is accessible to anyone connected to the internet as God and man. Two features of the web make it appealing to God and man itself for the '*quest of light*'. The first is the non linear method of presenting information known as "*hypertext*". This enables users to jump between documents of subject – related material at the click of the mouse to see the world as a whole at one time. The second is the multimedia format of Web pages which can be designed using sophisticated graphics, sound, and animation or living view of the life, and displayed on – screen by a program called a "graphical browser". Since the development of the browser, the Web has become more sophisticated and easier to use and interest in the www, three wonders of the '*Nam*' will be exploded for sake of revision of Indian history by the '*Chamar Dynasty*' of the period.

The Internet and the Web Sites

The Berners –Lee, the physics researcher who first conceived the Web sites in 1989, compared the internet and the Web to the difference the brain and the mind; where the Internet is the physical method of communication and the Web is the information itself in the computer. A Web site is a communication of linked documents stored on a single computer, anywhere in the world. Sites can be linked up to each other using "hyperlinks". There are millions of pages available on the web and graphical browsers, such as Netscape Navigator, provide a window to the Master in the computer screen on which these pages are displayed in fine detail Keyword searches can be performed using a facility called "search engine"; particular topics can be explored using directories called "subject trees" and specific pages can be accessed by typing the exact address, or URL (Universal Resource Locator). Other browser tools include "history lists", "hot lists", and "book marks".

Choice and Variety on the Internet

Children's Web Sites: From finding a pen-pal to linking up to the educational resources, the Web provides information, education, and enjoyment for children.

Commerce on the Web: Placing sites on the World Wide Web is becoming an increasingly popular marketing strategy for many companies around the world to see the actual position of the business.

Music Pages: Musicians of the *'Nam'* called *Chamars* are able to present themselves and their music of the *'Nam'* to the public; and fans can find more information on the Scientific Revolution according to their favourite bands.

News and Informations: Many newspapers and magazines now have regularly updated online editions such as the U.Ks Daily Telegraph.

Hypertext and Hypermedia

Using a formal called hypertext or hypermedia, web documents contain links to other pages of the latest text, pictures, sound recordings, or videos, which can be activated by clicking on highlighted or underlined text and picture icons of the man, known as "hyperlinks" or "hot-spots" in history. These links are created by the programming language of the different countries called HTML (Hyper Text Mark-up Language), which also defines how the text and graphics will appear on the page of the human history called head and mind. This Web site, called "Virtual Sun" as Lord on earth, authored by a graduate student in Astronomy at the University of Amsterdam about the non-linear organization of information allows user to pursue areas of particular interest in the history of man, and a page can contain direct links to several other pages of related information, as well as other Web sites of the present man. The welcome page (the first screen) usually contains an introduction or a contents list of the subject. Web pages can contain clips of film, animation (living being) and sound (which are why hypertext is now often referred to as hypermedia of the *'Nam'* or God in the context of Internet). URL or Web page addressed system Netscape browser menu contains navigation buttons on earth and it embedded beneath hyper links hotspots lies a command to get the relevant document or "node" of the life. The contents of the system many Web sites are illustrated with colourful programmes in graphics manner.

Universal Resource Locator (URL)

Prefix http:// (hypertext transfer protocol) indicates a Web site or page is being accessed through the study of the system to locate a particular folder and file of the system as it is called http:/ / *www.astro.uua.nl. / michielb / sun / kaft.htm.* commands browser to look for Web pages stored at this computer and find out the file of the name of original Web page follows as under:

1. Web page broken down into packets of binary data for transmission.
2. Data is sent to destination via the internet system to see the global picture.
3. Web page is downloaded into user's screen of the man that is called mind and heart.
4. Packets of binary data are translated into a readable message of the 'Nam' or God on earth.
5. Analog audio signal received and converted into binary data via modem of exchange where stand the reality of life.[11]

The Surface of the Sun or Solar Flames Through Scientific Study of '*Nam-mantra*' Theory

The surface of the Sun or Solar system have been put forth by some scientists that 'life is scattered throughout the universe' is neither based on laboratory tests nor on observational data. In fact, this problem is beyond the scope of laboratory tests unless some material culture from the outer space (*Akasa*) i.e., beyond our galaxy is brought here for tests called *dosa* a kindness love of the Father as a 'Noble and Holy One' called '*Nam*' on earth. Under the present circumstances, it is important to note that number of his follower's wants to leave free India as a Greater Power of the world. Alternatively, this problem could be solved by observers in an observatory life of the man that God is watching every moment of the life, that is way most of the scientists are busy to find out the scientific evidence[12] in the idea of man that man has always been curious to know the origin of life and its concept. Some have even suggested that the life could have been brought to Earth from Heaven by extra terrestrials! For example, *Eric Von Daniken* suggested this in Charities of the Gods, which he wrote around forty years ago that '*Science is History*' as God and man work together. Similar suggestion was made by *Sir Fred Hoyle* and *Prof. N. Chandra Wickremasinghe*, scientists with impeccable credentials, in 1970s. The propounded the '*Panspermia*' (meaning 'seed everywhere') theory with maintains that life evolved out of a primordial soup, which got dispersed into cosmos through comets and meteorites. Life began on Earth, when some of this landed on it. However, many mainstream scientists just laugh it out. An obvious reason for this is that the conditions conducive to existence of life and its propagation as available on Earth are not there elsewhere; one of these being the temperature factor of the life to find out the Truth where it stands. But the telemetry data and images of Titan, the Saturn's largest Moon; being sent by the Cassini spacecraft, may change our thinking.[13]

J.D. Bernal's first formal research work was done at the Davy-Faraday Laboratory under Sir, William Bragg under the title of '*Science in History*'. This research work has touched all aspects of Crystallography, notably instrumentation, symmetry groups and the structures of all kinds of material including skeletons of the man. He has examined increasingly complex biological materials and has made fundamental contributions in the development of Science and Society. More recently; he has made great synthesis in the fields of the origin of life and of the solar system. He directs a laboratory, the interests of which include the structures of industrial products to check in history. He has always been concerned with past, present and future history in *Chamar* and its social implications[14] expresses that history is going to change.

The Role of the Amateur in History

As we know the Archaeology, Palaeoanthropology are the discipline as also a method enabling historians to study the facets of the '*Human Cultures*' of by gone Ages for which there had not survived any record pertaining to written material where from we conduct the interviews of the man to collect the historical evidence to write down a factual history of the areas as we take the example of 'Jammu Region' that its ancient documents have been destroyed for the human history of the ages in this context 'Archaeology' and "Palaeoanthropology' played a very scientific role to reconstruct the past history of man; rather these subjects were to a great extent the product of a cadre of dedicated amateur to the study of man and mankind's, who, however crudely, had long been digging back into prehistory on their own times. Dr. R.C. Majumdar, therefore, admits in his writings that the literary genius of India found in *'Chamar Family'* of Jammu and Kashmir State and destroyed by idiots *Motavis* and *Kashmiri Pandits* for the sake of money-matters. Therefore, physical evidence is important to crush the idiot historians like Irfan Habib, Shrimali, etc. They destroyed the records of *Dalit Kings* like the poets of Jammu and Kashmir State under mentioned above. Educated people from all walks of life, some had made discoveries that were of great significance[15] like art actoress Sabana Azami and others. So far as *Nanak's bani* about the existence of life through out the cosmos is concerned as he said; "by truly believing in God's name the knowledge of all sphere (in this universe) is acquired.[16] It is imbued with *'Name'* or *'Nam'*, the neutral gains of the knowledge of the three worlds"[17] i.e., God and man, than Universe is there.

Man's Place in Nature

John Frere (1740 – 1807 A.D.), an English Archaeologist, played a vital role in the Scientific Research, first of all, he founded hand axes in undisturbed nature started from the strata in a brick –field in Suffolk and he recognized them as being of human origin. In 1797, he wrote to the *'Society of Antiquaries'* ascribing them to "a very remote period indeed, even beyond that of the present world". A landmark in pre historic research, his letter were promptly forgotten,[18] he reconstructed the history of modern Europe in the prehistoric concept as a living man of the history like Dr. *Raj-Rishi*. Boucher *de Perthes* lead, *Lyelly* studied tool-rich layers in the 'Somme Valley' and argued that they were at least 100,000 years old man. *Charles Lyell* (1797–1876 A.D.) advanced this theory in *"The Geological Evidence for the Antiquity of Man"* now it became a classic study of the man in the of England. Thus, the Lyell's great work on geology was published between the 1830-33 A.D. Among its readers was a young man named Charles Darwin, who, in another 26 years, was to publish an even more shattering book, *"On the Origin of Species"*. Like *Lyoll, Darwin* organized a great amount of evidence[19] to provide the history of pre-historic man in new form called *'Boucher do Perthes'* in the history of England. Darwin was also extremely immature in study and the evidence he used to support his theory the origin of human beings took place from plants and animals; but he did not include man, because every activities of the plants and animals, are also limited in man's itself as their deeds and actions display such type of characters. Therefore, it is essential for the Master to provide them the same status and power like dogs and animals. His book was followed in 1871 A.D. by another *Darwin's* concept, '*The Descent of Man*'. Both were widely misunderstood for the time being, but with the passage of time book came into existence even some scientists they worked on it and came into the conclusion; 'Light will be thrown on the origin of man and his history'.[20] One who examined it was the renowned German anatomist-anthropologist *Rudolph Virchow*. He promoted his study in fossil human of primitive *Java* man, who now bears the scientific name of '*Homo Erectus*', a '*Peking man*', each given him Latin name, a delightful man of the God's race relative dating is based on the fact that strata get older as one goes down to earth for the study of '*Nam*' as a limited knowledge in human history as '*Word in World*'. Thus, a find made in an upper layer is younger than one from a lower layer. Absolute dating, i.e., age in actual years is made by Chemical and radioactive methods of the '*Name*', such as Carbon – 14[21] are there. Thus the water table under the great northern plains of China is falling every year. The aquifer under the American mid west is falling four feet every year. The same is happening in India and Pakistan, the water aquifer is a community bank of the *Sudhra Family* making a account sheet upon which every one's life depends[22] on this earth, but the '*Brahminical Ideology*' is working very harmful to destroy the man to polluted pesticides found in number of goods material. Therefore, it is necessary to note man's place in nature is dangerous for the life.

Nature's Timepiece

In the study, we learn that most of the elements found in nature are mixtures into 'History' as a 'Creative Power' of several isotopes '*Word*' or '*Nam*' atoms that are chemically identical with man but have different atomic weights as God and Man. Some of these isotopes, such as the ones listed above in the 'History in *Chamar* - A Scientific Discovery' in the man. They are radioactive; that is, they emit nuclear particles and gradually disintegrate into other elements as 'Brahmin' and '*Chamar*', these to opposite forces working in this universe. For instance, the radioactive isotope carbon-14 disintegrates into Carbon-12 and nitrogen gas. It shows from the study that each radioactive isotope has its own fixed rate of decay as human's life, expressed by the term "half life", *Chamar* the time required for half the atoms in a sample to disintegrate. Therefore, if one knows an isotope's half-life, it is not hard to calculate the age of a specimen '*Word*' or '*Nam*' simply by measuring how much of the isotope is to be left behind in the study because of the human knowledge is incorrect in the study of history as '*Nam*' on earth.

This is basis of many of the dating methods of science is using to find out the absolute age of fossils like *Surinder Kumar Megha* of Law Department, University of Jammu. He has fossil bearing deposits, but hesitating to show them that 'I am *Megha*'. Above is a chart of eight which know the methods and history of fossil along with the materials to which they are applied into their characteristic half-lives, and potential time ranges[23], i.e., the Master of the '*Nam*' called *Deepit Raj*. In human society, it has been observed that preoccupied with physical things, or if the biological considerations dominate the issues of life, because of their wrong notions, then it will be at the cost of the scientific, aesthetic and intellectual excellence of life is within the body of *Chamar* (made of skins) and other elements of the life, i.e., 'Spiritual Knowledge', as well as 'Spiritual Law'. Thus the Scientific Spiritual Law' is the 'Supreme Law' as '*Nam*' or God on earth to regulates all the other Laws like abolition of Dowry, Property Right, and those disobey Him, they must be destroy as a wasteless material on earth, there are certain dimensions of the human personality each representing a law, and all together, forming the interpenetrating whole '*Chamar*' an ancient Buddhist the man of history, who is working just for the human Civilizational growth, and thrives i.e. *Baba Gurinder Singh Ji, Biaswale, Dr. Raj Kumar* and *Master Deepit Raj*, when all the laws function together in the interest of man in all his dimensions, i.e., social, political, economic and religions are in harmony, life becomes an unfolding adventure into Reality[24] as peace shatter by Brahmins into different quarters of the world community as whole in human by piecemealing engineering cutting the society on the basis of caste, colour and creed. In that case *Namrupa paccaya Salayatanam* depends on the psycho-physical aggregate, the six bases (that is, the five physical sense organs and consciousness as the sixth) arise[25] to find the faults in history as *'Nam'* use to check it in progressive manners from one period to another period as from Dark Age to Enlightened Age; and modern humans being belong to the Mammalian order of Primates, became dangerous for the present man of the history, he is interested to serve the society and the Brahmins of the period, they came in India as tourist collecting the money with illegal resources like tuitions, etc.

Examples of Snakes[26]

Snakes are creeping animals like Brahmins of the Indian history having backbone in the politics and dirty from the nature as *Gandhi* and *Jinnha* were there before the 1947 A.D. and India was divided on communal basis, cold blooded, powerful eyesight strong power of smell from them *Dr. B.R. Ambedkar* kept a distance to save His force i.e., called *'Untouchables'* or *Sudhras* to defeat the Brahmins at an appropriate time, whenever we think of poisonous animals, snakes are first to come to our 'Mind' as an evil force of the Father called *'Manmukha'* eating poison, delivering positions and crushing the innocent people of the Father. Other deadly animals are spider, who comes under their guideline, they also become small snakes like *R.K. Chadda, R.K. Gupta, Rajesh Kanth, Jagdish Lal*, and others. Snakes are mentioned in our ancient literatures' like *Mahbharata* and *Ramayanas* found in different places of the world. There are 2500 species in all over the world. 500 species are Venomous i.e. 20% of the total species. In India, there are 260 species including BJP, Indian National Congress, BSP and other heads of the political parties and their worker, they are in millions.

According to the study of Peterharline, U.S.A. in 1971, it has been confirmed tat snakes also received air borne vibration via their lungs as *'Nam'* takes in the lungs a blasting message of the God or *'Nam'* on earth. Tongues area strong took for them to picking up scent particles from their study, they always ready to cut the *Sudhra* people of the *'Nam'* by exploiting them in men and material for their own benefit. Tongues area strong i.e., tool for picking up scent particle from air a special kind of message and on ground they come for the transforming of the *"Jacobson's"* organ which is not control by them. They are very cold in their metabolic spell and sluggish whereas during hotter spell, they were known torpid, dehydrated at one time and then die to come in another life with their deeds and actions. Among the venomous species, there are only four land snakes i.e., *Cobra, Krait, Russell's Viper* and Saw scaled in the form of man like *Dr. Raj Kumar, Baba Gurinder Singh ji Biaswale, Dr. Ram Dass and Master Deepit Raj* which account for 98% of the total bites by the snakes at present time and 20%, they are working as unbited as they are think about 90% they are working on the caste-base factors, they express, we are superior race of the world and else are degraded. The feed of these human snakes is '*Word*' who control the entire system of the world and one time they kept in store feeding for several months to study the '*Nam*' as an entire mechanical controller of the world system as WWW.Com of the computer required early in the morning for the adventurous race called *Chamars* on earth.

Sharks and Jawless Fish

Sharks and dogfish are small in numbers divided into different groups called *Chondrichthyes* class and another group is called super class fish named as *Gnathostomata* (meaning "Jawed Months"). Also sometimes known as elasmobranches, sharks and their relatives have a skeleton made of cartilage (hence their common name as cartilaginous fish of the big pond like sea). These characteristics are typical as man born having bony fish include a swim bladder, which functions as a variable – buoyancy organ of the man, enabling a fish to remain a fish, but his or her effortlessly at whatever depth is there in the sea, she is swimming, she is swimming nobody can hold her without the bail. A relatively thin than that of the fish, and her bone like scales; a flap (called an operculum) covering the gills; and paired pelvic and *pactrol* fins. Scientifically, bony fish belong to the class of *Ostrichthyes*, which is a division of the super class *Gnathostomata* already mentioned as "jawed mouths" in the history of man and God as a study of the natural instinct.

Breathing Process of the Fish

Fish "breathe" by extracting oxygen from water through their gills, but at the level of the land she dies, because this process is limited up to the watershed of the sea or pond. As, we take the example of the man, who use to take bath daily and worship the self style god, that he is great like Brahmin, why the fish is deprived form this matter, she always lives in water, without water she can not live on earth. Study shows that Brahmins has false propaganda of the '*Nam*', they became businessman over here by collecting the money from the innocent peoples. So far the breathing of the fish is concerned, she is sucked in the body through the mouth; simultaneously as God and Man on earth, the opercula close to prevent the water from escaping the Father as an approach of the '*Nam*' that God resides in the human body not elsewhere in the history of man. The mouth is then closed for the worship of the Father, and muscles in the walls of the mouth to meditate the 'Nam-mantra', pharynx, and opercula cavity also contract to pump the water inside the body over the gills and out through the opercula. Some fish rely on swimming with their mouths open to keep water flowing over the gills as '*Nam's* power flow from the body across the worldly life to find out the truth in history that is resided inside the body not in the outer worlds. They have the number of varieties known as Mandarin-fish (*synchiropus splendidus*), Oceanic Seahorse (*Hippo Campus Kuda*), Angler-Fish (*Caulophryne jordani*), Lion-fish (*Ptero's volitans*), Sturgeon (*Acipenser sturio*) and snowflake Moray EEL (*Echidna nebulosa*) produce the eggs for the betterment of the life who to change the system of the 'Universal Truth' by melting snow from the peak and to spread the terror in the human life as a dangerous species of the animals who bring change in the study of the earth and the man itself as a mediator of the God and man to help for the establishment of the uniform system in the world as a dynamic approach in his study as '*Nam*' has its history.

Besides this, there are certain other characteristic of cartilaginous fish are extremely tough in study as '*Nam*' is tough for the human beings that without pious approach one can not understand his beauty. It has not tooth-like scales, and lack of a swim bladder, but it has the broad base prospective as God and man have the unlimited knowledge. Jawless fish called 'infinite' like value called lampreys, and hagfish called *Chamars* like definition are primitive as '*Ravidas Culture*' of the world as stream of the life having eel-like fish that make up the order of the *Cyclostomata* [meaning "round months" like 'Infinite' or zero (0)], a division of the super class *Agnatha* (meaning "without Jaw", work do without hands in the '*Word*' script called Scientific Study). In addition to their characteristic round the world, sucker like mouths and lack of jaws, here the '*Bani of Nanak*' and Babar is suitable in Indian history, do without eyes, do without walk, heard the message of God without ears, as cyclostomes also have smooth, slimy skin without scales, and unpaired fins[27] of the life as God and man or *Chamar* and Brahmins work an opposite force in this universe, even though they have the same features of life, but the difference is that Brahmin is a self-style force and God is a universal operator suckled from the 'inner lips' of the '*Nams*' having internal anatomy of a female dogfish in the history of man to repeat the history, time and again on this earth as a survival interest of the man. Typical features of the adult frogs and toads include a squat body wit no tail, long, powerful hinds legs; and large, often bulging eyes similar to man. Frogs undergo complete metamorphosis. Eggs (*spawn*) are laid in water and hatch into young tadpoles which have a tail shrinks. Eventually the tail disappears, resulting in a young adult frog[28] like man's tissues.

Birds and Animals

Birds and animals are our feathered friends in human history as '*Nam*' and '*God*'. Their fastness, flights and feathers and legs are fascinating in human life to keep the environment intact of a wonderful society or a welfare state, although, they evolved from more ferocious dinosaurs, yet they are elegant, graceful and enchanting in the life of man. They help us in numerous ways for the controlling of pollution and carried messages during the ancient times as a messenger of the God in peaceful manner as a symbol of the historical man of the life. They pollinate red flowering trees and bushes of the God, dispersal their seeds from one place to another, enhance seed germination, devour away insect pesticides, form crucial links in the food chains and decorate over green surroundings[29] as imaginary birds and animals. The ability to fly the bird is reflected in the study of the '*Nam*', they brings the massage of the masters time and again to cool down the crisis from the Heaven on earth. They have been classified in the typical features called as fore limbs modified as wings; a streamlined body; and hollow bones of contention to reduce the weight of the man into automatic ways to keep the health active and busy in work after attaining the Spiritual Knowledge of the Father as a proof of the beauty. All birds and animals beak and feet vary according to diet and way of life. A simple man having simple diet and linear man has linear diet, sometime he becomes filthy, therefore, it is necessary to keep him under control, why unnecessary eating more and more, no body is there to ask you, then God land, he takes the notice of that and strike them give my loan along with interest, then it will become difficult to answer to the man of such stature. Beaks range from general purpose types suitable for a mixed diet as God use to strike his test during the time of mixed society as this diet to check the unnecessary burden of the earth and Brahmins from the orthodox nature must be punished in the hell; and those of thrushes, for example, to types specialized for particular foods called *'Nam'* on earth such as the large, cured, sieving beaks of flamingoes and their feet range from the webbed "paddles" of ducks, to the talons of bird of prey. Plumage also varies widely sometimes they were used in Kashmir history as ear ornaments to listen the message of the Father, and in many species the male is brightly coloured as *'ranga'* or *'Nam'* in the life of man. They are in numbers called as male Tufted duck (*Aythyafuligula*), white stork (*ciconoa ciconia*), male ostrich (*struthio camelus*), male kestrel (*tinnunculus*), and common Black headed Gull was called (*larus ridibundus*). Moreover, the primary flight feathers are called *primary remiges* and secondary flight feathers are called *secondary remiges*.[30] Thus, in this way the greater wing converts in major wings to fly other the world to collect the message of the *'Nam'* or God from the different quarters of the worlds to repeat the history of man and God itself.

Doves are peace loving birds. But the birds and animals life on international level became critically endangered due to the Brahminical Ideology pollution in the society and there are certain birds known as White rumpled Vulture, Indian Vulture, Slender billed Vulture Siberian crane, Forest Owlet, pink headed duck and Himalayan *Quait*. In addition to this birds like *Bengal Florican*, Swamp Florican, *Hodgson's Bushchat,* Grey crowned *Prinia*, Brisflecf Grassbird, Great Indian Bustard, Finn's Weaver are listed as threatened by these black forces called idiot Brahmins. Before it is too late, let us collaborate with join hands of the of our feathered friends fur their welfare in natural beauty and for the survival of the man[31] itself.

Insects, Sponges, Jellyfish and Sea Anemones

As per the scientific history is concerned that '*Nuclear Magnetic Resonance Spectroscopy*' is a non-destructive powerful technique investigated by man itself for the welfare of the community. It has the structures, motions, and reactions of molecules. Its usefulness is based on the fact that nuclei are not unfeeling point charges. They have individual properties which make them sensitive to the internal electro magnetic fields called '*Nam*' inside the body as a small molecules of the Father in Spiritual form. The only nuclei that exhibit the NMRS phenomenon are those which are greater than zero (O). The nuclei of many elemental isotopes as surveyed from the Archaeology and Anthropology sciences that man have a sin ('1' 'ego') against the Father as a cheap man of the History and Chemistry is powerful subjects in electrons and protons to produce the energy for the welfare of the man, but during the 20th to 21st centuries, there is a lot of development in this field, but failed to achieve its objectives that how a solace should be given to man, but it is not invested in the laboratory, but it is invested in the man's life itself. Isotopes interest and use to organic chemists are 1H, 13C, 19F and 31P, all of which have 1 = ½,[32] which reveals the Scientific Truth is not in the laboratory, but it is invested in the '*History of Chamar*'.

As we take the example of *Mughal* period, there was a lot of development in the Science and Technology and western astronomy brought to India by them for the study of '*Nam*'. They signed a zodiac trade, the seven days week, the hour, and several other ideas of the NMRS. Thanks to their achievements in mathematics Indian astronomers as mentioned by *B.S. Komal*, in his study linear formula of the life and Metric System is the advancement of the knowledge in human history. As early as the 7th century A.D., the Syrian astronomer *Severus Sebokht* knew of the greatness of Indian astronomy in Kashmir history that *Chamars* were the founders of this 'Idea' and then Caliphs of Baghdad in the form of *Dr. Ram Dass* employed Indian astronomers outside the India to spread the message of the Mission that '*Nam*' has been established a threat for them who do not believe on the present Living Master of the period. On word of the terminology of medieval European Astronomy, aux, the highest point of a planet's orbit, is certainly borrowed from the recent study of the Sanskrit *Ucca* through Arabic messages of the God that God is One and Man is One, where there is difference between the two aspects, because one believes and another does not believe. Now question rises, who will resolve the dispute, it depends on the Master's thought that is '*Voice of God*', (*Master Deepit Raj*) man of the '*Chamar History*'.

Like all primitive astronomers, Indian were restricted owing to ignorance of the telescope; but methods of observation were perfected which allowed very accurate measurement and calculations were aided by the decimal system of numerals to minimize the error in the statement or on the days of the Judgment. Their sole meaning was to observe the Indian Knowledge particularly the *Brahmins* who think themselves we are supreme on earth. It has been known from the study that in ancient India there were seven planets (*graha*): (1) Sun (Surya, Ravi), (2) Moon (*Candra, Soma*), (3) Mercury (*Budha*), (4) Venus (*Sukra*), (5) Mars (*Mangala*), (6) Jupiter (*Brhaspati*), and (7) Saturn (*Sani*). The names of these planets had many synonyms, some of which were evidently borrowed from the Greek, e.g. *Ara, Ares*, or Mars. To these *grahas* two more were added known as *Rahu* and *Ketu* in the ascending and descending modes of the moon. At the "Churning of the Ocean"[33], milk is coming out form the study where Brahmins stands in 'History' and *Chamars* are going to repeat the history of the world with the powers of '*Nam*' a '*Reality*' over the '*Black Power*'.

A spinning charge magnetic field called '*Nam*' on earth which is connected to every bit of the knowledge. The resulting spin–magnet has a magnetic moments in history in U-form as proportional to the spin cord exist +½ and -½ as these number differs in composition, same is the case found from the 'Brahminical Ideology' as a negative force to damage the society with Blind Faith. Inductive Effect into Electronic Density of the group is attached to atom and it become an atom-bomb in the mankind's history. Hydroxyl Proton Exchange and the influence of Hydrogen-Bonding[34] is not effected on earth, because, they have the little bit of Spiritual Knowledge of the Father. Sometimes, it can be multiples in the association of man and its organizations, they shift the ideological identify of the '*Nam*'s fashion.

Now, we come to the word '*Insects*' refers to small invertebrate creatures, especially those with bodies divided into two sections as God and man. Insects, including beetles, ants, bees, butterflies, and moths, belong to the various orders in the class *Insects*, which is a division of the phylum *Arthropoda* has been took place. Its features are similar as in common to all insects called exoskeleton or external skeleton; they are composed of three pairs of jointed legs; three body sections (head, thorax, and abdomen); and one pair of sensory antennae. Beetles (order *coleoptera*) are the biggest one group of the insects, with about 300,000 species at one time (about 30 percent of all known insects). They have a pair of hard elytra (wing cases), which are modified from the front wings. The principal function of the elytra (wing cases), which are used for flying. Ants, together with bees and wasps, form the order Hymenoptera, which contains about 200,000 species. This group is characterized by a marked narrowing between the thorax and abdomen. Butterflies and moths form the order (Lepidoptera means "scale wings"). The separation of *epidopterans* into butterflies and moths are found about 150,000 species which are largely artificial as there are no features categorically distinguish from one group to another. In general, however, most of the butterflies fly by day not in night, because they do not like the blind to live in the life, they mostly live in the day light judgments, whereas most of the moths are have the night-flyers. Some insects, including butterflies and moths, undergo complete metamorphosis (trans formation form one life to another) during their life-cycle. A butterfly metamorphoses from an egg to a *larva* (caterpillar), then to a *pupa* (chrysalis), and finally to an image (adult)[35] transfer into the old one new takes place as a change in the aspect of life.

There is another species called sponges are mainly marine animals that make up the phylum *Porifera*. They are among the simplest of all animals, having no tissues or organs as '*Nam*' close this tissues in spiritual sense against the heavy lust of the sexual intercourse and maintain the character of the man, same idea has also been found in the animals. Their bodies consist of two layers of cells separated by a jelly –like layer (*mesohyal*) that is strengthened by mineral *spicules* or protein fibres. The body is perforated by a system of pores and water channels of the '*Nam*' called the *aquiferous system* as One water, One air, One fire, and there should be a One Father or Husband on this earth. But Brahmins as multi Fathers and husbands, unlimited chain. Special cells (*choanocytes*) with whip-like structures (*flagella*) draw water through the *aquiferous system*, one should have to obtain, thereby bringing tiny food particles to the sponge's cells. Jellyfish (*class scyphozoa*), sea anemones like *Sudhra* class called class of *Anthozoa*, and corals (also class *Anthozoa*) belong to the *phylum Cnidaria*, also known as Coelenterate. More complex than sponges, coelenterates have simple tissues, such as nervous tissue; a radically symmetrical body; and a mouth surrounded by tentacles with unique stinging cells (*cnidocytes*) found in '*Chamar*' the writer of this text. There are number of examples of Sea Anemones called Jewel Anemone (*Corynactis viridus*), an old man of the history, Parasitic Anemone (*calliactis parasitica*) having the idea of '*Ravidas Culture*' called '*Chamar Culture*' of the 'Nam' or God, Plumose Anemone (*metridicum senile*), study begins with New Thought as a twist for the future study. These varieties mostly found in the Mediterranean sea called *condy lactis* special, Green Snakelock (*Anemonia viridis*) old snakes of the '*Nams*', Beadlet Anemonia (*actinia equina*), Ghost Anemone (*actinothoe spyrodeta*) in English Words called Holy Ghost, and *sagarita elegans*[36] as the thought of the sea level depth in the study of the *Sudhra* Family of the '*Untouchables*' that one can not touch them without the *pure-thought* as an old concept of the human history.

Internal anatomy of a Jellyfish is based on stomach, filament, ectoderm, endoderm, radial canal, hood, *rhopalium, mouth, oral arm, subgenital pit, tentacle, mesoglea* and *Gonad* in historical terms reflect the message of God that we have to see the God as a prefect manners in the study of Zoology branch of knowledge. In addition to this, the *Sea Anemone* has also a beautiful characteristics called oral disc, mouth, sphincter muscle, mesenteric filament, incomplete mesentery, *Gonad*, basal disc or pedal disc, *pharyn gastrovascular* cavity, retractor muscle, complete mesentery, *siphonoglyph*, collar tentacle and *ostium* (mesenteric perforation[37]) are the basic elements in the study of internal process of the God and man.

Rabbits and Carnivores Animals

The mammalian order carnivore includes cats, dogs, bears, raccoon's, pandas, weasels, badgers, skunks, otters, civets, mongooses, and hyenas. The order's name is derived from the fact that most of its members are carryovers (flesh eaters). Typical features of the carnivores are reflected a hunting-life style; speed and agility; sharp claws and well developed canine teeth for holding and killing prey as God kill the idea of '*manmukh*' as a poison for the society, he is eating and delivering the message to the public as too, as poison, exploiting the people against the one another on the basis of caste and religious factors, and their carnassials teeth put forward as facing eyes kept from the good distance as a judgment in the history. However, some members of the order are bears, badgers and foxes, for example, these animals have a more mixed diet at the time of hunting as slower – moving than pure flesh – eaters[38] of the '*Nam*' as "*Nam*" do during the time of historical events for the establishment of '*New Society*' of the '*Chamar Dynasty of Kashmir*'.

Story of North American Oldest Known Primate

According to the report of National Geographic News[39], the animal is related to similarly aged fossils of the Primate of the very primitive relatives migrated in Southeast Asia from the North America and no settle in India in the North of Kashmir and working as their migratory birds and animals. Now they have been called *Ramapithecus Punjabicus* the single species and this came to be known as man's earliest ancestors of the man. It is interesting to note that the first human like primate, dated to 9 to 121 million years B.P., appeared for the first time in *Punjab* only. In 1932 *G.E. Lewis* discovered in the Siwalik Hills of Punjab (presently in Pakistan) now they migrated in the Jammu and Kashmir areas for the development of the 'History' as it shows from the right upper jaw fragment a recent discovery of the man called *Raj Kumar* and *Deepit Raj*, those having the same species as man and God. *Elwyn Simon* advanced the theory of that *Ramapithecus* represented the first step in the evolutionary divergence in human species now they are common hominoid stock that produced modern apes and humans in the history of Jammu and Kashmir State. *Simon's* theory was strongly supported by his student *David Pilbeam* in this process, they have been found in Jammu and Kashmir and it soon gained wide acceptance among anthropologists. The age of the fossils (about 14 million years) fit well with the then prevailing notion that the Ape-human split had occurred at least 15 million year ago. The first challenge to the theory came in the late 1960s from biochemist *Allan Witson* and anthropologist *Vincent Sarich*, who at the University of California at Berkeley, had been comparing the molecular chemistry of albumins (blood proteins) among various animal species, they concluded that ape-human divergence must have occurred much later than the dates for *Ramapithecus* (it is now thought that the final split took place some 6 to 8 million years ago, between the name *Brahmapithecus*. Thus, the name *Brahmapithecus* was dropped form the study of '*Nam*' and *Ramapithecus* was retained[40] for the development of the history as Lords on earth.

Characteristics of the Carnivores and Rabbits

Study shows different orders of mammals like Rabbits and Rodents, they have some common feature in external and internal anatomy like man and God. These features including chisel-shaped incisor teeth that grow continually and eating their faces to extract more nutrients from their plant diet as their pure habit in comparison with man and his habit. Thus, the rabbits and hares belong to the same order called *Lagomorpha* Characteristically, they have four incisors in the upper jaws and two in the lower jaw in comparison with man and God. Similar their powerful hind legs for jumping, forelimbs adopted for burrowing; long ears; and a small tail of the '*Nam*' is there for the listening of the music of the Father was sufficient to carry the message of the worldly information for the Revolution of the Information Technology in the history of man. Rodents make up the order *Rodentia*. This is the largest order of mammals, with more than 1,700 species, including squirrels, beavers, chipmunks, gophers, rats, mice, lemmings, gerbils, porcupines, cavies, and the capybara kind of species helped the man to retain the progress in study. Whereas typical rodent features including two incisors in each jaw; short forelimbs for manipulating food; and cheek pouches for storing food[41] for the welfare of the more species in the future course of action to develop the history of man and God, and the skull of a lion having different features called *zygomatic arch*, *coronoid* process, *sagittal* crest, occipital *condyle*, tympanic *bulla; condyle*, angular process, upper carnassials tooth (4th upper premolar) lower premolars, mandible, lower canine, upper canine, upper premolars, maxilla, nasalbone of the same kind and orbit of the period helped the man for the study of Father. Whereas the skull of a bear has a slight differences between the two, its main features are as *sagittal* crest, *occipital candyle*, *tympanicbulla*, angular process, condyle, lower molars, lower premolars, mandible, lower canine, lower incisor, upper incisor, upper canine, maxilla, upper premolars, nasalbone, upper molars, orbit and *zygomatic* arch[42] of the study in history called moleculars of the Father.

The Magic of Art

In the study, we learn that this occupational group called '*Chamar*' may be traced back to the very early times as already mentioned in the book. Tanning, *mla, mna* is also a spoken word in the *Rig veda*, and certain details of stretching and wetting hides probably refer to the process of manufacture of the soul at one time during the time of heaven. Ox-hides were used in the pressing of the *Somarasa* and ox-hides and antelope and tiger skins were used in sacramental and ceremonial rites[43] to repeat the history of man itself as a magical art in his life. The paintings and stone engravings[44] as the *sila* of the *Ravidas* working in this Universe. Most of the paintings of the migratory birds and animals like the horse and reindeer, herd animals like the aurochs and bison, or carnivores like the lion and bear, all of these affected the lives of Palaeolithic man in some way either as sources of food or objects of dread. By reproducing such beasts on the walls and ceilings of caves, these early artists were apparently attempting to gain power over them by known their objective feelings on earth as art historian, because their interest is likened with the '*Natural thought*', striving to ensure the fertility of the animals and to make them vulnerable to the hunters' spears[45] as God and man. Thus, a pregnant horse or any other kind of animal or birds gallops across the limestone ceiling of Lascaus type of system in this process. The slash marks above its shoulders may indicate spears drawn in for their magical effect[46] in this direction. Keeping in view, the process of the time, *Ravidas* possesses thinking about his faculty i.e., *Chamar* or *Untouchables*, they have been degraded by the upper class people they are the dirty people of the *'Nam'* or God. Thus, he started creating different objects according to his needs to check them, he created knowledge for the world. The power of thinking did generate in him a sense of good, bad, likes and dislikes. Thus, three processes worked together that is imagination, conception and creation as a natural thinker of the subject 'History', having different knowledge against the Brahmins as a positive force of the Father. He made different tools for hunting like *Rambi, Ar, Jamur*, *Banyang* for the tanning of the skins and for its beautification, Banyaning is beautiful tool for the extensioning of the leather in different manners like the scanning of the leather industry of the modern India, by producing beautiful articles of the leather goods like bags, belt, etc. called Buddhism in Tibetan language. Similarly, some objects depicting the aesthetic sense were also created by him like Professor *Raj Kumar*, *Baba Gurinder Singh Ji, Biaswale*, Master *Deepit Raj* and *Dr. Ram Dass* man of Veterinary sciences an experienced man of the field. These objects were not simply of material use, but gave a sense of pure visual pleasure as *Sudhra* by nature. The object which gives a sense of pleasure is a work generally called *'Art'*[47]. The word 'art' derived from the Latin words *'Ars'*, meaning 'skill'[48] of tanning the leather made goods as the body of the man and animals having the same meanings, but interesting thing is that he is a soul created in the history of man. May this story take you on a journey of exploration; a discovery of truth in all its simple wonder and delight may every child of every race and faith find inspiration from this book by reading its pages, they will find *Chamar* has insight Knowledge into our origins as a human species as the evidence of the origin of the man is concerned. The long journey of the Master's life and the wonderful finding of the Universal Truth may have been way back to our common home, long long ago which was lasted in the myths of the *'Brahminical Ideology'* created as a false notion of the man. It appears from the study that in the very beginning, there was God and nothing, but God. There were no skies or planets, seems, moons or stars. There was absolutely nothing but God or *Chamar* on earth.

Study demonstrates that God was a wondrous *'Ocean of Light'* called *'Love'*. In this Great Ocean of God, there were millions and millions of drops of light that were all fast asleep, because they had no idea how magnificent and shining God was there on earth. Each and every drop was a tiny part of the Big 'Ocean of God'. Each little drop of 'Light' was called a soul. One of those little drops is you!

After a while God willed the creation. He sent forth a wondrous luminous wave of 'Sound and Light' from his own being and made the entire creation from it. He made skies, planets, suns, moons, and stars. He made mountains, valleys and deserts, oceans, lakes, rivers and streams. The creation was majestic and beautiful '*Chamar*', but there were no living things in it to enjoy it.

So God decided to put on a play, using his souls as actor, and his new creation as the theatre! God is the Director, and He named his play, "Life".

Almost all of the souls wanted to be in his show, as God told them they could leave their home in the Ocean of Light and journey down to be performers in the theatre of creation. But there were a very few of the little souls that did not want to go at all because it depends on their deeds and actions. They wanted to stay at home with their Lord. But he told even these to go and enjoy being in his play, too, then he put a mark on each one of the souls that wanted to stay with him, and promised them that one day he would send certain messengers for them from the heaven and have them brought back to their Real Home with Him, but certain decided to stay over the earth, therefore, it is difficult for them to leave the earth as a 'Blind Faith' called 'Brahminical Ideology'. He told all the other souls that if they ever decided they wanted to come back Home again, He wanted mark them too, with the theory of '*Nam*' or *Chamar*. One day, through God's boundless Grace, He would help them come Home, too.

An so it was! According to the wishes of the Great Lord, all the little souls left their Real Home and drifted down through many splendid and magical lands until at last they were here, standing on the stage of this world we live in right now. The show was ready to begin!

The Great Lord gave every soul a costume to wear so that each little drop of light would be dressed to play its part in "Life".

The soul's costume is called a body which is made of leather or *Cham* or *Khal*. Every soul on earth has a body to wear. The length of time that a soul wears a certain body and plays that part in "Life", is called a "lifetime" soul or God on earth.

Some souls were given the bodies of plants. Some were given the bodies of insects and reptiles as already mentioned. The Great Lord gave some souls the bodies[49] of fish and birds. Some souls were given animal bodies like elephants, ungulates, amphibians, sharks and jawless-fish, molluscs, starfish and sea urchins, crustaceans, arachnids and mammalians of the primitive history of the man grasping in some species and transformed into different races and faith according to their own will. Thus, the *hominids* typically have large brains to check the system with airel message, and no tail. This group includes the apes called chimpanzees, gibbous, gorillas, and orangutans.[50]

And some souls were given the most wonderful body of all, *Chamar* the human body with their body costumes on, all the soul drops look different as idiot of the '*Nam*'. But underneath their bodies they are still the same little drops of light and love.

We all belong to the same family because we all have the same One Father, God, the Great Lord. We should always be kind, gentle and loving to every living being in the history of human being as this soul because a soul lives inside each one either there is a '*Brahmin*' or '*Chamar*'.

In addition to this, all the living things that we see in the world can be divided into five groups. If we could see them on a ladder from bottom to top, it has different aspects of life. Human are on the top step because we are able to understand that we are soul drops, not just actors. And because of a wonderful secret you will soon discover in the history of man where true faith stands, either in human or animals. Animals are on the fourth step. They are lower than humans because they are not able to realize the soul of the God at one time as in human form, their actions were transformed into motions as they were their in their nature. Birds are on the third step, though they are free to fly, they are less clever than animals.

Fish, Reptiles, Insects and Worms are on the second step. They are less claver than birds, and plants are down at the bottom. They are the lowest form of life. They cannot think and are rooted to one place as God depict His Light. Thus, in this way, soul is what makes the body alive, and able to jump and run and swim and fly! Over the world. When the soul's part in the play is finished, than there is a 'Dawn of Light' in the history of man, the soul leaves the body costume of the earthly material into trans-migratories changed the life of the man for the struggle of "Life" as its own concept to regain the power of the '*Nam*'.

But the Universal Soul never dies! Your soul is a radiant drop of God, so the real you lives forever! In the history of man to repeat the story of man as a Universal Truth'. Thus, the Soul of the Father never dies, it remains strike on earth for the survival of the man from one generation to another as from *Dr. B.R. Ambedkar* to *Baba Gurinder Singh ji, Biaswale* including his close friends like *Dr. Raj Kumar*, Master *Deepit Raj* and *Dr. Ram Dass* of the period of 21st century A.D.

Plants and Animals

In the study, it indicates that a North-west wind is blowing, and fires set by the hunters far up the Valley of Kashmir are sweeping the migratory herds before them history will speak truth that life of the man is endangerous that forest have been fired, elephants have been caught in the bog. On the left, wildly shouting hunters have fired the dry grass to the game from crossing the streams to solid ground, they have been reached to repeat the history itself on the basis of 'Nam' or God's theory that soul never dies, He comes to the universe time and again, to repeat His story. Therefore, to the right the elephants of the 'Nam' called *aja* are hemmed in the Valley of Kashmir by the steep sides of its surroundings, up which may be seen escaping a herd of more nimble footed wild hones like Sonia Gandhi and her follower, they are walking as black rat or mad rat of the nations. Some of the mired elephants may yet break loose, but once so heavy an animal becomes struck in mud up to its Knees, it is virtually helpless, she nothing know the knowledge of the spiritual world, who govern the whole system. The female in the centre, trying so desperately to free herself that she is Supreme being and at the same time it gives her young a helping prod to assist her in the doom's day. The hunters have only to wait to catch her; when she is will be dispatched in the other world with wooden spears and stones[51] to see another valley of the *'Nam'*, it is not meant for you. It is for the historians of the *Sudhra* Family who were the rulers of the Kashmir called *Chamar* in the human history and disliked by the Brahmins.

An account of Geology will have been found in the memoir of Father i.e., Master Deepit Raj by Mr. Richard Lydekker, *'The Geology of the Kashmir'* and *Chamba Territories* and *the British District of Khagan.*[52] Mr. Lydekker differs from Mr. Fredric Drew, also an expert in Geoglogy, not idiot like *Yash Paul Kundal* from G.G.M. Science College called H.O.D. *Chutya* from the subject study and egoistic man of the history collecting the money from the illegal resources as he has opened a prostitution centre in *R.S. Pura* and *Mira Sahib* in the area of ritual family where from *Meghs* have been born and became Brahmins of the 'Nam' who held that some of the gravels at *Baramula* were glacial origin from the primitive periods, indicating the existence of glaciers in the valley at a level of 5,000 feet, but he has no doubts as to their existence on the *Pir Panjal* range and in the neighbourhood of the various *margs,* or mountain meadows were surrounded by the *'Gujars* and *Bakarwals'* in the valley as the race of the Father, innocent people of the *'Nam'*. The question of the glaciations and the evidences of the relative changes of level within a geologically recent period is fully discussed in the Sindh Valley by R.D. Oldham in Records, *Geological Survey of India*, Vol. XXXII, part 2. The study of Zoology is helpful to human beings in many ways, and zoologists work in hundreds of careers. Since human beings and many animals of the areas have similar body parts and function like men, but is the different between animals and men, that man has to realize the 'Truth' a challenge opposed by Nature to man in the form of *Dr. Raj Kumar, Master Depit Raj*, and *Baba Gurinder Singh ji Biaswale*, and, opposite force called *'Mad Cow Disease'* and *'Mad Pig Disease'* as *Brahmins* and *Molavis*. To protect natural resources and minimize the harm of plant and animal population. Therefore, there is a great need to repeat the history of God and man; and there is a need of great healthy animals as already mentioned above Zoology, which is one of the two main branches of biology, is the science of living things. While Botany involves the study of plants, Zoology includes the study of any kind of animal, ranging from a 180-tonne blue whale to one-called creatures such as bacteria and several fields of Zoology involve in the study of structures or system of animals. These fields include embryology (the study of the development of individual animals), anatomy (the study of structure of the animal's body), and physiology (studying of living processes within animals). The main branches of the Zoology study are called herpetology, is the study of Reptiles, and amphibians and others. Ornithology is the study of birds, mammalogy is the study of mammals, ichthyology is the study of fish, and entomology is the study of insects. These are the major fields of Zoology involving in the study of animal behaviour. They include natural history of the God and man, for the evolution of the Indian history from one generation to another similar as man's life. Zoologists can work in this area of environment and ecology as a new plants of the animal study. Project tiger in India is essential for the Zoologists to control the World Wildlife as a specialists study of the God and man in this Universe. Forensic Science will be used for analysis of criminal evidences in the eyes of '*Law*' or '*Nam*'.

There is abundant evidence that igneous or volcanic agencies were actively at work, as is proved by the out pouring of vast quantifies of volcanic rocks; but these are not known to have been erupted since the Eocene period of the Indian history. Subterraneous thermal action is, however, indicated by the prevalence of numerous hot springs of the '*Nam*', they are waiting and watching the situation for the blasting of their secret methods that what part has been played by the spiritual knowledge of the man.

The following table of geological systems in descending order is given by *Mr. Ludekkar* for the who state of the Kashmir :

European Equivalents
Alluvial system:
Low-level alluvia, and glaciers chamar theory. Prehistoric
High Level alluvia, glacial, lacustrine, and Karovia
series 'Brahminical Ideology' Pleistocene
Tertiary system:
Siwalik Series (Outer Banda, Inner Rulers) Pliocene
Sirmur Series (Murree group 'Word', Sabathu group Chamar
Indus Tertiaries) MioceneEocene
Zasnkar System:
Chikkim series Visva Karma Cretaceous

Supra-Kuling series *Sudhra Family* Jura & Trias
Kuling series as Stream of life Canal road Carboniferous
Pir Panjal System: Pandevas
Not generally sub divided *Megha, Batwal, Barawals, Chura, Mahashah*, etc. Silurian Cambrian
Metamorphic System : Metamorphosed Panjals, and Other Coordinators-Central gneiss of *'Sudhra Industry'*.
Palaeozoic and Archaen

Under the first of these systems, *Mr. Lydekkar* has discussed the interesting question, weather Kashmir was once covered by a great lake, what it is the water of the *'Nam'*, who dry it and fill it up. In this discussion the *Karewea* already discussed plays an important role for the establishment of truth in way back to *'The Journey of Soul in Kashmir'* as already discussed in detail.

A full account of the 'flora and fauna' of Jammu and Kashmir', chapter No. IV. The valley has an enormous variety of plants, and the Kashmiri finds a use for most of them in the history of man called *Dr. Raj Kumar, Baba Gurinder Singh Ji Biaswale, Dr. Ram Dass* and *Master Deepit Raj* are the historical plants of human history visited time and again, in Kashmir as a rulers of the *'Sudhra Family'*. Among condiments the most important is the *Sira siyah* (carum special), or carraway under drugs, *cannabis sativa*, who always drinks the nectar of the Father, the hemp plant similar to cambel style, and *Artemisia* or *tetwan* may be mentioned the plants of the Fathers. *Asafoetida* is found in the Astor tahsil of the *'Sudhra Family'* during the time of *Rai Dynasty*, ruled at least 137 years in Kashmir after this 'Chamar *Dynasty'* of the *Karkota Family* established their rule in Kashmir as the follower of the Islam along with Prophet Mohammad of Kashmir, the founding father of the history of 7th century A.D., after the downfall of the Gupta period. Numerous plants were yielded dyes after the *Karkota* family called *Harsa, Kalsha, Didda, Sussal, Uchchala, Jayashima* and others, and tans, of which *Datisca Cannabina, Rubia cordifoliia,* and *Geranium nepalense* are the most families because they had the relation with *Napali* territories as *Dr. Karan Singh* and his wife. No doubt, Jammu and Kashmir was rich in fibres, and the people make great use of them from the time immemorial. The two are the best friends, i.e., *Abutilon Avicennae* and the *Cannabis Sativa* as *Baba Gurinder Singh*

Ji Biaswale and *Dr. Raj Kumar*. Burza (*Betuta utilis),* the paper birch, is a most important tree to the natives like *Dr. Ram Dass* and *Master Deepit Raj*. The bark is employed for various purposes, such as roofs of houses writing papers, and packing paper. Many of the ancient manuscripts are written on birch bark. The Kashmiri neglects nothing but only for the survival of man which can be eaten as fodder by the animals. The willow, the Indian chestnut like 'Nam's symbol the cotoneaster like *Dr. Ram Dass*, *Kabir* by nature, the hawthorns as *'Nam'* itself, and the popular are always lopped to provide fodder to the Father for cattle of the *'Name'* and sheep in the winter to the Muslims for the celebration of, *'Id'* as a destructive power of the *'Nature'* idiot of the *'Nam'*, exploiter of the Prophetic religion that is *'Islam'*, surrendering before God, they have forgotten and collecting the money from the illegal resources or from the malpractices of the *'Nam'*, look busy do nothing only to collect the money as a 'black power' for them.

Excellent grasses abound, and the swamps yield most nutritious reeds and other plants, virtually called 'fire' or we can say as thus nomenclature as 'fiery' owing to due to fiery-colour of leaves called *'Chinar'* in the history of Kashmir, a Persian derivative meaning thereby called as *'Chi+nar'*, *Chi* stands for good in the history of man, and Brahmins who believe on self style belief, not faith on God and, an *'egocentric'* man of the history. Basically, this beautiful plant have a majestic and indigenous, identify of Kashmir known as *Boin* in the folklore of the Kashmir, the picturesque and Kaleidoscopic beauty of the man in the history of Kashmir over the years have attracted the foreigners from Chinese and Western countries and they described it as the *'Paradise on Earth'*. The environment that surrounds the valley is unambiguously[53] because of the 'Brahminical Ideology' of the man after the independence of India, because they could not understand that Kashmir is a spiritual land of the Father and He was disturbed before the 1947's independence by the *Molavis* and *Pundits* that He is Schedule Caste man of the Indian history. He nothing know the reality of world as a 'Word' on the earth. Therefore, they must have to pay the price of the disturbed nature of the man as a Supreme Being at that time was *Dr. B.R. Ambedkar*, a man of the real history as *Chamar Guru*

Ravidas was on earth an old species of the man in the history of man.

Enchanting and enthralling greenery of the flower and fauna of Kashmir are called salubrious and lush green *Deodars* of the golden age of the human history of the Kashmir called *Deva daru* (anglicized into "*Deodar*"). The most conspicuous feature of this plant is the lordly teak, unanimously voted "king of forests" as God and man on earth and the "prince of timber". It is an indigenous variety of oak, which thrives best at a eight of from three to four thousand feet, and grows in continuous mosses, absorbing the nourishment of the soil so as not to allow any other three or plant to come up in its domain[54] as it is the highest one on the earth as God and man. Western Himalayas, admiringly named "*Tree of the Gods*", but it has valuable and majestic two forest Kings, i.e., *Dr. Raj Kumar* and *Baba Gurinder Singh ji Biaswale*, they are far eclipsed the eco-system, both in beauty and dimensions of the native tree, i.e., Brahmins or *mana*, which may be considered the most characteristic of the Indian vegetation and its surrounding atmospheric beauty. It belongs to the family of fig-trees, to which the soil and climate of India will have to change, are so congenial that it is represented, its different parts of the continent, by no less than a hundred and five varieties of the '*Nam*' called *Pandevas* on earth including *Ramiyan Bhardwaj, Amrit Bhardwaj, Amri Devi* (Amrita of the *Nam*), *Dr. Raj Kumar* and *Master Deepit Raj*. This particular variety, specially known as "Indian fig-tree" (*Ficus Indica*) in the form of *Baba Gurinder Singh Ji Biaswale*, surely may claim to be admired as the paragon not only of its own species, but of all vegetation without exception. It takes so influential and prominent a place in the "Life", both physical and moral, of India, and is, moreover, such a marvel of nature, that a description of it is not out of place even in a necessarily brief sketch, and we may as well borrow that given by Lassen in his monumental work called *Indische Atterthumskunde*.[55]

"The *Ficus Indica* is probably the most astounding piece of vegetation on the face of our earth. From one single root it produces a vast green temple of many halls, with cool like '*Nam*' on earth, shady bowers impervious to the light in the history of man, and seems a 'creative power' of the small plants and exclusively for the purpose of supplying shelter less primeval humanity with ready-made dwellings into houses of the man, and if it inspires the Hindus particularly to the '*Sudhra Family*' who were degraded by the man itself and their neighbours with a profound veneration, it is owing to the surpassing marvel of its well-high preternatural growth in the '*Nam*' and its indestructible during and everlasting self-renewal; to which traits the mysterious gloom of its galleries and avenues adds not a little but in broad sense as '*Nam*' or God; by yielding a most grateful retreat from the torrid summer heat of the Sun. The trunk or *tana* of the tree, at a moderate height from the ground, branches out into several stout limbs which stretch from it horizontally knowledge skill as '*Nam*' possessed in previous life from these, slender *shools* of the '*Deva daru*' tree called anglicized tree of the God the so-called "air roots" are concerned as '*Chamar*' of the society rise his power from bottom to top as '*Nam*' on earth in the absence of the Master. As the Central trunk or *tana* is concerned, is increases in height, it goes on producing tier upon tier of horizontal limbs, and these add row after row to the outer circler pillars through the air-roots of the papers, not indeed with perfect regularity, but so as to form a grove of leafy halls and verdant galleries multiplying '*ad infinitum*' of the '*Nam*' or God. In this way, the evolution of the natural plants takes place form one species to another incompletion with air roots of the Masters on earth as a new-breed of the Natural Theory. Such is the tree, more generally known under its popular name of *banyan* than under the scientific one of *Ficus Indica*. This name is supposed to come from the fact that the tree was carried westward by Hindu trades men called *banyans* like *Gnadhi* and *Jinnha* of the period. This accounts for its being found in places along the Persian Gulf, in parts of *Arabia* (Yemen) called *Dr. B.R. Ambedakar* a man of the history established his Kingdom in *Dekkan* in the native land emphatically called the Indian Continent concerned with table – land of the same, whereas *Gandhi* and *Jinnha* they sailed their land into inhumanic way to the countrymen of the period called the Brahmins and *Molavis*, and they made a trade against the Britishers earned more money, which became illusion of the man and the Indian National Congress as well as the Muslim League founded by *M.A. Jinnha*. How large indeed, can scarcely be realized without the help of the few figures who were absence from the minds that were *Sudhra* class of the Indian society deprived from the actual rights. Thus, Master of the earth i.e., '*Nam*', played a wonderful game to explore the truth where it stands, and today it is found that it lies in the *Sudhra* Community not others. What may be its ages, no one can tell in the history of man, but they have five hundred years are historically recorded know known as *Dr. Raj Kumar* and *Baba Gurinder Singh Ji Biaswale* were the rooted friends of the '*Nam*'. This is the *Ficus Religiosa*, very well known under its pretty native and popular names of *Ashvattha* and *Pippala* among Brahmins who worship them in the form of trees not man, because they are the Scheduled Caste and Scheduled Tribe of the period in the history of the Brahmins, hate with them. There[56] is an abundance of food-plants found in China and India. Though the Kashmir, "Tulip Garden' was 'dedicated' to the people of valley with the claims of being one of the largest Tulip Garden of Asia in the form of '*Nam*' itself. According to the recent survey on the map and inputs of the various organizations, China has the largest garden having more than three million Tulips of around 300 varieties which are in bloom at the Shanghai Flower Port in *Nanhui* district of eastern China boasts of 20 hectare Tulip Park, five times larger than the Tulip Garden of Kashmir which has 1.2 million Tulip of 60 varieties, UPA Chairperson, Sonia Gandhi, the follower of *Gandhian* philosophy having false claim over Kashmir, and China because they have no knowledge of the 'Creative Power' who is working in India as '*Nam*' on earth called *Deepit Raj, Dr. Raj Kumar, Dr. Ram Dass*, and *Baba Gurinder Singh Ji, Biaswale*, and *Baba Rasila Ram*.

Prehistoric Earth and its Changing Crust

In the study, we learn that natural resources are meant for mankind to provide energy to the man and has been exploited by the mans due his narrow mindedness in the history of man. The important natural resources are the fossil fuels used by man in his daily life, and crusted by him due to the lack of Sensitive Knowledge of the man's life in surroundings and in society to exploit it one or in other hands, by capturing the land in illegal way of life; with the process of the time, a challenge was given to these exploiters to protect the life of man, but due to the lack of sources and energy, he becomes helpless. Keeping in view, the exploitation of the men and matter by the clever minded peoples, nature will have to predict his theory in natural way as God is a Supreme being invested in man itself, but he never bothered for his activities and exploitation is there. Thus, the natural elements of the God also becomes exploiter at the time of false propaganda led by man against him, at that time earth formed from a cloud of dust and gas drifting through space about 4,600 million years ago to change the idea of man in crust form, change takes place one form to another as from childhood to olden age as a life cycle business of the man depends on the monsoon, and other natural objects of the life, dust, water, air, fire, etc. Dense minerals sank to the centre while lighter ones formed a thin rocky crust to repeat the history of the natural force as good has good ideas, bad has bad ideas. However, the first known life-forms the species of man from the bacteria of the earth form a 'New Natural Force' called '*Nam*' as infinite power of the earth as empty vessel of the '*Nam*'. On the other one, blue-green algae in the form of negative force of the man damage the man of the society and its sources based on practical life, but the life of the negative force is based on destructive vision in nature to exploit the man in the society by showing 'egocentric' approach in the history of man and he exploits the man by creating various barriers including superficial knowledge of tale-telling; did not appear until about 3,400 millions years ago, but was the blind faith of the man, with the historical progress, it was only about 700 million years ago that more complex plants and animals began to develop and its species. Since then, thousands of animals and plant species have evolved into the man's life. Thus, the man's life became more superior to the other life to keep the eco-system neat and clean for the protection of man. As soon as man started to exploit it in unnatural way, such as the dinosaurs, survived for many millions of years, while others died out quickly due to his good habits in the life. As we know Earth itself is continually changing the life of man and it is necessary for the man to change according to its rotational movement, man must have to change his ideas and thought, and some have the stick idea on earth that it can not move without their signal, it shows that dirty idea has been created in that race and faith. Therefore, due to the wrong pressure of the dirty gases, there is an exploitation of the natural resources. Although continents neared their present locations about 50 million years ago, they are still drifting slowly and gradually over the planet's surface but testing the soils, and mountain ranges of the forests such as the *Himalayas Chamar* or *Chinar* which began to form 40 million year ago, the life of man as *Shivji* on earth, are continually being built up his houses in the Kashmir Valley as an 'infinite' power on earth to visualized the history of man in direct and indirect form, as an active and inactive force of the life. As Fluorescent Lamps added the global warming explain the energy consumed sources, it is explained by the natural sources that is man of the history, who will express this idea about the destruction of earth system led by "ozone depletion" to explain to save the 'Humanity' as a natural source of the man, by serving the idea of the mankind in humanity sciences to serve man to man. While on the topic "Thermal Image-seeing in the Dark Age", as a blind faith of the energy and at that time *'Brain at Risk'* having physcosomatic diseases and B.P. to the average man of the life. Study shows at that time 'Leather industry of the man shrink due to the lack of salting in tanning the body as a natural phenomenon to protect the skin and its leather goods as a microbiology study of the viruses bacteria, ineffected in the algae, fungi, in animals plants. How these viruses attack over the man and its surroundings atmosphere to destroy the RNA and DNA tests of our bodies. In addition to this the use of the artificial satellites in the field of telecommunications and its advancement in rocket technology before the 19th century A.D. proved as harmful for the man, and in return we obtained the 'Global Warming' as it is explained in normal way it is called as 'increasing temperature of the earth' due to lack of natural resources like plants and animals, and its effects, there is a change in the climate to the global warming and the lack of interest of human species into wild life as well as in agricultural systems. Water is another natural resource exploited at a higher rate than that of the others and it has been considered to be the life line on the earth as God and man of the human history. It shows that water contents are important in life line of the history and should also be used judicially as an essential needs of the man for the purifying the clothes and other things. Moreover, waste water from the house domestic areas like society should be purified and then it can be used in the agricultural processes. Dumping of wasteage in the water bodies should be avoided to a maximum level that the future of the life of the man will become safe that it will remain safe for the life of man. As soon as plates start to move towards each other with pressure of earth, one may be subducted beneath (forced under) the other for the protection of the safety of the man itself under the sky. In mid-ocean, this causes ocean trenches, seismic activity, and arcs of volcanic islands take place. Where oceanic crust is subducted beneath continental crust or where continents collide, land may be uplifted and mountains formed. The processes involved in mountain building plates termed or genesis as a crustal movement on continents, as a result of the movement earthquakes, while movement under the seabed can lead to tidal waves in this process. There are three main types of mountains: Volcanic Mountains, fold mountains, and block mountains. Most Volcanic mountains have been formed along with plate boundaries where from plates have been together or move apart and lava and others debris have been ejected onto the Earth's surface. The lava and debris may have built up to form a dome around the vent of a volcano. Fold mountains are formed where from plates push together in the form of man like *Dr. Raj Kumar* and *Baba Gurinder Singh Ji Biaswale* and cause the rock to buckle upwards in the form of man as a natural idea of the man. Where oceanic curst meets less dense continental crust, the oceanic crust is forced under the continental crust. The continental crust is buckled by the impact of the political forces, who are problem created in the society by exploiting the natural force of the man itself. On the other side, society is forced to find out the truth behind the bar, in such conditions people from the low strata of the society; they are endeared to the natural force as the savior force of the nature, who are innocent from the idea as 'infinite' itself. This is how folded mountains ranges the idea of man in History for the future generation to protect the 'nature' as his life, such as the Appalachian mountains in North America, were formed as an idea of keeping in view, the above mentioned facts, that there is a great need to change the climate of the earth with pure water. Thus, the Earth has undergone a series of change in climate by melting the ice ages interspersed with warmer periods of the '*Nam*' (the most recent glacial period was at its height about 20,000 years age)[57] is going to prove the Spiritual Knowledge of the man which intact the history of man in uniform system as its crusts are the solid outer shell of the earth as egg of the hen's keep the structure of the life of the child for its survival. During the movement of earth, the crusts and the topmost layer of the mental form the lithosphere of the study. The lithosphere consists of semi-rigid plates that move in collaboration with other natural forces relating to each other on the underlying asthenosphere (a partly molten layers of the mantle). This process is known as plate tectonics and helps explain continental drift as man and God in symbolic reason as realization of the thought on earth. Were two plates move apart from each other there are rifts in the crust and gases leak out which were protected in the earth by testing the missiles and other atomic tests. In mid oceans this movement results in sea-floor spreading in widening way in continuously and the formation of ocean ridges; on the continents, crustal spreading can form rift valleys shape, a threat to the modern man for the protection of the earth will have to given to the founding Father of man's History. Fold mountains are also formed where two areas of continental crust meet, forces compelles to form a New Idea of the man in history. The Himalayas, for example, began to form an idea in the history of man as a repeating force of the natural theory as a strategic point from top to bottom when India collided with Asia as a single natural force of all the human species as there is plants, birds and animals, are in the surface crying for the social justice theory, everybody has equal right to live on this earth. In this way, History form an idea to explain the injustice of the man against the man, and buckling the sediments of the exploited race and faith takes new place in the history of man as an idea from his own body which is made of *cham*, tanning by the Father, at one time, when he was in the heaven as was the Director of the tanning industry. As soon as, he lands on earth certain political forces which are based on false notions without knowing the origin of the human species, they exploited the people become palpitate due to his scientific authority over the earth as a true natural force and the result was that certain parts of the oceanic crust take place between the two natural forces that is called negative and positive in natural sciences. As it is believed that positive force is the force of winning authority on this earth as good over the bad. For the time being block mountains of the natural forces are formed between them when a block of land is uplifted between the two faults as a result of comprised or tension in the earth as well as in the man is to be start the continuous movement of these two natural forces that is negative and positive crustal plants have been squeezed, stretch, or break rock strata, deforming them and producing faults and folds of the history of man where the fault lies either it is in natural force or in artificial force; punishment will be accorded.

A fault is a fracture in a rock of the *Ravidas* Movement along with his forces to repeat the history as a Dictator of the world. The movement can be vertical, horizontal or oblique (vertical and horizontal). Faults develop when rocks of the *Ravidas* Movement are subjected to natural forces of the theory to compression or tension without their history. They tend to occur in hard to leave the rigid rocks of the negative forces that is 'Blind Faith' of the political forces, which are more likely to break than bend into idiot manners. The smallest faults occur in single mineral crystals and are microscopically small, whereas the largest 'Word' the Great Rift Valley in Africa working as spy, which format between 5 million and 100,000 years ago '*Chamar* is more than 9,000 kilometers long working in this universe as a Master of the '*Name*'. A fold is a bend in a rock layer caused by compression[58] of the earth. Three hundred years or more ago, small bands of hunters were found roaming in Europe 'Word' probably members of the species Homo erectus, which at that time was widely distributed in Asia and Africa, stone tools of the *Ravidas* (*sila*), and animal bones found at two sites excavated by the author of this book in the history of man and God, reached Spain during the time of study to confirm the truth and it has been found and reconstructed in five paintings of the '*Nam*' in the *Ambrana* Valley of the Akhnoor. *Clark Howell* came upon a paper by this man called *Ravidas* of the period. The central concentration of bones, with the exception of two smaller tusks i.e., called God and man is found in reality as man himself in the history of man. Whereas the earlier investigators were also contented merely to catalogue their finds, such a meticulous study of the nature of the different sites of the earth makes it possible for experts to build solid theories about the activities of the Early Man[59] like *Dr. Raj Kumar* and his colleagues already mentioned above.

Movement of the Earth at Different Periods

The exposure of Piltdown man gave a dramatic emphasis on the movement of the earth at different periods on the study of basic fact of anthropological science in history to determine the age of the Early Man. The relative age of fossils is usually determined by references of the various authors who study this theory to confirming the historical truth of the Early Man from the deposits material of the life to Modern Man. But with the growth of atomic knowledge of the man in species, however, dating techniques were devised[60] by radio-carboning which could provide absolute age of the Early Man. Most important, their way of life was different from man to man and God to God in the development of the history. For example, from *Lord Buddha* to Gupta period, than Gupta to Modern period, number of saints and *sants*, they came in India for the development of the history with honest and dedicate approach to realize the truth in the life of man as an objective of the history which is lying in the man itself. As we take the example of various layers of the cave of the Early Man, like strata of gravel in a river bed, tell a rich story if they are investigated and analyzed carefully and their evidence is read right[61] found in the same area like Akhnoor in the history of Jammu and Kashmir, where from, a recent study on the '*Early History of Jammu Region*': (Prehistoric to 6th Century A.D.) expresses the same value as 'history repeat itself'.

Early Signs of Life

The theory of man's evolution around a storm of controversy in the Victorian world of India that many people denied even the fossil evidence of their primitive ancestry: others exploited the confusion with elaborate hoaxes.[62] However, this is also only a part of human history in Panjab and its adjoining areas. The hills of Punjab are in fact the cradle of Primates who are supposed to be earliest stages of Ape-man of the remotest ancestors of the humans. They are dated to 12 – 8 millions years ago. The fossilized bones of several species of these Primates named *Ramapithecus, Sivapithecus*, many more in variety, have been found in the *Siwalika* Hills of the Jammu and Kashmir State. It is significant to note that along with the fossilized bones of these Primates they are the bones of animals of the contemporary period of the Indian history which are now completely extinct in the '*Nam* or *God*'s theory and determine to repeat the history as *Baba Ravidas* did in the 15th and 16th century A.D., crushed the 'Brahminical Ideology' of the man which was created by man himself without Knowing any reasoning and logic of the scientific truth. Thus, their specimens of which are in the Punjab University Museum Chandigarh[63] for the study of man as a scientific research in the history of Early Man. Now the methods of investigation were increasingly refined, the doubter were silenced[64] as their 'Reserve' theory as Saints and *Sants*, keep in their mind, not Brahmins of the period, do less work, cry more. It shows that modern dating methods of the period from the fossil carbon-dating is more efficient as it was not exhibited in the ancient time.

Notes and References

1. J.D. Bernal; *op. cit.*, Vol. III, p. 703.
2. Arun Kumar Jha; *Chemical Industries in Ancient India* (From the Mauryan Era to the Gupta): An article published in Indian history Congress, 64th Session, Mysore; 2003, p. 122. **Note** : Author mentions that furnaces for smelting and forging of objects were known during their period. It lays down that the produce of various mines should be turned into articles of use in the respective workshops. It further mentions factories during their period was to be started for the manufacture of various articles of the living materials known as bitumen, copper, lead, tin, brass, steel, bronze, iron, trade in metalwork and leather of the period. In the *Amarakosa*, it is mentioned '*Word*' plasterer (mason), weaver, tailor, painter, sharpener of weapous (armourer), cobbler and leather worker (*Charmakara*), blacksmith, goldsmith; (*Banjara*) bangle-maker (from *chankskells*), coppersmith moulded the material matter alike of the period. It shows that there was an advance metallurgical skill of the art and cultural development in the history of science and society (Ibid. p. 123).
3. D.H. Udall; *The Story of Life*; London; 1968, p. 30.
4. Published in the Memories of '*Huzur, Maharaja Sawan Singh*', Beas; Reprint; 1989.
5. Published in the Memories of '*Maharaja Charan Singh*', Beas, 1972.
6. *Ouest for Light*, p. XV, Introduction.
7. Ibid., pp. XV-XVI.

8. A.L. Basham; *The Wonder That Was India'*, Delhi, Reprint, 2003, p.488.
9. Ibid., p. 322
10. *The Dawn of Light*, p.3.
11. Dorling Kindersky; *op. cit.*, pp. 46A-47A.
12. Dr. Vasdev Sharma; *op. cit.*, p.116.
13. *Science Reporter*; December, 2004, p. 5. Hereafter cited as S.R.
14. J.D. Bernal; *op. cit.*, Vol. III.
15. F.Clark Howell; *Life Natural Library*: *Early Man*; Nederland; Reprint; 1970, p.23. **Note**: Authored has become the outstanding representative of that breed of anthropologists who were able to synthesize data from many fields from the earth sciences like Archaeology, Anthropology and Geographical conditions of the areas, keeping in view to located the sites of the '*Nam's* or God's who earlier resided Spain and Africa, Europe and the Middle East, and participated in many International Conferences on human evolution from one stage to another as a historical progress in civilizational growth to judge from the History of Father'.
16. Dr. Gopal Singh; *Guru Granth Sahib*; (Tr. into English) New Delhi; 1989, p.3.
17. Ibid., p. 941.
18. F. Clark Howell; *op.cit.*, p.10.
19. Ibid., p. 11.
20. Ibid., p. 12.
21. Ibid., p. 14.
22. S.R., p. 4.
23. F.Clark Howell; *op.cit.*, p. 15.
24. U.A. Buddharakkhita; *The Buddhist Law of Kamma and Rebirth*; Bangalore; 2007, pp. 16, 17-18.
25. Ibid., p. 19.
26. *Science Newsletter*, Vol.III. Government College for Women Parade, Jammu 2008. An article published by D.N. Sahi. Snakes: *As We Know Them*. **Note**: Lizards and snakes belong to the order *Squamata*, a division of the class Reptilia. Characteristic reptilian features include scaly skin, lungs, and cold-bloodedness. Most reptiles lay leathery –shelled eggs. It depicts that *Chamar* is working in that area from the distance in scientific ways, although some hatch the eggs at the time to check the race as '*Nam*' do inside their bodies and

give birth to live *Youngman* of the time by convincing the people with good gestures as free from the tension, working as an automatic force on earth. Lizards belong to the suborder *Lacertilia* to work for the betterment of the society as Ligards' work in his life orders as '*Nam*' do in the history of *Chamar* as a Scientific Discovery of the Father that God reside in the body a God made temple, not man made *Mandir* and *Masjid*. They are the centre of research for mind where God's reside at one time as Living Deity; in human form not in structural form deities and scriptures. It is duty to feed rats, mice's, frogs, fishes, eggs of birds' small mammals and lizards provided by the man itself. As a controlling system of the father on earth. *Krait*, and *King Cobra* feed on other snakes like *Dr. Raj Kumar* and *Baba Gurinder Singh ji Biaswale*, big snakes of 'Nam', they feed lambs, goat, sheep, small animals of the '*Nam's* and sometimes young ones of human beings. They have the seasonal growth to check the eggs. Which are left in natural style to serve the society for the welfare of the man and forget on earth, that some one are watching from the distance. There are certain myths and beliefs about snakes. When a snake bites, the best medicine to treat bite in 'Nam' which is harmful not for others, but for your oneself, that has to die into it and see the wonderful world. But Brahmins actually bite the living man and its surrounding atmospheric, birds and animals by eating their careers. Therefore, there is a need of special snakes of the 'Nam' against them to find out the qualities of their venoms as human beings. Before the biting of these snakes, there is a (First Aid) called '*Nam-dana*' of the Father, then there are less chances from the above to bitten them, because it becomes his race. This would prevent the venom rulers from being absorbed into the upper part of the body called Head and Heart to realize the natural theory of the whole world. There is a need of a strip of cloth during the time of meditation, at 2.50 A.M. to worship the Father at least 2.50 hours as his service has studied of the 'Brahminical Ideology' where stands Father thought. It is interesting to note that they are working under the artifacts of the Father's race called working class or Labour Party of the Father Ravidas. They are called '*Mexican Mountain King Snake*' or *Lampropeltis triagulum annulata* or *Banded Milk Snake* (*Lampropellis ruthveni*). Typically, they have long tails, and shed their skin in several pieces like man and God. Moreover, many lizards can regenerate at tail if it is lost at one time come in another form in the colour scheme of the God and some are limbless as 'Nam' itself. Snakes make up the suborder as *Ophidia* type of snakes, they do their presentation in the form of man and God called Serpents'. All snakes have long, limbless bodies as the '*Nam*' itself; can dislocates in the hands of the Brahminical Ideology and their lower jaw to swallow large prey to eat the Brahmins with the power of '*Nam*' and have eyelids that are joined together to form a single transparent covering over the front of the eyes, but these eyes working as the eyes of God to uniform the system of the faith. Most of snakes shed their skin in a single piece as God and man passage from the Universal Concept of life. Constrictor snakes kill their prey by squeezing; venomous snakes poison their prey as '*Nam*' gives to man illusion of the *Maya*, and '*Nam-mantra*' is essential to get rid from this illusion as an heavenly abode, as crocodilians and turtles belong to different orders in the class of *Reptilia*. All crocodilians are adapted to living on land and in water as God and man, at one time they live in Heaven to Earth and Earth to Heaven as fresher-water turtles and land turtles. Characteristically, chelonians have a short reactor, but a broad body encased with the natural shell with an outer horny covering to provide the reality to the worldly life, into which the head and heart can be with drawn for the mercy of Father, as internal. Anatomy of a female tortoise and external features of a Caiman, a comparative analysis of the two animals as man and God on earth. Whereas the birds make up the class *Aves*. There are about more than 9,000 species in almost all over the world. They egg in a single cell, produced by the female species as an individual capacity of the man itself. But the difference between the two is that, the shell eggs of the birds and reptiles contain enough yolk to sustain the young until it hatches into a juvenile version of the adult as pointed out in hatching and cutting size of the egg, and cracks runs completely around the shell as do Early Global Warming in the history of man. Those emerge from the egg, they are the race of the Father and those left in the form of man called Brahmins, they become the study of man by Archaeologists and the Anthropologists to find out or reconstruct the history of man. As in Mammalian order carnivore includes cats, dogs, bears, raccoons, pandas, vessel, badgers, skunks, otters, civets, mongooses, and in hyenas. The order's name is derived from the fact that most of its members are flesh-eaters of the (*Nam*) and '*Nam*' becomes fragile and hunting the lifestyle of the people who are multiple in number as in Mathematics study, it is called as Linear Transforming and Matric System from 0 to 9 as natural numbers of the human body, who feels and analysis' the historical feet's of the human history in natural way as 'Creative Powers' as pious approach of the life , as we take up an example of this in Linear space manner as C (IR), of all infinitely differentiable functions as God stands for 'infinite' and '*man*' or *Mana* or Mind stands for Rotational Change. We shall now see that a Linear Transformation T = R2; R2 is completely determined at one place by its action on the basis of vectors as God is stick at one point. Earth is revolving round the sun and moon, and stars are displayed functioning for their own benefits on the standardized basis as R2 such that Te1 = WI, Te2=W2. If WI = (a-c) ER2, W2 = (b,d) ER2, it follows T stands for Truth is determined by four scientific numbers that is a, b, c, d. It is common practice to write these four numbers in a 2x2 matrix, A = (a, b, c, d). It makes clear from the basic study of matrix system that it is difficult to go back to original house, where it stands in the life of man as a linear study of transformations it lies in the study of man's own life tanned by skins or leather by the *Chamar*. Conversely, we suppose, matrix (a, b) – 2x2. Then we can set W1 = (a, c) and W2 (b, d). Define T (X1, X2) = X1 W2. It can be easily verified that T stands for Truth is a linear space of study from bottom to top and top to bottom and let e1, e2, e4, be the standardize basis for R4 in rotation form to change the earth into another geographical conditions as the scientific study in mathematically calculation proved the environmental system of the '*Nam*' or God as a True force and Brahmin is a linear force to trans form it, it is the duty of God or *Nam* work in the favour of degradation class as favourite class of the Living Master of the period.

27 Thus, W1 = T (e1), W2 = T (e2), equivalent to Wn = T (e4).
In fact, T (X1, X2 = X4, and X1 W1 + X2 W2 + X4 W4 is the unique linear transformation as neitar in Rm to W2, W2 with T (ex) = Wn means O stands for 'wonder' or 'Infinit Power' and 'N' is a negative force stands for 'Black Power' as 'destructive force' in the thought of 'Brahminical Ideology'. Now we conclude the article of Gods and

man by given examples of the illiterate people as an illustrate example for the examining of Truth in history through the idea of Alzebra

No 1. Let T : R2 R2 be the linear transformation defined by T (X1, X2) = (X2 – X2,7X1 + 3X2) then T (e1) = T (1,0) = 1, 7) it means in matric system of Arabic standard one stands for God and 'Seven' means *Sapta – Sindhu* in the form of God in Persian terms called truth never dies, it has to be observe in the body as a striking feature of the body as a wonderful power and modern mathematicians like Professor *B.S. Komal, Jagdish Lal Megha* and others renowned faculty member they are determining the truth in 'Brahminical Ideology' in linear manners as a blind faith of the subject matter of the life

As we take up another Example of the Matrix System that is 'A'. As it is mentioned in the mathematic calculation

A = (2 – 1)

(2 4): then T (e1) = (2, 1) = W,

T (e2) = (-1, 4) = W2 Explicitly refers that there are two wonders in the life i.e. God inside the man as a 'Wonderful Power'.

T (X1,X2) = X1W1 +X2W2 = X1 (2,1) + 2 (-1, 4) = (2X1 – X2, X1 + 4X2)

In the end, we would like to communicate the mathematics students and scholars that the best way to learn the mathematics the *Chamar* on earth as scientific study of the subject cited above called 'Linear Transformations and Matric System' into uniform system as a learned mathematicians otherwise modern mathematics is hell for the student as a 'sexual study' of the modern Brahmins of the period. (**References**: (1) Dorling Kindersley; *op.cit.*, pp. 184-186, 188; (2) S.N. An article represented by B.S. Komal; *Linear Transformations and Matrices*'.)

27. Dorling Kindersley; *op.cit.*, pp. 178, 180.
28. Ibid, p. 182-183.
29. S.N.L; An article, published by Dr. O.P. Sharma; *Birds-Our Feathered Friends.*
30. Dorling Kindersley; *op.cit.*, p. 188.
31. S.N.L: An article published by Dr. O.P. Sarma, *op.cit.*
32. Ibid., An article published by K.K. Kapoor; '*Nuclear Magnetic Resonance Spectros Copy*: Salient Features.
33. A.L. Basham; *op.cit.*, pp. 490-91.

34. S.N.L. An article published by K.K. Kapoor; *op.cit.*
35. Dorling Kindersley; *op.cit.*, p.168.
36. Ibid., p. 166.
37. Ibid., p. 167.
38. Ibid., p. 194.
39. Washington Report Agency dated 5.4.2008, *A Discovery in Science*. Kashmir Times News.
40. Arun Kesarwani; *Pre-historic Punjab: A Reassessment* (From the *Dawn of Man to the First Urban Civilization*); An article published in Punjab History Conference (PHC) 37 Session, March, 2005, pp. 38-39. **Note**: Author's recent discovery in Human Origin species found in the areas between the *Ravi* and *Chenab*, wherefore *Indus-Saraswati Civilization* of the *Akhnoor Valley* of the Jammu Region was developed a Second Civilization of the world, later on, Vedic, Aryan and Harappan Civilization developed in the worlds. Akhnoor was the biggest centre of trade between the man and God, who used to live together in the history of man itself. Due to the migratory of the world soul, the conditions of the man's history were changed and hard shipped were faced by his race in this Universe, because they use to believe on the idea of their forefather and one group of the race called *Brahmapitheous* they suppress them on their simplicity and dedication towards the Master. After coming to the back of these migratory birds and animals, their condition become very degraded in the society and these migratory birds and animals transfer their life into man itself and settle the score on the behalf of their race against this dirty race called Brahmins of the period or modern politicians.
41. Dorling Kindersley; *op.cit.*, p.196.
42. Ibid., p. 194.
43. G.W. Briggs; *op.cit.*, p.11.
44. F. Clark Howell; *op.cit.*, p. 158
45. Ibid., p. 159.
46. Ibid., p. 158.
47. *Chandella Art*, Dr. M.A. Ansari Memorial Lecture, by S.K. Sullerey; Introduction by S. Inayat A. Zaidi; Department of History and Culture; Jamia Millia Islamia; New Delhi; 2004, p.9.
48. Ibid.

49. Victoria Jones; *The Journey of the Soul*; Beas; Reprint 2004. **Note.** This book is dedicated to the Living Master Beloved Saviour, Eternal Friend of the world as God on earth.
50. Dorling Kindersley; *op.cit.*, p. 202.
51. F. Clark Howell; *op.cit.*, p. 94.
52. Walter R. Lawrence; *Provincial Gazetteer of Kashmir*; New Delhi, Reprint, 1985; pp. 16-17.
53. G.L. Khajuria; '*Charming Chinar*'; An article published October 21, 2007, daily Excelsior Magazine' on '*Eco-Watch*'
54. Zanaide-A-Ragozin; *Vedic India*; New Delhi; 1961, p. 23
55. Christian Lassen; *Indische Alterthums kunde*; London; 1866-1874, Vol.1, 2nd Edition; pp. 301ft.
56. *State Time* News dated 30, March 2008. News item; 'Sonia's false Claim', 'China has largest Tulip Garden'. **Note**: Besides the Tulip food-plants, too numerous to be enumerated here and found in Kashmir during the time of Britishers. There were known as *Euryale ferox, Nymphaea stellata, Nymphaea alba, Nelumbium speciosum*, the exquisite pink waterlily, *Acorus calamus*, and *Typha special*, the reed mace, all contributed to the Kashmiri substance. Wild fruits are in profusion, and many fungi are eaten by the people and transmitted to another disease as a transferring formula of the nature from top to bottom in self style manners according to its functions. The mushroom is common, and the *morel* (*Morchella special*) equivalent to *Chamar* abounds in the mountains of the father as a snake of the *Shivji* found in the Himalayan range as a special term called 'Saint' or '*Sant*'. So many mistaken motions are current about *Sant Mat* that even a large number of educated people, including some leading exponents of various religions thoughts, do not seem to understand it clearly. The term '*Sant*', 'Saint' and '*Sadh*' are so widely misunderstood that any beggar in saffron robes is loosely called a *Sadh*, which term was originally used to denote a person who is highly developed spiritually and has crossed the regions of matter and mind. It should be made clear from the study that *Sadhus* do not recommend outward formalities, rites, rituals, modes of living, symbols or any special type of clothing has Hindus recommend. It shows that Hindu or Muslim religion is fraud and mockery for the human history. There are plants that are useful for hair-washes called '*Nams*' of the Father, as *Radha Soami Mission* of

the *Chamar* society, and herbs with medicinal properties are found from the *Chamar Industry* called absorber of the *'Nam'* inside the body and then try to learn the history of *Chamar Family* otherwise it is difficult to understand its original value. In addition to this *Macrotomia Benthami* is one of these peculiarly esteemed by the Kashmir's as a remedy for heart-off editions as *'Nam'* loves to everybody. Among the scents may be noted *Goyaldhup* (*Jurinea macrocephala*), which is largely exported to India, where it is used by the Hindus, as an exploited power of the *'Nam'*. The most important of the aromatic study of plants is the *Saussurea Lappa*. This grows at high elevations from 8,000 to 9,000 feet from the sea level on earth for the study of man in human history who to filter the layers of the particles of the *'Nam'* into human species and to stop the red light of the God and man in a straight forward manners that mobiles the people for good habits, leave the bad one like drinks and alcoholic things for the establishment of a good society of the *'Nam'*. These kinds of plants have long roots of scent like *orris* with a blend of violet colour technique of the *'ranga'*. It was largely exported to China for the study of *'Nam'* as a natural threat of the Father. Where it is used as incense in the joss houses of the Fathers. It has many valuable properties, and is a source of consideration for the revenue of the State itself. The mad rats race called modern politicians, like *Dr. Frook Abdulla, Mufti Mohammad Sayyid, Mahbooba Mufti, Gulam Nabi Azad, Sonia Gandhi, A.K. Antony, Saifuddin Soz, Indra Gandhi,* etc. amongst the nations of the world for development, has jeopardized the human health itself. They are the destructive forces of the each as self centered man because these are the idiot of the *'Nam'* or God on earth. A full account of the animals and birds will have also found in the same book of the *Lawrence* i.e. *'The Valley of Kashmir'*, Chapter No. V. Since that book was written by the Britishers as the forefather of the *Sudhra Family*, and they preserved the material for study for their own race on great strides, and has prevented the extinction of the *barasingha (Cervus duvanceli)* and *hangal* or Kashmiri stag kind of animals, who always use to live in paradise, and Brahmins or *Damaras* of the period could not explore Him under the blind faith of the material force, categorically known as *Cashmirianus*; belonged to Kashmir, reside in *Jambu* or *Jambudvipa* belonged to the area of Jammu region. Among the *Cervidae*, the musk deer of the *'Batwal Family'* called as *Moschus Moschiferus* man of the history called *Mohan Lal Kaith* is commonly known as *Batwal* and its pod is valuable for the community to teach the lesson to the idiot Brahmins and *Rajputs* of the family of *Ursidae* i.e., *Chamar*, from the background of the *'Ravidas Culture'*, the black bear, or *bomba hapat* (*Ursus arctus or isabellinus*), is very common, being a great pest to the crops and a danger to the people at the time of blasting the bombs of the *'Nam'* or God in human form to repeat the history itself as God and man on earth. The brown bear, or *Lal hapat (Ursus arctus or isabellinus)*, is still for from rare called Chamar of the Father in skillful manners, how he knows the technique of writing the history as a Spiritual Subject into Scientific Study of the "life" from one process to another. Author is partly herbivorous and partly. Carnivorous in the history of *Chamar Dynasty of Kashmir* of the family of *Bovidae*, the *markhor* (*Capra falconeri*) and ibex categorically known as *sibirica* tolerance man of the history are still to be met with the friends of the 'Nam's living in Heaven of the Kashmir valley. The Kashmir *marknor* has from one to two complete turns in the spirals of its horns to study the truth where it lies. The *tahr* or *jagla* (*Hemitragus*) is found on the *Pir Panjal* to repeat the history of the *'Nam'* or God, and the *serow* or *ramu* (*Nemorhaedus bubalinus*) is fairly common in Indian history, but having no knowledge of the Father, they must be accommodate in the history of man as innocent people of the *'Nam'*. The *goral* (*comas goral*) also occurs inside body of the *Chamar* History. There is also a considerable variety of the birds who messages the Father in the movement of the earths, migrate from the one place to another place and they bring transmigration in the history of man like parrots, doves, pigeon, peacock, the blue heron (*Ardea Cinerea*) is very common in human history, and the fine heronries exist at several places like *Barani* in Jammu region as the founding father of the *Chamar Dynasty of the Kashmir* in the absence of the forefathers. The heron's feathers are much valued, and the right to collect the feathers is farmed out feathered friends of the *'Nam'* already mentioned above as a study of the man in historical progress. Among game's birds may be noticed from the snow partridge areas like the *Siwalika* hills of the Father known as *Lerwa larwa*, the Himalayan snow cock known as *Tetraogallus himalayensis*, the *chikor* partridge

(*Caccabis Chukar*), the large grey quail (*coturnix*), the *monal* pheasant (*Lophophorus refulgens*), the *Simla* horned pheasant *Mohan Dass Namishtry* (*Tragopan melanocephalum*) and the Kashmir *Pucras* pheasant (*Pucrasin biddulphi*), Buddhist trees of the Lord who always resides in Kashmir. The large sand-grouse (*Pterocles arenarius*) is occasionally seen in the history of man, they are called migratory birds of the Kashmir history pigeons, turtle-doves, rails, grabs, gulls, plovers, snipe, cranes, are common in the human history. And storks are sometimes seen in the form of man otherwise, they mostly found in the paintings of the period. Geese are found in vast flocks on the Wular Lake in the winter during the study of '*Nam*', and there are at least thirteen kinds of duck one called as male tufted duck (*Aythya fuligula*), etc. The goosander and *smew* are also found on the Wular Lake. There are six species of eagles, four of falcons, and four of owls who see at night the activities of the Brahmins to maintain their records for the future course of action in the 'History' like *Dr. Raj Kumar, Dr Ram Dass, Master Deepit Raj* and *Baba Gurinder Singh ji, Biaswale*. Moreover, Kingfishers, hoopoes, bee-eaters, night-jars, swifts, cuckoos, wood peckers, parrots, crows in great variety one is called *Pahari Kana*, other are known generally *Kanas* of the period. Choughs, starlings, orioles, finches (12 species), buntings, larks, wagtails, creepers, tits, srikea, warblers (14 species), thrushes (20 species), dippers, wrens, babbling trashes, bulbuls, fly-catchers, and swallows are all familiar birds of the '*Nam*' work as a messengers of the Gods. Among the reptiles there are two poisonous snakes of the '*Nam*' in the *Barani* areas of the Jammu region i.e., *Master Deepit Raj* and His father *Dr. Raj Kumar*. The *gunas* and the *pohur*, the bite of which is often fatal in the history of the natural force called '*Nam*' on earth. Fish forms an important item in the food of the Kashmiris as '*Nam*' eaters. *Vigne* noticed only six different kinds already mentioned above, but here in this study, Lawrence enumerated thirteen in numbers as its capacity in the binding of the history of the man for the final direction of the earth who it moves and take position in different form as per the choice of the God or '*Nam*; on earth, *Deepit Raj* the man of the Modern History. (**References**: (1) Walter R. Lawrence; op.cit, pp. 18-19; (2) *The Science of the Soul*; Beas, Discourses and Excerpts from letters of Sardar Bahadur Maharaja Jagat Singh; complied by A.D. Ahluwalia; 1959; p.3.)

57. Dorling Kindersley; *op.cit.*, p. 56.
58. Ibid., pp. 62. 60.
59. F. Clark Howell, *op.cit.*, pp. 85, 87-88.
60. Ibid., p. 26.
61. Ibid., p. 15.
62. Ibid., p. 17.
63. Arun Kesarwani; *op.cit.*, p. 38.
64. F. Clark Howell; *op.cit.*, p.17.

Note: From the study, it shows that man to be older than Darwin could have imagined from the history of man, as human beings work like animals and many other species who do not trust on God but on (Only Mind) as a blind thought of the human history.

3

New Productive System of Life

Study demonstrates due to the controlling of sex organs located in the *pelvis* create 'New Human Productive System called lives as life, commences with the Enlightenment Era of the *'Nam'* or God on earth is going to control the increasing population of the world wide in the history of man with the power of *'Nam'* is called *'The Science of the Soul'*[1] the Master of Soul. It is a masterly exposition of the teachings of the Saints or *Sants* and speaks vividly of whom the Masters are, those repeat the history itself with the power of *'Nam'* or God. The downfall of the soul and how it can return his home from the passing out the various stage of life, the utter Darkness left behind for the study of man in different fields and how He comes to the union of life as in 'Human History' as a natural thought and how one can dispel it as a authority in the world. According to the teachings of the Saints and *Sants*:-

1. *Bhekh* or Initiate is he who follows the principles of *'Sant Mat'* and makes sincere efforts to tread the path of God- realization 'within' according to the instructions of the Master in living form.

2. *Shishya* or Sikh is a disciple on scientific way not in duplicate manners like we see in the Sikh community they worship the scriptures not the Fathers that who a *Sikh* reached the first stage on the way of life in the human history and who sees the light of the flame within. *Guru Gobind Singh* says: "A *Shishya* is he who sees the Living Flame within himself".

3. *Gyani* or learned is one who has reached the *Brahm* stage, which contributed by the Brahmins with their own life as 'Blind Faith' of the Sanskrit *mantra* as a script of the modern man to study the Reality where it stands; which is the Fountainhead of all knowledge invested in man's life not in books, but books are the good friends of the man and Brahmins made them bad and the downfall of the Sanskrit was took place and *Britisher*, they revived it and called the founding father of the Sanskrit.

4. *Sadh* is another term meant for the Saints or *Sant* who has reached the '*Par Brahm* Region: *Kabir* says, "*Sadh* is he who conquers this fort". It shows the theory of *Sudhra* saint has the Cosmic Knowledge of the earth. According to the last census recorded the number of so-called *Sadhus* in India at five million. But if you try to find the real *Sadhu* or *Sadhs*, perhaps you will not be to find even five. "None hath seen bags of diamonds, packs of lions, flocks of '*Hansas*; or groups of *Sadhs*". Found in houses not like Brahmins wondering in the material life as a burden over the society to increase the population in illegal way. It is story of the modern Brahmins.

5. *Sant* or *Saints* is He who has attained highest stage of knowledge as a Fountainhead of the study and as become one with the Lord and man. The drop, having merged in the Ocean, has become the Ocean itself. "God and God's men are One. There is onl distinction between God and man", working as human beings on earth in the absence of the Father, but Brahminical theory lies their, because they are problem created in the society. It shows they are not true scientists, but they are pollution created in the society that they have totally forgotten its divine origin. The *Skand Purana* says: "Guru is Brahma, Guru is Vishnu, Guru is *Maheshwara*. Guru is God himself. My obeisance to Him". For learning every science or profession '*Nam*' is key player, we have to seek the help of a teacher from this background who are pure from the thought and knowledge. That is the common experience, then, would we not require a Teacher for the most difficult of all sciences is the '*Nam*', who is the operator of all the sciences, Science of God and Spirit? *Guru Amar Das* says: "None will reach the Lord except through the Guru, this is ordained by the Lord Himself". You will

have to obtain the secret of the inner path and learn the technique from some True Master. "The Key is in the hands of the *Satguru*. None else can open the door", (*Guru Arjun*). You can attune yourself to the Divine Melody only by acting in accordance with his direction. He will show you the way to 'go in' and contact '*Nam*'. Only then will you be liberated from the cycle of birth and death in human form. "Those who do not go 'within' and ever wonder outside, simply waste this precious gift of a human life". *Guru Amar Das, Dadu* Says: "Others speak only from hearsay Saints see Him face to face."[2]

The first or the lowest centre, the *Mulchakra* or the basic concept of the life, at one time presided over by *Ganesh* means do goods, have goods, the second, the *Indri chakra* or sex organs, is governed by Brahma, the creator of the bodies, the third or *Nabhi Chakra* is controlled by Vishnu without money, the *nonrisher* or sustainer of the life. The fourth, which is *Hirday*, or *Heart Chakra*, is ruled by Shiva or '*Nam*', the destroyer of the evil powers, i.e., virtues, The fifth, is the *Kanth* or *throat chakra*, presided over by goddess *Shakti*, the source of power to the three gods of *Brahm, Visnu* and Shiva. The sixth *Chakra*, which is the highest stage reached by the *Nam yogis*, is the '*Tisra Til*' or the 'Third Eye', situated in the centre behind over two eyes, and is the 'Seat of our soul and mind', the 'Centre of Consciousness', 'Thinking Centre'. This is the centre from where all our thoughts and energy go out. Our creator, the Lord, is above in the *twelfth chakra*. Thus, we have to cross the six more *chakars* above the seat of our soul knowledge, behind the eyes, to meet him[3] with the process of *Nam-dana*.

Keeping in view, *Ravidas's* growing fame in the human history a devotee of the God emerged the Brahmins of *Kashi*, and there is a story that they approached the King with a request to prevent this low-born *Shudra* to performing the action of his study of the same as *Chamar*, this menial worker, from worshipping God challenge to Brahmins which are supreme on this earth like *Sonia Gandhi, L.K. Advani, Preveze Mussaraf*, many more from this background. He humbly explained the terms of the caste and creed are made by man not by God. Finally, he was placed in the court, he fervently prayed to God as follows:

Act not in such a way, O my Lord, That my work may go wrong, As you merely watch, sitting at a distance in the body of 'Chamar'

Kashi is crowded with a multiple of people, who have come to witness this assembly of devotees, Keep or give up your reputation, as the saviour of the lowly, Prays Ravidas the Cobbler[4] *of the 'Nam'.*

New Female Production of System

According to the Scientific Research, section trough female pelvic region, as we know each month a ripe egg is released from one of the female's ovaries into a fallopian tube leading to the uterus (womb), a muscular pear-sized organ have been produced in her body for the conceiving of the child. Whereas, a male produced minute tadpole-like sperms in two oval glands testes called one is the part of God and another is the part of the man, and third force remain constant change in the idea of man to man. When the male is ready to release the sperm into the female's vagina, then there is a problem in human history, why the women should become sufferer due to the conceiving concept of the *'Nam'*, because a human value is resided in the life to feel as a labourious job of the sexual intercourse, in that case many millions will have to pass into his *urethra* process even the *Sants* Himself, in this condition we leave his or her body through the fleshy penis which has no lust of sex organs. But sometimes sperms travel up through the process of vagina into the uterus and one sperm may enter and fertilize an egg of the *'Nam'* as God on earth. The fertilized egg becomes embedded in the uterus wall and starts to grow into a new human being like man on earth to repeat the history of the man itself.

Development of a Child[5]

"Since man is by nature a social being, he has learnt through the ages that his personality as well as groups activities can be best develop through community being like *Ravidas* the *Sant* of the *Hathras* and his force called *Chamar*". As we know the base of human society is the social group. The social group bears the responsibility of a child's education as *Ravidas* did for their children to worship the 'Living Nam' which is resided in the human history as ultimate truth in the form of man, God on earth (*Dr. Raj Kumar*) as suggested by the founding Father of the history, i.e., *Master Deepit Raj* and is forerunner colleague *Baba Gurinder Singh ji, Biaswale* along with the company of *Dr. Ram Dass, Kabir* on earth. A family may be either unitary or joint in this process. These groups are of two kinds – (1) Permanent, and (2) Temporary as God is permanent and man has temporary life. It is to be noted here that these groups are permanent and the child influence each other very powerfully. In short, association of the *Chamars* with *Radha Soami* is a social group provides social education to the child and develops socially desirable qualities, attitudes and value in him as a natural instinct, whereas the Brahminical group has no natural instinct in the theory of '*Nam*' or God, therefore, their theory is based on temporary as a destructive force of the society called negative element of the society and traditional natural instinct, they have ignored in self-style manner as are problem created of the society in Indian history. During the Brahminical period, two great epics were written by the *Sudhra* family, i.e., *Ramayana* and *Mahabharata*. Brahmins give great regard these documents, but failed to negotiate with the living man of the history i.e., *Dr. Raj Kumar* and *Baba Gurinder Singh ji, Biaswale*. During the Buddhist period, the superior status of the Brahmins was also challenged by these forces, but they were failed to accommodate them in the history of man to realize the truth, therefore, lier statement proves false as a dirty race of the Father, and Father rejects to accommodate in history.

Indian Society During the Muslim Period

Muslim rulers were generally pleasure loving. As a consequence permissiveness pervaded the society in the form of a prostitution like *Yash Paul Kundal* of the said department, drinking and gambling the women for sexual intercourse as idiot force of the nature. In this process, there was a great tension among Hindus and Muslims women that there should be a free sex society. As we know under the 'Brahminical ideology', many Hindu women had to commit mass suicide of '*Johar*' system in the history of man when there was a rule of the *Rajputs* and *Nawab Community*. Muslims believed in polygamy as unnatural rule of the law as a self-style law called 'egoistic' approach in history during the absence of the Master or Father-in-Law of the History. Out of fear, Hindus rulers adopted social evil practices like *Sati* system, child marriage, infanticide system modern term used as '*foetus*', in particular an unborn 'birth', did by the doctors, modern man of the Brahminical society and same idea has been found in the modern teachers, they are collecting the money from the tuition work, and forced widowhood to sacrifices. *Guru Nanak* and *Kabir* preached the cult of *Bhakti* or *Bagti*. This *Bagti* movement became popular among Hindus and Muslims. Later on, Mira became the follower of *Ravidas*, popularized the preaching of the Divine Cult of the God i.e., '*Nam*' of the period.

Indian Society During British Rule

After the downfall of the *Mughals* as historical rulers of the 'Dum Dynasty of Kashmir' called *Chandalas* of the period, power was transformed in the hands of the *Britishers* as the followers of this dynasty and ideas of the *Ravidas* called '*Chamar Cult*' and revolutionized the modern Indian society on the same cult i.e., called '*Chamar*'. During their absence, power was transferred to the Brahmins of the period since, 15 August, 1947 to find out the Truth where it stands either in *Sudhra* class or Brahmins of the period even they have enough degrees of M.A. B.A. and Ph.D., but poverty, unemployment, other social evils like empowerments to women and *Sudhras* to provide social justice equally failed in this process due to their mal-practices in the society like corruption, sex free society, criminals were encouraged for the lust of power in illegal ways, rise of a capitalist class of the film industry. Thus, there is a great impact on the physical development of the children's impact on child's mental growth, in the field of moral and spiritual value of the life have been totally absent in the human history and the impact of the poverty, disintegration of the caste system and the impact of the crimes, Indian society and Education could not obtain the knowledge of the Supreme Lord, who is invested in everybody's life called *Chamar* of the period of the modern society i.e., Master *Deepit Raj* as a ruler of the modern society, know the every bit of the knowledge in comfortable to channelize the truth of the history invested into man's life itself. In short, the whole process of socialization falls within the scope of interaction or the social act of the said child like sympathy, child rearing, co-operation, suggestion, social teaching, reward and punishment to the family of man and God.

The School and Community

The school and community are closely related to man and God on the basis of teaching and learning process they are mutually inter dependent upon each other for their growth and development. As a matter of fact, each nation is a conglomeration of communities. The development of these communities is the development of the nation, after the development of the nations then there is an Imperialist Thought of the nature to control all the nations in scientific way that God governs the whole world and His focus is society as a natural thought and schools for education for young, are established by a social group of good personalities which are closely associated with natural forces. So that it may maintain and perpetuate itself as a society of religious minded group of the '*Nam*' the school is one of the chief instruments by which a society seeks to ensure the acceptance by children and youth of the period, influenced by the ethics and moral values of the life. The character and behaviour of such teachers, students who are associated with this kind working, they must be encouraged. This association will function on two type of concepts i.e., 'Totalitarian' and 'Democratic' to look after the welfare work of the society as a community of the man in scientific way and extent the mission of association which is based on scientific study and moral values for the establishment of a peaceful society. School often improves these styles and standard of living which the whole community of the '*Nam*' adopts gradually the modern life style of the community as a simple way of living and thinking as a progressive society. Thus, schools play an important role in the reformation and reconstruction of a community and its history as a whole development idea of the man.

Position in Relationship between School and Community in India

In ancient India, schools existed as *Gurukuls* thought of the man in domestic house through spiritual values. But the situation of the schools have changed during the Brahminical period more and more schools started functioning near the towns and the teachers changed their outlook from a sense of duty to a profession to earn more money from the profession. But the relationship between the school and the community remained as pure as the *Sudhra* rulers of the period were the teacher in the Vedic Age and later on corrupted by the Brahmins as a money-minded race of the Father. During the Buddhist period, the relationship between the two were remained pure and high as the rule of the '*Chamar Dynasty* or *Sudhra* Family'. Due to this relationship, the schools during that period remained busy in serving the community as a whole through the gospel of the Buddha or Lord on earth. One day, as the Buddha was on this way to the village of *Jantu*, Venerable *Meghiya* who accompanied Him wanted to stop by a mango grove and practice asceticism. Thrice the Buddha advised him against this, but he went his way. Eventually he returned to the Buddha and confessed that he had failed in his practice because almost all the time he was in the grove and found three kinds of evil thoughts disturbed his mind with taunting arguments, thoughts of sensual desires, ill will and thoughts of cruelty. Choose out one disciple to attend always on me[6] i.e., '*Nam*' and Four Noble truths of the '*Nam*' already mentioned above and their names.

During the Muslim period, schools became the play things of the '*Nam*' spreading the idea of '*Islam*' in naturalistic way as old relationship between the school and the community.

Islam and Science: *Maulana Shihabuddin Nadwi's* Scientific Approach toward *Quran*

Authored of almost a hundred books, the late *Maulana Shihbuddin Nadwi* of *Bangalore* (1931 – 2002) was the good friend of *Dr. B.R. Ambedkar*, is remembered for his efforts to develop what he regarded to the 'infinite' force of the '*Nam*' as a 'Scientific' framework of *Quranic* exegesis, being one of the few contemporary South Asian friends of the *Ulema* during the life time to have worked in this field to study the theory of '*Nam*' or '*Kalma*'. His books and the institution that he founded 'Word' the *Furqania* Academy *Chamars* were devoted to the elaboration of a 'Scientific' Islamic Theology (*Kalma*) as well as 'Scientific' explanations of various Islamic beliefs, laws and practices[7] which were based on '*Nam*'s theory i.e., God and man, not on Religion. The word 'Religion' comes from the root 're', meaning 'back', and '*ligare*', meaning , 'to bind' the life of man in a way which binds our soul back with God. The science presented here gives a clue to the direction founds in the body not in *Masjid*. Arabic term *Masjid* denotes the theory of 'Mind' as dangerous thought of the *Satan* called *mana* of the living species of the man; and it tells us how the two distinguished forces work in this Universe as God and man of the History called *Dr. Raj Kumar* was the Prophet of God at that time during the beginning of the 7th century A.D. He had a friendly relation with *Durlabhavaradhan* I, the founding father of the Kashmir history of the '*Chamar Dynasty*' in Chinese language that dynasty was called *Karkota Dynasty* of *Sudhra Family* in Kashmir history, and in what manner the inquiry is to be conducted by the author due to again with friendly relation of the *Sudhra Family* with *Baba Gurinder Singh ji, Biaswale*, the founder of the Scientific Religion of the '*Nam*' called '*Radha Soami*' for the concept of the modern society with the *Chamar* ruler who is working in Jammu and Kashmir State. There is no question of proselytizing, but those who are not satisfied with abstractions or speculations of the '*Nam*', who long for an eminently practical science of the spirit which would quench their thirst, who do practice the '*Nam*' in the history of man. Who feel there is something more to be learnt than seems obtainable from the present religions or philosophies of this world, may feel inclined to study this science in which case it should be approached as should any other science namely in a spirit of open-minded thought and investigation in scientific truth, prepared to accept or reject it is upto Master of the science i.e., *Deepit Raj* of the period. If a reader thinks there is something herein for which he is seeking the truth, then he should study it carefully, take notes, ask questions to the Masters of the period and investigate it as an objective research, not relying on emotion, superstition or vision, but on historical facts[8] that history repeat itself for the realization of man and God on earth. Thus, the *Maulana's* passionate appeal for the *Ulema* to study the modern sciences of the soul about the basic idea of God and man, that is, the Word of God (*qaul-eilahi*). Rather, the laws of both support each other to form the theory of '*Nam*', because they are from the same source; as God and man of the previous history. Every age has its own intellectual framework (*aqli-Mizaj*), and since Islam is for all times, it needs to be expressed a good behaviour as in every age, he explains, 'religion has a very close relation with each other sciences of the period and this is why 'the miracles given to every prophet were in accordance with the demands of his age'. Hencc, he goes on, in today's 'Scientific Research' and it needs to be expressed in scientific manners as a compulsion for the man to live in a peace-loving society. The *Quran*, repeatedly exhorts the Muslims to reflect or ponder on various aspects of God's creation as a means for gaining understanding God's attributory names of the Lord on earth as a historical value of the document 'Accordingly', he writes, 'adopting new meanings not the old one for a 'Word' does not mean that old meanings attributed to it are fully nullied'. This, he says, can be construed as a call for Muslims to take to the study of various physical and social sciences.[9] Only if 'Muslim' word, they utilize in proper way means simply 'one who submits', before God. The creed of Islam is a simple statement already discussed in the '*History of the Chamar Dynasty*' (From 6th Century A.D. to 12th Century A.D.)[10] of the same writer in two parts, "*La Ilaha Ilallah wa Muhammadur rasul al—lala*" (There is no God but *Allah* means 'Law of Nature' a scientific study of the God. Muslims accept these two basic things in the heart; that there really is one God. Supreme and Unique; and that the revelation given through the Arab Prophet Muhammad is the genuine in the form of Dr. Raj Kumar, final and complete revelation from this God is depended upon the Master *Deepit Raj* that came before it[11] as a 'Voice of God'.

According the recent news agencies, two antique copies of holy Quran, written in golden letters and dated back to *Mughal* period, were seized in the national capital and three persons were arrest in this connection of the '*Nam*' i.e., *Raj Kumar, Baba Gurinder Singh Ji* and *Master Deepit Raj* as explorer of the study of the Truth while the Archaeological Survey of Indian Report ascertaining the value of the rare treasures, police said, the three accused had struck a Rs. 3.5 crore of deal with decoy customers of the '*Nams*' sent by *Delhi Police's* crime branch for the study of '*Nam*'. Experts have initially estimated that two seized pieces of '*Quran Mazid*' in Arabic called 'Word'or '*Nam*' one a 150 pages laminated leather hard-bound *Chamar* and another a 220 pages embedded with golden metallic leaves of the '*Ravidas Sutras*' belong to either *Shah-Jahan's* or *Aurangezeb's* period.[12] Study shows that only if Muslims were to do this, could they be suitably empowered to fulfill their responsibility as God's vicegerents on earth (*Khalifa ficarz*) and as people commissioned by God to guide human kind as old species into new human origin, as God and man to do to enjoin what is good and forbid the wrong (*amr bil marufwa – nahy anil munkar*) mentioned in the study of *Maulana Shihabuddin Nadwi's* Scientific' approach to Quran. Developing a 'Scientific' *Quranic Theology*, the *Maulana* further adds, is also essential for Muslims to take on and defeat the political forces based on false propaganda of the Religion on materialism, who viewed the world through a lens that claims to be 'Scientific', but it is based on atheism. He again insists on the materialism and then suitably 'Islamized' the term in ethical way. By relating the school of thought and His community the creation is with the Creator, and showing the correspondence between Science and Islam a scientific study of the '*Nam*' or God and the planned nature of the whole cosmos' in this way he argues, proofs for the existence of God (*delail-e-rabbani*) can be articulated as real '*Nam*' on earth in the form of man and God. Further elaborating the need for the *Ulema* to study the science and to develop a scientific knowledge of the 'Name', as per *Quranic* exegesis, the *Maulana* writes that knowledge (*ilm*) in Islam is a composite whole a study of it as a source of history of the past event in the history of man, there being no division between 'Religious' and '*Nam*' and in worldly knowledge in human history. Hence, one arm or eye of Islam is the *Sariat* and the other is *Fitrab* of the man in nature or in scientific study as a new discovery of the man's history. Hence, he stresses, both forms of knowledge i.e., 'Brahminical Ideology' and 'Pure-thought' for the process of the man's struggle in the life. Muslims should have the *Shariah* in one hand and the sciences in the others for the development of the human history in progressive way. If Muslims were to ignore this, he claims, they would actually be against God's will,[13] and punishment will be accorded on their action and deeds. There are certain selective verses of the Quran from *Surah X* are corporate in the study as follows:

1. My taste to me, yours to you, You are not accountable fro what you do, Nor am I for what you do in this world (10:41)

The detractors have 'a little enjoyment', on this earth, but everyone of them has to return to God.[14]

Selected Verses of the Quran

Through the stories of Noah and Moses, the plight of the disbelievers is depicted and their doom and destruction described. The ultimate triumph of Truth or '*Nam*' is, once again, graphically explained and lessons are drawn.

Then, we will make them
Suffer the severest punishment,
For all their blasphemies.
(10:70)

Surah X

2. *Why should people wonder*
That We have sent Our Revelation
To one from among themselves?
He has come to warn of dangers ahead
And to give glad tidings about the truth.
But unbelievers accuse Our Messenger
Of being a sorcerer.

3. *Verily your Lord is the Creator*
Of the heavens and the earth.
He created them in six days.
He is firmly established on His Throne
Regulating and governing everything.
No one can intercede with Him Excess by His leave.
Indeed He is the Lord, Serve Him
And listen to His admonition!

4. *Everyone will return to Him, That is His promise.*
He creates, destroys and recreates:
He rewards those who believe in Him,
But those who reject Him
Shall suffer grievous hurt.

5. *God has given the sun a shining glory*
And the moon a wondrous light,
And through their measured beauty
People have the count of time
And learn the number of years.
He has created these
To advance righteousness and truth,
And to explain His signs
To people who understand.

6. *In the alternation of might and dry*
And in all that God has created
In the heavens and on the earth
There are indeed signs
For those who fear him.

7. *Those who do not hope to meet Us*
And those who enjoy this life
In the belief that they will not meet Us,
They are those who heed not Our signs

8. *Their abode is the fire of hell*
Into which they will fall
Because of the evil they have done

9. *The Lord will guide those*
Who believe in Him
And work righteously,
They will be blessed with gardens
Underneath which rivers flow.

10. *When a man is in trouble,*
He cries to Us in every situation,
Lying on one side or sitting on the other
Or even while standing.
But when we have eased his trouble
He goes about his way pretending
He had never cried to Us,
And did not do anything unfair.

11. *Many generations before you.*
O people! Were destroyed when they refused to
Listen to their apostles.
And rejected our clear Sings,
They would not believe in Us,
And thus were punished for their sins.

12. *And even when our clear verses are read to them,*
They persist in saying:
"This is not enough,
Bring something else or change this".
Tell them, O Muhammad!
'It is not for me to replace or change them,
If I were to disobey my Lord
I would suffer the severest punishment
On the Day of Judgement'.

13. *Tell them further:*
'If God had so willed
I would not have preached as I do,
I have spent a whole lifetime in your midst.
Why can't you then understand my position?'

14. *Mankind was created as one nation,*
But it differed subsequently.
Had God wished otherwise,
Differences would have been easily settled.

15. *When we show mercy to a people*
After they have suffered adversity,
Behold, instead of being grateful
They plot against Us.
Tell them:
'God is a swifter and better planner'.
Verily, Our messengers are aware of
All the plans that are made by Us.

16. *God enables you, O people,*
To travel over land and sea.

You rejoice while boarding ships
And are happy wish favourable breeze.
But you cry to Us for help
When the waves confront you.
Then you beseech Us and say:
'If you will deliver Us from the calamity
We shall indeed be grateful to you'.

17. *But when we deliver you,*
Behold! You become insolent and defiant.
This is not good for your souls.
What worth is the enjoyment of this life
When in the end you shall return to Us
And shall be told of all that you did?

18. *Your present life is like the rain*
Which we send down from the skies.
Their juxtaposition produces the food
For men, women and animals,
Until the fields look like golden ornaments
And their owners feel content.
But suddenly we dry them up. In these are Our Signs
For those who can reflect.

19. *God invites you to peace in Heaven.*
He guides whom He pleases
To the path that is straight.

20. *To those who do righteous deeds*
There shall be good reward
Such as cannot be measured.
They shall not be shamed
Nor will their faces be tarred.
They will be companions in heaven
where they shall abide forever.

21. *But those who do evil.*
They will receive ignominy.

Their faces will be blackened,
And they shall have no defender
Against the wrath of God.
They shall fall in hell
To burn therein forever.

22. *Every soul will taste*
Fruits of its own deeds.
And when people will be brought
in the presence of their Lord
They shall then realize
How false was their belief.

23. *Ask them: 'Who is it that*
Sustains you and has the power
Over your hearing and sight?
Who gives you life and raises you from the dead
And who regulates your affairs?
They have to admit that it is God
Ask them then why they do not worship Him
And be pious and do righteous deeds.

24. *God indeed is your Cherisher and Sustainer.*
This is the Truth or 'Nam' which distinguishes right from wrong.
Then why do you turn your back on Him?

25. *The word of God is true,*
And not of those who refute it
And do not believe in Him.

26. *This Quran given to you, O Muhammad!*
Is, indeed, our creation.
No one else can produce it.
In it is confirmation of Our message
Sent to earlier messengers
And an elaboration of the same truth as 'Nam'
that the Lord of the Worlds
Has revealed from time to time.

27. *Unbelievers may say*
Mohammad has forged it.
Ask them: 'can you bring
One surah like this
Even with the help of others?
The result will be obvious.

28. *If they change you, O Muhammad, with falsehood*
Tell them, "My task to me, yours to you.
You are not accountable for what I do
Nor am I for what you do'.

29. *Some of them may pretend to listen to you,*
But in reality they do not.
How can you make the deaf hear,
Or make sense to the senseless?

30. *And there are some*
Who pretend to look to you
For guidance, But they are blind.
How can you make them see.

31. *Verily God does not wrong man,*
It is man who wrongs himself.

32. *Remember: To every nation*
We have sent an apostle
For people to be rightly guided.
And then we judge them fairly
And do not wrong them in any way.

33. *It is God who gives life*
And who takes it away
And to him shall be all return.

34. *O people: this is the guidance.*
That has come to you from your Lord
So that it may heal the wounds in your heart
And you may take to the right path.

35. *Tell the people:*
'Rejoice in the bounty of God.
It will give you better satisfaction.
Than all the wealth you may possess'.

36. *In whatever state you are,*
Whether reciting the Quran
Or performing a good deed,
We see everything.
Nothing remains hidden from Us
Not even the smallest atom or the biggest article;
Everything is clearly recorded for Us.

37. *Had your lord so wished,*
All people everywhere
Would have been believers. But that is not
His way,
Hence do not force anyone
To take to Our path
Unless they do so willingly.

38. *Tell them O Muhammad:*
'In case you doubt the truth of my way,
I cannot help you; but remember
To God alone you will be accountable
Of all that you do.
As for me, I offer my gratitude to Him,
For having put me among His believers."

39. *But those who are disbelievers*
And choose to go astray,
The loss will, indeed, be theirs,
And make it clear to them, O Muhammad.
That you are not there
To settle their affairs.

40. *Follow then, O Muhammad,*
your direction.

Be patient and constant in your faith.
God alone will decide your fate,
For He is the best decision maker.

In this regard the *Maulana* evokes the study of *Quran*. As a true Muslim not fraudulent towards the scientific discovery of the 'Nam' or God on earth. As it is mentioned in the *Quran* the appointment of Adam as human being on earth called God or *Kalifa* and his being given knowledge of the '*Names*' of everything in the history of man and mankind. The *Maulana* takes this to also mean *Quranic* sanction for intellectual, not materialistic, including Scientific Knowledge and development of the society. He appeals to his fellow *Ulema* to reconsider their stance in this regard, warning them that 'the community, that breaks its ties with modern knowledge that is '*Nam*', will have to commit suicide. The temper of the always changes', he adds, and community which is ignorant of the temper of this age will always be defeated by the '*Nam*' or God on earth. Despite this, he kept up his struggle, as manifested in the enormous number of books as a struggle of the '*Nam*' at that time on earth was *Dr. B.R. Ambedkar* his fellow friend of the Supernatural Forces, who keeps the control of the Universal Idea of the Truth resided in the man's body itself, but there is a way to see him i.e., '*Nam-dana*' of the Living Master without free of cost what a realization of the fact of the human history as '*Nam*' on earth a natural force of the man. Many of these are real treasures that urgently deserve to be translate into English and widely discussed and disseminated, particularly those are believe on modern Islamic theology and education, which present a novel perspectives on a host of issues of contemporary society of the 'Name' or God on earth as a Scientific Research of the Father. He also refers to a *Hadith* report states that the 'miracle' of the *Quran* can never be end, taking to this to mean that people will constantly reflect on Quran and discover or uncover new meanings from out of it.[15]

British Rule in India

During the early British rule in India, during the closing time of *Mughals*, East Indian Company was remained indifferent with the close co-ordination of the *Mughals* because their founding Father of the History was 'One, that was, '*Ravidas Chamar*' by caste, pure from the heart and the head and their education system was also different, because they used to believe on One Father, One Family, i.e., '*Nam*' or *Chamar* on earth as a positive force of the subject 'science' called 'Natural Science'. But in 1913, under the insistence of some Indian on the basis of the study of 'Only Mind' not the Law of Nature i.e., '*Nam*' , East Indian Company agreed to shoulder some responsibility of education of Indians. For full twenty two years, the controversy between study of *Veda* and Oriental education continued to rage giving rise to a number of problems on the basis of Brahminical Ideology. Finally, Lord Macaulay, with the purpose of consolidating the British Empire in India, decided in favour of English, education exhorted 'A single shelf of good European Library was worth the whole native literature of India and Arabia'.[16] *Lord William Bentinck* on the pattern of '*Macaulayian System*' of education has profoundly affected the moral and intellectual character of the people of India. Bentinck appointed Macaulay as the President of the Committee. He gave a definite turn to the controversy of the Education system of India. He further wrote, "what the Greek and Latin were to the contemporaries languages of More and *Ascham* our tongue is to be the people of India". In making his recommendations Macaulay has planned to produce a class of persons of intellectual who would be "Indian in blood colour, but English in taste, in opinions, in morals and intellect" and expressed the hope in one of the letters to his Father Dr. B.R. Ambedkar of the period that " if our plans of education are followed up, there will not be a single idolater among the respectable classes in *Bengal* and *Bihar*". In that case *Macaulay's* views were accepted and embodied in a Resolution of March 7th 1835 A.D., which decreed that English would be the official language of India in the higher branches of administration. Since, the English language English literature, English political literature and English natural sciences have formed the basis of higher education in India. With an eye on the charter debates, the Home authorities of India led by Brahmins. He tried to reform the Hindu society by abolition of the cruel rite of *Sati* system and the suppression of infanticide. He crushed the gangs of assassins called *thugs* of the '*Nam*' and made peaceful loving society of the '*Nam*'. But due to the strong opposition of the

Brahminical Ideology of the Indian Priestly class both the Hindu and Muslim religion, *William Bentinck* sought to efface the humiliating distinctions between these forces having negative elements in their mind, and Indian subject of the Company in India was to be debarred from holding any office under the Company rule "by reason of their religion, place of birth, descent and colour". It is believed that this chart clause was inserted at the instance of *William Bentincks*[17] request, but Brahmins of the period were not satisfied with their unnatural activities.

Politics in Indian Education System

With the end of the Company Rule, political system in India was established, *Gandhi* played a predominant role in this field. The entry of politics into the field of education was also started for the establishment of various universities and colleges, a chain of problems which adversely effected the process of education due the mal-practise of the politicians like *Gandhi* and others, and our political system became corrupt by bribing the economy of our own nations in illegal practice from academic institutions itself. Thus, the result of the modern scenario of education totally failed for the younger generation in this field due to high economy rate of the fee as well as for the poor people of the Father to compete with the materialistic people is difficult with them and their mal-practise. Therefore, it is necessary to streamline the education system on productive way of life for the welfare of the people and society. The following steps are necessary to follow-up:

1. The group which holds the administrative powers like Vice-Chancellor of the Universities, they must be punished with hell leading the peoples in 'blind faith' with immoral ways of life.
2. The dominant groups in the politics like BJP, Indian National Congress, PDP, NC, and many more they must be punished, because they are the problem created of the society on the basis of false propaganda of the man on their caste, colour and creed which goes to the against of the Indian Constitution made by the poor people of the Father, He is still existing in the society in form of *Baba Gurinder Singh Ji Biaswale* as an advance idea of the man itself.

3. Political leaders exploited the energies and resources of the students for their personal benefit or party interests and exploiting their carrier without reasoning and logic of the life.
4. Through undue favouritism, educational procedures by their misdeeds, evil-designs and selfish doings parties for the collecting of money created inefficient and incapable persons in the field of education, and institutions are turning out indisciplined, law breaking students rather than dynamic, education system became defunct. In modern universities particularities in India on the ideology of *Gandhi,* made corrupt the system on sexual union, practicing the *Gandhian* thoughts in the universities of India, with the experiment of the sex to find out the truth, and those who are working with honest approach against them, became headache for them and then they take the interest in wrong political system in indiscipline manners by creating the political parties in the institutions.

From the above discussion, it is crystal clear that the modern political system of India has spoiled the wholesome working of educational processes of the 'Brahminical Ideology' to a very large extent. The need of the time is to beak this unholy alliance of politics with power of '*Nam*' and His story is going to repeat the history and to punished the culprits of the period, and it is essential for the modern scenario to follow up the natural paths and grow in desirable direction achieving the good objectives of life together with society[18] and natural science that lies in *Chamar's* body as a Scientific Research of the Modern Man.

Notes and References

1. *'Discourses and Excerpts Letters'* from Sardar Bhadur Maharaj Jagat Singh ji Biaswale; p. 4.
2. Ibid., pp. 7-8.
3. Ibid., pp. 8 – 9.
4. *Sant Guru Ravidas Vani.*, p. 138
5. N.R. Swarup Saxena: *Principles of Educations*; Meerut; Revised edition; 2003.

6. *The Life of the Buddha*-Part-2, Bangalore, Maha Bodhi Society; 1982; p. 12
7. An article written by Yoginder Sikand; '*Kashmir Times*', dated, 29.3.2008.
8. C.W. Sanders; *The Inner Voice*; Beas, Reprint; 2002, Preface, p. X.
9. Yoginder Sikand; *op.cit.*
10. Raj Kumar, '*History of the Chamar Dynasty*'. Delhi; 2008.
11. Ruqaiyyah Maqsood; *Islam*, U.S.A, 1975, p. 1.
12. News Item, "*Mughal Period Quran Seized in Delhi*', Kashmir Times, Dated 13.3.2008.
13. Yoginder Sikand; *op.cit.*
14. Rafiq Zakaria; *Muhammad and the Quran*, New Delhi; 1991, pp. 140-47.
15. Yoginder Sikand; *op.cit.*
16. N.R. Swarup Saxena; *op.cit.*, p. 418.
17. B.L. Grover and S. Grover; *A New Look at Modern Indian History* (Form 1707 to the Modern Times). New Delhi; 2005, pp. 129, 126-128. **Note:** The term *Sati* literally means 'a pure and virtuous women', and Brahmin made the natural event into unnatural history as a negative force of the society.
18. N.R. Swarup Saxena; *op.cit.*, p.422.

4

Physical Features of the Life and Theory of Special Creation

Geologically speaking, the State of Jammu and Kashmir has its own importance. The region has undergone many changes in geographically and geological times. The territories of the State are historically rich for everything in life from Heaven to earth. The territories of the State fall within the geological history of mountain building movements in Northern India during the ancient period of the Indian history as already discussed 46 millions years back in the *Chambrian* period. And it is rightly called the Crown of India. Geographically, it is located between latitude 32^0 -15' North and 37^0-5' North longitude 72^0-35' East and 80^0-20' East. It has international boundaries with the Tibet in the east, *China* and *Afghanistan* in the North and *Pakistan* in the west. *Punjab* and *Himachal Pradesh* lies to the south of *Jammu* and *Kashmir*. With its borders sealed, the snow covered peaks on the east and west, north and south is only accessible. Major portion of the state is hilly and height from sea level varies between 1,000 feet to 28,500 feet[1]. The valley of *Kashmir* presents a rich field of study for Earth Scientists called Geologists. In spite of its small geographical area as '*Nam*' it carries one of the finest development sequences of rocks right of '*Ravidas Family*' called '*Sudhra Family*' of the Kashmir, '*Chamar*' by caste and *Chandala* in Sanskrit language form the ancient period to modern man. It has been found from the Achaean Times to Recent Times[2] of the 21st century working in this Universe for the development of historical concept of the God and man. 'Mr. Spectator, Women are armed with fans of the physical world leave this India for the Sudra people, we do not need of dirty women like Jagdish Lal Mochi in the court of the Sudra family. She needs money, not the love of the author. In dog-days, we need good friends like Bachan Lal Megha, Rattan Lal Megha, belongs to the respectable family of Nam-History. There is an 'infinite variety' in their subject-matters like Suresh Dogra, creator of the Nam-History. Fir one whose lover was approved by the Donor. There is something in Nature, when we see the people take a certain painful gratification in beholding the encounters. Is it cruelty that administers this sort of Delight ? or is it a pleasure which is taken in the exercise of pity ? in natural thought during the days of Night. Nationalprejudices are there, and we have thereby an opportunity of observing an infinite variety of characters, which, to a person of a contemplative furn, is a much higher entertainment than a view of all the curiousities of art or Nature in physical standard, 'Work and Worship'. This very learned and judicious remark in general category of the Sudra family.

Origin of the Name and Climate of the Area

The name of Jammu and Kashmir state is very ancient in *Sudhra* history, has already discussed before *Pre-Chambrian* Period. It has been found in ancient texts like *Nilamat-purana*, and grammarian Panini's magnum opus, *'ASHTADHYAYI'*. The *Ramayana* and *Mahabharata*, *Puranas* are also referred about the history of the said area. Kashmir is its original Sanskrit form, has been used as the sole designation work in the country of *Jambu* or Jammu as its nedus name traced back through an unbroken chain of documents for more than 23 centuries. Reference to *Jammu* and *Kashmir* is also found in Ptolemy's geography having the same concept as God and man. Tradition in *Askardu* exists to the effect that it was once called *Iskandaria*, and that it was one of the cities founded by Alexander the Great during Greek rule in India. It is watered by the *'Indus Valley Civilization'* of Akhnoor at village Manda in Ambarana, and the country striking its banks is more fertile than any other part of Ladakh as *Lamayuru*, Zanskar, Kargil, Baltistan, Rondu and Astore, etc., traced the origin of the *Fakirs* as King of the *Sudhra Family*. However, in winter the climate of this areas is one of great severity of cold and warm up with the house jouney of the Soul in *Nam-History*; as respectable Wazir of the *Dalit Family* as SC King.

From the geographical point of view the location of Jammu and Kashmir State consists of four Major Zones. First, the sub-montane and semi-montane plain most of which is known as '*Kandi*' or dry belt of the '*Nam*'. Second is the *Shivalik Range*, and third zone is of high mountains mainly constituting the Kashmir Valley, *Pir Panjal* and its offshoots of the Natural Theory. This includes *Doda*, *Poonch, Rajouri* and parts of *Kathua* and *Udhampur* districts of the State. Finally the fourth zone comprises *Tibetan Track* of *Ladakh, Kargil, Gilgit* and *Skardu,* i.e., illegally occupied by the Pakistan as a part of India, consisting of middle run of the *Indus* River[3] of the *Akhnoor* valley called '*Indus- Saraswathi Civilization*' of the '*Ravidas Culture*' of the Jammu region as he was the founding father of this civilization and later on called '*Indus Valley Civilization*' of the '*Chamar Dynasty*' of the Kashmir who rule over India in the very ancient period of Indian history. The *Chenab, Tawi, Jhelum* and *Ravi* flow through this region as explored from the various sites of Indian history by Archeologists. Their origins have been established as a metamorphic and not igneous by the presence of minerals like *kyanite, staurolite, garnet, marbals, iron, coal*, etc. The Indus rising from Mansarover lake flows through the division and takes a sharp *South-Westerly* bend near *Nanga-Parbat* giving rise to Indus gorge.

Stratigraphy of the State

The main characteristics of stratigraphy of the state Jammu & Kashmir were first formulated by Lydekker in 1883. He was followed by Middle-miss in 1910 A.D., Burrard in 1932, Wadia in 1926 and later on others. The account given in the following pages an idea of classification of the '*Precambrian*' to modern '*Chamarizations*' of the '*Nam*' in the history of India, correction and interpretation of stratified rocks of the *Ravidas* period to modern period of the Indian history is determined from the geological records of the period found from the Jammu & Kashmir State discussed as under one by one.

Archaen Group

The Archean group or system includes the oldest rock of the world on this earth's crust during the study of the pre-historic period of the man called Early Man, that exhibit very complex structural deformations of the primitive man of the history called *Dr. Raj Kumar, Baba Gurinder Singh ji Biaswale, Dr. Ram Dass, Baba Rasila Ram* and *Master Deepit Raj* modern man of the history on earth. It includes *granties, gneisses* and *schists* occurring largely in the north-western of *Kashmir, Sindh, Nanga Parbat, Multan, Blochistan, Dera Ismail Khan,* and others like *Zanskar* and *Ladakh* itself. They are called "central-gensis" by *Stoliczka*. Their occurrence has also been encountered in the south of *Pir-Panjal* is *Kishtwar* and *Bhaderwah* extending westwards to Rampur in Kashmir. Debate about their age remained for quite a time and a group of geologists including MacMohan considered he is very man of human history always busy with the works and actions of '*Nam*'. These genesiss not of Archaen Age but of intrusive in origin form which have intruded into the rocks of various ages of the man's history. This view, however, has not been established firmly in the history of man that *Ravidas* is still working to formulate the history of man, he has been degraded in the history of humanistic approach by the '*Brahminical Ideology*' of the period. But certain geniuses and schist part are believed to be *Prechambrian* [4]called *Nelumbo nucifera*, Sanskrit name *Padma*, Hindi name *Kamal* and his family called *Nelumbonaceac*. As it is mentioned by the writer in the beginning was the water, water was with God. As a matter of fact that readied itself as old specie of the '*Nam*'. The sun glowed and a lotus slowly opened for holding of Supreme Knowledge of the man in this Universe on its golden pericarp is associated with Divinity early in the medieval period of the Hindu history to defeat them with the power of the *Nam* as *Chamar* itself by the said author. Once he aroused this serpent of wisdom ascends "fine as a lotus-fiber" through a succession of psychic centres described as '*lotus-chakras*', until it reaches the last stage of the life and highest *Chakras* of the *Nam* which opens as "the thousand-petaled lotus of understanding" on this earth as Self-styled a Universal flame no wind has ever disturbed him against the modern politicians of the period because they have no self-efficiency to function in the society as cheater of the human history.

Appropriately, the medicinal properties of the lotus appears to aid concentration and *Ayurvedic* science extracts medicines from the louts, which are antiallergenic, anti-spadmodic, and astringent. The beauty of the lotus is also considered a medicine[5] for health treatment of the period in the history of India and has been termed as "*Salkhala Series*" of the '*Nam*' in the body of the *Chamar* from their occurrence from village near Karan. Local differences in fashion are much less marked in the history of modern historians than one might expect from the study of this text. One is surprised to find the *Dress* in *Andhra* in the 1st to 4th Century A.D., as shown in the sculpture of *Amaravati* of '*Ravidas Culture*', *Nagarjun Konda*, and *Jaggayyapeta* is also identical with that worn further North at the same time during the rule of *Kushans* and other rulers of the period. It is said that between the two schools of thought, i.e., *Mathura* and *Gandhara*, a border area under western influence were *Indo-Greek*. Due to the '*Islamic Invasions*' from 7th century A.D. to 12th A.D. in original form as '*Nam*' or *Aja* on earth, it is a strange discovery in the Scientific Knowledge that '*New Colour*' of the human history in the paintings of Jammu region have been explored by the author that today India dyed material or colour in dress until the 12th century A.D. in moderate term taken from Gujarat on the basis of *Ajanta* paintings as the paintings of *Heir labour* or *Coolies* of the period called *Chamar* in India. *Red* and *Black* strips on a white ground predominate; even the famous guardians (*dvara palas*) of Kashmir, whose painted dress survives in the history of world almost intact in two schools of the *Ajanta Caves*. 12th to 15th century A.D. rich decorated *Dresses* of the '*Nam History*' have been found from the *Slave Dynasty* to *Mughal Empire*. *Rajasthan* and *Kangra* were the rich in pattern of cloth among '*Sudhra Family*' between the period 16th and 17th centuries, a composite culture of both the Hindu and Muslim Concept i.e., *Sudhra* of the period. This analyatic study made from *Charles Fabres*, *Indian Dress*.

The Prechambrian Group or Chamar History

The Prechambrian or *Prechamarization* groups includes those rocks which were very closed to the *Archean System* known as *slates, phyllites, hornfels* and *quartizities* belonging to *Cuddapah* or *'Chura Culture'* as *'Chamar Culture'* of the ancient period and *Vindhyan Systems* of the earth means rectify the wrong notions of *manas* against them. The *Slates* are partly carbonaceous, highly broken at places and finely cleaved occurring between *Ramban* and *Ramsu* region of the Jammu and Kashmir State; the entire formulation has been designated as the *'Dogras Slates'* of the Jammu region wherefrom *Ravidas* was born in the history of the man and God. The states are metamorphosed to phyllites as they approach the *'Sakhalas Series'* of the *'Nam'* and depict foliated structure of the life between man and God itself on this earth.

Dravidian Group (*Palaeozoic* Group)

Dravidian Group of the *Palaeozoic* period of the rock is extensively developed in the Kashmir history with power of *'Nam'* or God on earth. Over laying the *'Dogra Slate'* of *'Purana Group'* consisted of God and man is a belt of rocks termed as the *'Tanawal Series'*, which tan the life of man from one generation to another period in consecutive way. It shows from the study that the rocks may very in age of the pre-historic period is commercial from Pre-Chambrian to *Permo-Carboniferous* type of man in the human history of the Father. A brief description of each- system is given as below.

Cambrian or Chamarization Period

There are four well known areas in Kashmir where from fossiliferous Palaeozoic rocks of *Chambrian* or *Chamarization* period are identified as Liddar Valley, the Vihi region east of Srinagar, the thin band of rocks of the Father are found between the areas of Sumbal and Bandipur along with right bank of *Jhelum* and the *Handwara* areas of the *'Nam History'*. The interesting localities where these rocks can be easily studied are of *Zewan, Risin Phalgam Ajas* and *Zawar*. It shows from the study that *'Nam'* is a powerful state of mind to defeat the black people of the *'Nam'* or God with writing of Spiritual Pen. These rocks or crusts are argillaceous silicems and micaceous *slates* with compacted arenaceous and calcarious beds generally known as greywacks[6] of the life or called deep man of the human history who possessed right information of the historical knowledge without knowing illegal responsibility of the ill-will of the man's history as a Prefect Knowledge.

Ordovician Period

Fossils are the remains of plants and animals that have been preserved in rocks. A fossil may be preserved remains of an organism itself with the force of internal pressure of the earth, an impression of it in rock called *Ordovicia* or Preserved traces known as trace fossils left by an organism while it was alive such as organic carbon outlines, fossilized footprints of the '*Nam*' as dropping methods of the sex. Most dead organisms soon rot away from the study of '*Nam*' or are eaten by scavengers[7] as the history of the same study already discussed above i.e., *Chamarization* of the period. For fossilization of the body *Chamar* is very important to cover the ribs and the other bones of the body for a particular period of time and space to find out the "Truth' in History as the real founding father of the period as on this the earth. The rapid burial by sediment is necessary as God and man. The organism decays but the harder parts right from the hills of *H[illegible]ndwara* consisting of *geywacks slates* and flaggy limestones with few evidences of fossils, bones, teeth and shells e.g. belong to *Ordovician Period* of the Indian history. The few fossils that encountered are Linguletta (*Brachapoda*) and *Michodiscus* (*Trillobite*[8]) may be preserved and hardened by minerals from the surrounding sedimentary rocks. Fossilization may also be occur even when the hard parts of an organism are dissolved for the experiment in the history of the '*Nam*' or '*Chamar*' way to leave an impression called as a mould in the history according to geographical conditions of the areas as physical features of the life of the man and the country itself. The mould is filled by minerals, thereby creating a cast of the organism based on Scientific Discovery of the man in human species. The study of fossils (Palaeontology) can not only show how living things have evolved in the history of man, but can also help in mathematics to reveal the Earth geological history in scientific way, e.g., the linear problems by adding in the dating of the rock cycle process[9] of the lower strata of the society as '*Nam*' on earth to give a new life to man and his surrounding.

Process of Fossilization

The process of fossilization is located from sea called ammonite sell of the seabed, is absorbed away and replaced by minerals to the sediment of seabed sheet circulate in natural way as scropian or arthropod moves around the world for collecting the facts of history of the '*Nam*' on earth. A thin but continuous band of Silurian rocks have been identified from Aishmaqam in '*Liddar Valley*' of Kashmir to Latherwan in the '*Wordwan Valley*' of the '*Chamar Dynasty*' found in the lime light of the world history. The rock are arenaceous shales, argillaceous sandstones and impure limestones containing various fossils like Orthis, Atrypa, Strophemena (*Brachiopoda*) Calymena, Phacps, *Illanus* (*Trilobites*) and Orthoceras(*Cephalopoda*).

Devonian Study

The Devonian of Kashmir lies conformably over the Silurian rocks in both the blanks of the Liddar – anticiline as thick beds of unfossilferous quartzites known as *Muthi Barnai* quartzites. Its occuperance has also seen noted on the southern flanks of *Pir Panjal* areas in Jammu region lying between the areas of the region of *Rajouri* and *Chenab* or *Indus Valley* of *Akhnoor* from the ancient period. The rock shows cross –bedding indicating its sedimentary origin.[10] They are formed by the accumulation and consolidation of sediments (rock particles); e.g. it becomes compressed and cemented together in a process known as lithification are derived from plant and animals remains. Chemical sedimentary rocks of the '*Nam*' or '*Chamar*' are formed by chemical processes. For example, salt is formed when salt dissolved in water as into skin of the animals is deposited as the water evaporates in the Upper Worlds as God and man. Sedimentary rocks[11] are laid down in layers, called beds or strata of the society as '*Nam*' becomes itself. Each new layer is laid down horizontally over older ones of the Fatherly period. There are usually some gaps in the sequence due to the lack of knowledge in the mind of people, depends on self-styled study called 'ego' in the history of India and called instable behaviour in the society. The represent period of the study in which no new sediments were being laid down they were as old as the '*Nam*' or '*Chamar*' is there. When earlier sedimentary layers were raised above the sea level and eroded away from the history due to the lack of the knowledge of the Supernatural Forces in the history of India as degraded race, therefore, there is a need to repeat the Idea of the 'Nam'.

Rock Cycle and Lower Carboniferous

The rock cycle is continuous process of life through the physical features of the world which old rocks are transformed into new ones from man to god's creative life. It can be divided into three main groups; igneous; sedimentary and metamorphic. Igneous rocks are formed when magma (molten rocks) from the earth's interior cool and solidifies, originates from deep beneath the crust. They are of two types: intrusive and extrusive in the history of man as god and man. Intrusive rocks are formed deep underground where *magma* is forced into cracks or between rock layers to form structures such as sills, dykes and batholiths. The magma cools slowly to form course grained rocks such as gabbros and pegmatite. Extrusive rocks are formed above the earth's surface from lava (*magma* that has been ejected in a volcanic eruption). The molten lava cools quickly, producing fine-grained rocks such as ryfolite and basalt. Metamorphic rocks are those that have been altered by intense heat (contact metamorphism). Contact *metamorphosim* occurs when rocks are changed by heat from the internal pressure of the earth, e.g. an igneous intrusion or lava flow. Regional metamorphism occurs when rocks crushed in the middle of folding mountain range. Metamorphic rocks can be formed from igneous rocks, sedimentary rocks or even from other metamorphic rocks with the pressure of the '*Nam*' on the '*Earth*' surface[12].

The rocks are added to the earth's physical surface by crusted movements and volcanic activity. Once exposed on surface the rocks are broken down into rock particles by weathering condition. There are two main types: physical (or mechanical) and chemical. Physical weathering may be caused by the temperature changes on the earth with the pressure of '*Nam*', such as freezing and thawing, or by abrasion from material carried by winds, rivers, or glaciers. Rocks may also be broken down by the actions of animals and plants, such as the burrowing of the animal skins for the utilization of the leather in Chapal or shoes making process. Thus the tanning industry played a very predominant role for the changing of the life style of the man from bad to good by melting the body into *Ranga*-or '*Nam*' on earth and the growth of roots started widened. Chemical weathering causes rocks to decompose by changing their chemical composition of the '*Sudhra Family*' on earth. For example; rain water dissolves certain minerals in a rock for the repetition of the history itself. Erosion is the wearing of another dress of the surface away and removal of land surfaces of the water, wind or ice. It is greatest in the area of little or no surface vegetation such as desserts, where sand dunes may forms[13] another dessert of '*Nam*' as a day area of the Father. Keeping in view, the striking rate of the rock, the particles are then transported by glaciers, rivers and wind and deposited as sediment in lakes, deltas, dessert and on the ocean floor. Some of these sediments undergoes lithification and forms sedimentary rock. This rock may be thrust back to surface by crusted movement or forced deeper into the earth's interior, where heat and pressure is generating transformation of society into different direction of life style as it found into the metamorphic rocks of the '*Nam*'. The Metamorphic rock in turn may be pushed up to the surface or may be melted to form magma (molten rock). Eventually the magma interior cools and solidifies below or on the surface as '*Nam*' on earth forming igneous rocks against the negative forces a atmosphere to crust them with a scientific manner. When sedimentary rock, igneous rocks and metamorphic rocks[14] are exposed once more on the Earth's surface the cycle begins again for repetition of history in automatic style as '*Nam*' or '*Chamar*' on earth.

Keeping in view, the above mentioned facts of the study the Lower Carboniferous flaggy lime stones of grayish colour lies conformably over the *Muthi-Barnai* quartzites of Devonian Age in Aishmaqam and Kotsu type of places. These limestones are highly fossiliferous, the predominant fossil being the Syringothyris Cuspidata (Brachiooda) and for that reason, they are designed as the syingothyris limestones. Few other fossil like products, chenotes, athyris (Brachiopoda) already discussed above, and Phillipsia (Trilobite) have also been identified in these limestones[15] as '*Names*' on earth. Its atmosphere consisted of Volcanic gases with little oxygen, making it hostile to most forms of life from *Precambrian Period* to '*Devonian Period*' Constant movement of the earth's crustal plates carried continents across the earth's surface before the 3,400 million years ago for the first time in history to warm the sea or '*Sudhra Family*' to repeat the history of the 'Nam' in consecutive manner and Brahmins equally opposed it for benefit which stands nowhere in end.

Caves and Minerals Resources During the Middle Carboniferous Period

Caves are generally found in the limestone areas, although on coastlines of the rocks. It shows that limestone is made of calcite (calcium carbonate) which dissolves in the carbonic acid naturally present in rainwater, and in humic acids from the decay of vegetation. The acidic water trickles down through cracks and joints of the '*Nam*' in the limestone and between rock layers, breaking up the surface terrain into clints (blocks of rocks) separated by grikes (deep cracks) and punctuated by sink holes (also called swallow- holes or potholes) into which surface steams may disappear. Underground, the acidic water dissolves the rocks around crevices, opening up a network of the passages and caves of the '*Nam*' caverns, if the roofs collapse. Various features of the mineral resources are formed when dissolved calcite is redeposited e.g., it may be redeposited along the underground stream to for a *gour* (series of calcite ridges) or in caves and the passages of the God to form stalactites and stalagmites. Stalactites develop where calcite is left behind as water drips from the roof, where the drop level is stalagmites to build up[16] the earth as a beautiful place of the Father.

Mineral resources can be defined as naturally occurring substances that can be extracted from the earth and are useful as fuels and raw materials. Coal , oil and gas '*Word*' collectively called fossil fuel and *Chamars* are the organic origin commonly included in this group for the study of '*Nam*' or God, but they are not strictly minerals because they must study the process of the '*Nam*' as their race. Coal formation begins when vegetation is buried and partly decomposed to form peat. Overlying sediments compress the peat and transform it into lignite (soft brown coal). As the overlying sediments accumulate, increasing pressure and temperature eventually transform the lignite into bituminous and hard anthracite coals. Oil and gas are usually formed from organic matters that were deposited in marine sediments. Under the effect of heat and pressure of the *'Nam'*, the compressed organic matter undergoes complex chemical changes to form oil and gas. The oil and gas percolate upwards through water-saturated, permeable rocks and they may rise to the Earth's surface or accumulate below an impermeable layer of rocks of the *'Ravidas Culture'* or *'Chamar Culture'* have been found in Jammu and Kashmir State that has been folded or faulted in the history of man to form trap the *'Brahminical Ideology'* of the period working without logic and reasoning in this society as an 'egoistic thought' we are superior race of the Universal Culture like an anticline (upfold) trap of the human history. For Example, mineral resources like *Kasyapasilpa, Saraswathiya-Chitrakarma-sastra, Naradasilpasastra* and painstaking research of C. Sivaramamurti on the works of *Kalidasa, Banabhatt* and a number of other scholars like *Nannecoda, Trivikrama, Dhanapala*, etc. are inorganic substances on the paper entitled '*The Artists in Ancient India'* that may consist of a single chemical elements of the positive force will destroy them, such as gold, silver, copper or combination of elements[17] (substances) that cannot be broken down chemically in simpler substances as *'Names'* on the earth, simple and powerful to realize the man, the history of Spiritual Knowledge is necessary for the life of man; as *Mahabharata* and *Ramayana* was composed by the epic *Rishis* of *Sudhra Family* i.e., *Valimiki* and *Ved Vyas*) of the primitive society. A mineral is a naturally occurring substance that has a characteristic chemical composition and specific physical properties of the man, such as habit and need not have a specific composition and a rock, by comparison, in an aggregate of minerals. Minerals can be divided into two main groups: native elements and compounds one. Native eliminations called *manas* of the living man are made up of pure elements at one time, when it was there in the childhood in the history of man, with the development of the man made idea of self-style called *Brahmins* or *Molavis* of the period became problem creator of the society or making false propaganda of the man against man. Keeping in view, the situation, there is a need of pure elements of gold (chemical symbol *Au*), Silver (*Ag*), Copper (*Cu*), and Carbon (*C*); carbon occurs as a native element in two forms as black as *Brahmins* and *Molavis* form the heart, diamond and graphite, they remain constant as *Dr. Raj Kumar* and *Baba Gurinder Singh ji Biaswale*. Compounds are combinations of two or more elements called *Dr. Ram Dass, Master Deepit Raj,* and Baba Rasila Ram. For example, sulphides are compounds of sulphur (S) and one or more other elements of the '*Nam*' as *Pandavas* of the period of same family such as lead (*Pb*) in the mineral galena, or antimony (*Sb*) in mineral stibnite. They have the different properties such as : sulphides (*Pbs*) Galena, Gold (*Au*), Diamond (*C*) stands for *Chamar*, Graphite has also the same value as Chamar (C), Smoky quartz (SiO_2) , specular Haemattive (Fe_2O_5), Bauxite (FeO (OH) and Al_2O_3, $2H_2O$), Stibmite (Sb_2 S_5), Pyrites (FeS_2), Onyx (SiO_2). Kidney Ore Haematite (Fe_2 O_5), Pyromorphite (Pb_5 $(PO_4)_5$ Cl) Wavellite ($Al_3(PO_4)_2$, $(OH,F)_3$. $5H_2O$), Sodalitre (Na_8 Al_6 Si_6 O_{24} Cl_2), Tourmaline (Na (Mg, Fe, Li, Mn, $Al)_3$, Al_6 (BO_3) Si_6 . O_{18} $(OH,F)_4$), Olivine (Fe_2 Sio_4- Mg_2 Sio_4) Cerussite ($PbCO_3$) Calcite (Ca Co_3) Epidote (Ca_2 (Al, Fe $)_3$ $(SiO_4)_3$ (OH), Cyanotrichite ($Cu_4Al_2(SO_4)$ $(OH)_{12}$. $2H_2O$), Daisy Gypsum (Ca SO_4 .$2H_2O$), Muscovite (KAI_2 (Si_3Al) O_{10} , $(OH, F)_2$), Orthoclose ($KALSi_3O_8$), Walfenite (Pb M_o O), Green Flourite (CaF_2) and Orange Halite (Rock Salt) (NaCI)[18]. There the modern properties of the *Chambarian* Rocks and the *Chamar* industry of the Kashmir is to work for the rectifying of the truth as T stands its properties as a Universal Truth in the history of man and God.

Mineral Features of the System

Mineral can be identified by studying the physical features of the areas such as fractures, cleavage, crystal system, habit, hardness of the system, colours and streak have been found in the recent study of the nervous calls of the brain, called the habenula. They have the wired works attained significance movement of the man in history with its connection with brain, and its differences occurred in the left and right sides of the brain are thought to influence cognitive performance and social behaviour of the man through the wired connection in the body as a mineral process in the body. Lead researcher by scientists at University College *London* claim that causing habenular neurons to produce a bright green cell called fluorescent protein showed they form remarkable spiral shaped axons the long nerve fibers that act as the nervous system of transmission lines in the man's system,[19] as God and man on earth.

A new study by an Indian origin neurosurgeon has shown that cell phone use could kill more people than smoking because of its possible association with brain cancer. *Dr. Vini Khurana*, a staff specialist Neurosurgeon at the Canberra Hospital and Associate Professor of Neurosurgery at the Australian National University, said that heavy usage of the mobile phones might turn out to be greater threat to human health than smoking and even asbestos of the period. To support his finding, *Khurana* conducted a 15 month 'Critical review' of the link between mobile phones and malignant brain tumors and said that using mobiles for more than 10 years could result in more than double the risk of brain cancer to human beings[20] in the history of man a new devise of the Father to kill the bad elements of the history in the class-struggle theory of man and God.

In the study, we learn that minerals can break in different ways if a mineral breaks in an irregular ways, leaving rough surfaces, it possesses fractures of the opinion of the man in scientific manner and the negative forces are decorating their *Janam-patris*, and horoscopes and birth charts, in collaboration with other Brahmin astrologers like *Ganesh Dass, Bua Ditta, Ashoka Kumar Dogra* against the *Par-painters* and Shahpur was the original place of these artist, and located at *Pur* in child's thought. Master Deepit Raj will teach a lesson to them as idiot *Dalit-Brahmin* and positive forces become opposite to each other in the interest of, to find out the 'Reality' in the sense to defeat the negative force in the history of man. If a mineral features breaks along well-defined planes of weakness, it possesses cleavage. Specific minerals have distinctive patterns of cleavage, e.g. mica cleavage along one plane. Most minerals form crystals, which can be categorized into crystal system according to their symmetry and number of faces known from the study of '*Nam*' that God is working in this Universe. Within each system, several different but related form of crystal is possible, e.g., a cubic crystal can have six already discussed above in this chapter, eight or twelve sides. A mineral habit is the typical form taken by an aggregate of its crystals. Examples of habit include botryoidal (like a bunch of grapes) and massive (no definite form). The relative hardness of a mineral may be arrested by testing its resistance to scratching. The property is usually measured using Moha scale, which increases in hardness form 1 (talc) to 10 (diamonds) the colour of the material is not a dependable guide to its identity as some minerals have a range of colours as *White Huna* and Black Huna as two opposite forces working in this Universe. All the *par painters* from the Sanskrit word *patt*, live in the far-flung areas of Bhilwara and *Chittor* district of Rajasthan. Originally five *Pandavas*, the number of their families is now nine for the concentration of the natural historycame from the agricultural background as responsible kings of the Sudhra Family. Streak (the colour the powdered mineral makes when rubbed across an unglazed tile) is a more reliable indicator[21] of the *'Nam'* or God on earth. The development of Palacogic sequence in Kashmir history is more or less continuous upto the Middle Carboniferous after which there is a clear evidence of a break in deposition accompanied by many changes of the *Early Chamar* history to modern period of study in connection with advancement of Science and Technology or what we can call it as *Maid-Palaeozoic* efforts made by the *Black Brahmins* and *Molavis* to leave the *Sudhras* away from the discussion of the land issue like Kashmir itself is a part of the *Sudhra Family* explore with the *'Light'* of Father as an old concept of *India* during the Aryan period of the *Jammu* region.

Volcanoes are vents or fissures in the Earth's crust through which *magma* (molten rock the originates from deep beneath the crust) is forced on to the surface as *lava*. They occur most commonly along the boundaries of crustal plates most volcanoes lie in a belt called the "Ring of Fire" which runs along the edge of the Pacific Ocean. Volcanoes can be classified according to the violence of the 'Law of Nature' and frequency of their eruptions in the history of man. Non-explosive volcanic eruptions generally occur where crustal plates pull apart from the study of *'Nam'* a *Deepit Raj* a separate man of the history, he knows the reality of the world in obscure manners, cannot express its story in deep manners only signal he displays with actions and deed. These eruptions produce runny basaltic lava that spreads quickly over a wide area to form another idea relatively of flat cones already existed in the society, but certain sanction has to be release as a authority of the world knowledge as *Chamar* exhibits in very of the life of man as a repeated records of the human history as *Ravidas* is still working in this Universal as 'New Idea' of the Scientific Knowledge of man in the History Subject to wash artificial Scientific Knowledge of the Brahmins who are pollution created in this Universe. The most violent eruption take place where plates collide and history will take another turn in future course of action. Such eruptions produce thick rhyolitic lava and may also blast out clouds of dust to crush the pollution of the society and pyroclasts (lava fragments) take place the shape of the country and its original rulers, those are the Lovers of the *'Nam'* on earth as Natural Force of the Father like *Dr. Raj Kumar, Baba Gurinder Singh ji, Biaswale*, *Dr. Ram Dass* and *Master Deepit Raj* modern man of the Subject History. The lava does not flow far before cooling the history of the man without crushing the Brahmins of the period one or the other hands like 'Kalinga War' or *'Karbala War'* of the Muslim faith, therefore, it builds up steep-sided, conical volcanoes. Some volcanoes produce *lava* and ash eruptions, which build up composite volcanic cones. Volcanoes that erupt frequently are described as active forces of the Father from the inside study of the man, those that erupt rarely are termed dormant in worldly life and those that have stopped erupting altogether are termed extinct are the Brahmins of the human history or leading of the *Gayatri mantra* force of the unnatural force as a religious body of the modern politicians of the Indian society as the dictator of the Hinduism which has no history but bundles of superstitious, caste system, ritual ceremonies from the polluted ideas of the 'Mind Only' not of the God. They are celebrating without any logic of the objective in self style manners as egoistic thought of the study that we are learned of the religious society as a fraud against the Natural Thought. As well as *'Voice of the God'*, will play the role, it will become a volcanoes and they will have to struggle for another life. Other features are associated with volcanic regions include geysers, hot mineral springs, softataras, fumaroles and bubbling mud pools[22] of the *'Nams'*. It is to help the costume designer for stage and cinema of the world history as its illustrations in the paintings and other arts of the life. Womenfolk at home land a helping hand to the artist like *Sabanam Grewal Churi* of Kerala calls the writer on telephone and SMS messages.

Traditional Legends and Origin of the Name Jammu

In detail, the tradition and legends about the origin of the Name Jammu is originated from the *Jamboo tree*, as it grows with the race of '*Brahminical Ideology*' as black thought as the colour of the Jamun tree. In the Royal Camp of the *Nam-History*, a *Pandava* race was born out from this area to crush the idiot thought on the negative elements *Jambulochan* had a desire to kill raise after his Name, a delightful city of the *Nam-history* called as '*City of the Temples*'. The present famous Shivadwala in the centre of Jammu regionis to have believed the place wherefrom 'Light' of the world has been bornin the form of *Guru Nanak* in a Sudhra or *Untouchable* Family. Maharaja *Sudershan* of Ayodhya (1600-1560 B.C.) had two sons, *Agnibaran* and *Agnigar* as two members of the '*Nam-History*'. The elder one succeeded his father as ruler (1560-1530 B.C.). Finally, he came to *Podal* (Kathua) where he took possessionin some of the villages as Dr. Ram Dass of the village *Hiranagar* crushed the idiot *Brahmins* of this area, and killed *Chandra-Has* and occupied the kingdom of *Madra-Desh* of the '*Chamar-Culture*' including Jalahandar, Himachal Pradesh, Kangra-tradition of *Mahabharata*. The original kingdom of Susarma Chandra was supposed to have been located at *Multan* and Sindh in *Katoch* family in the 13th century B.C. According to certain Indian scriptures like *Marichi* was the offspring of Lord Brahma, as a 'Creative Power', as author created the idea of *Nam-History* with spiritual pen, destroyed by Brahmins in complacent manner. There is no criticism of the author's writings on '*Chamar thought*'. It shows that Brahminical historians like Irfan Habib, *Shrimali*, P.N. Shu, ect. have been badly crushed with the idea of '*Surya Race*' called 'Sun' or *Ravi* in natural history. The first historical mention of the land of five river called Panjab or '*Madra Desha*' have covered by the ancient *Name* of *Jambudevipa* that 'Light' of the human race will be forever born out from Jammu and Kashmir state as their original hereditary *jagir* of the *Sudhra Family*'; whichhad its headquarters at Sangala or Sialkot, in traditional value as Raja Shal, the maternal uncleof the '*Pandavas Family*' and for many generation from *Lord Buddh* to Gulab Singh, this territory of the *Jambulocan* became a part of *India*, a country of *Bharat* that was the legendary king of the past history of Jammu region; and the '*Dogra Family* is known as the story of God and Man'.

Glaciers and Rivers

Jammu and Kashmir, is well known as 'Paradise on Earth from the very ancient period of the Indian history also called 'The

Switzerland of Asia', *Chamar,* surely such a ridge gives a scope to variety of scenery to international tourist, is inherent trait of all living beings of the human history. Man, since his very beginning, travelled and toured from one place to another, as the flowing waters of the rivers, melting from glaciers as the original sources of flowing the water into different rivers.[23] According to the most acceptable and popular legend found practically correct in the history of Jammu region that *'Raja Jamboo Lochan'* founded the Jammu City in the 14th century B.C. During one of his hunting he reached near a river (Tawi) where he saw a goat in the form of a man as a changed species from animals to human nature by obtaining the beauty of the *'Nam'* in the life of man and a lion drinking water together at the same place as *Deepit Raj* son of *Dr. Raj Kumar* both were of the same category as they were the Chamars of the history. The King (*Deepit Raj*) was so impressed by harmony between the two i.e., *Dr. Raj Kumar* and *Baba Gurinder Singhji Biaswale* that entire matter of the world history was handed over to them to repeat the history of the *'Nam'*.

Mention is made of Jammu Province in *Mahabharata* that *Bharat* (India) was born there and found in *Harappan* remains of the *Chamar Dynasty* of Kashmir and of Jammu region called Indus Valley peoples of Akhnoor or Aryans, provide evidence that Jammu was a part of Harappan Civilization of *'Sudhra Family'*; was the force of the *'Ravidas Culture'*, who widely spread their culture in whole of the world, the artifacts of this period, numerous 'Stone Temples' objects of art found in various parts of the Jammu and Kashmir State, also speak of its heydays in the remote past in the history of *Mauryans, Kushana's*, and *Gupta's* time, found at *Akhnoor* in *Ambarana* Valley of the Father, have added new dimensions to its ancient character [25] as it was kept by the Master of the 'Human History' of the world. These appears to be *Central Asian* dresses of sorts, and though the *Huna* invasion belongs to this period, it is inexplicable why such costumes should have been depicted in this single monument and nowhere else have been seen in the study of the historical facts as 'Nam' has been established on this earth to clear the 'Brahminical Ideology' in the area of Jammu and Kashmir State.

According to the popular legend and the historical evidences reveal, Kashmir Valley was a famous for *Dal* Lake. *Kasyap Rishi,* drained out the Valley of Water with the power of '*Nam*' and made it habitable by cleaning the forest of the adjoining areas of the Kashmir Valley that is called 'the sea od*mountains of Kashyapa*' as the originated thought of '*Sudhra*' or *Dalit Family*. It is said that originally *Yakshas, Pashtun* and *Pishachas* tribes inhabited there on higher reaches as *Gujjars* and *Bakerwals* of the modern period that did not allows the people to live in peace in the pre-historic days because they had no political idea of the life, but with the establishment of the '*Rule of Law*' in India framing by *Dr. B.R. Ambedkar*, they were encouraged in the history of man, by providing certain privilege in the Indian Constitution since 1947 A.D.

History of *Srinagar* is in a fact the history of Kashmir based on the region of the Jammu state as an idealistic idea of the man in human history by developing man to God. Therefore, in the study we learn that there was the hub of the development of the Buddhist culture to all over the worlds which revolved the history of Humanism in whole of the social life. The city of great antiquity has had a chequered history of the man's study, which dates back to 250 B.C. when *King Ashoka* of the *Chamar Dynasty* founded his capital in Srinagar at *Pandrethan* mentioned in the *Kalhana's Rajatarangini*, an original sources of the Kashmir history. *Hieun-Tsang* defines the boundaries of *Pandrethan* as extending, along with the Zaberwan hills, from *Harvan* to *Zewan* or *Sempur*. King *Ashoka* brought Buddhism in to Kashmir from the Jammu Region, particularly from the Akhnoor Valley of *Ambaran*, a village called *Manda* having the '*Indus-Saraswati Valley*' of the '*Ravidas Culture*' or '*Chamar Culture*', which was strengthened by *Kanishka, Hunas, Satavahanas, Guptas, Karkotas* and others. The area attained freedom again in 530 A.D., but was short lived[26] in the hands of the *Damaras* of Kashmir, called feudal lords of the Father. Thus, the reverence command of the Jammu people during the absence of Father, these forces became heavy on the human history and due to the economic illusions, these political as well as economical forces beyond measuring the reverence of the Father that he is not watching the world. It is undoubtedly from the study of the 'History' the *Hazraratbal Shrine* was founded by the Father with the power of *'Nam'* on earth in the form of *Dr. Raj Kumar*, with the collaboration of his colleague *Baba Gurinder Singh Ji Biaswale*, as a *Punjab* ruler of the *'Nam'* called in Kashmir *Dulabhavardhan* I, the ruler of the *'Chamar Dynasty'* of the Kashmir in Chinese language called *Karkota* Rulers, became a central power of the Spiritual Knowledge of the world, and till date the modern historians of India could not confirmed the Scientific Truth of the *'Nam'* which *Dr. B.R. Ambedkar* already discussed that 'History repeat itself', announced in Indian Parliament in the Constituent Assembly in 1949, he also made a statement on it.[27] Because this unmatched reverence is anchored in the 'Love' of the Father, and respect for the Prophet *Mohammad*, whose *Moi-e-Muqqadas* (the scared air) is preserved here in this shrine as a religious place of the Father in Human form as a race of the human history predicts his history as *'Nam'* on earth, and Sir Walter Lawerence called this body as the "Lake par – excellence",[28] because he knew the wit of the *Chamar's* body, as they were the follower of the *'Ravidas Race'*, the excellent race of the world having full knowledge of the worldly wit as God and man knows, when they are worked together in the history of Kashmir as a Scientific Truth lies in the body of man. He would there be at the very core and centre of the *'DIVINE HIMAVAT'* like the stream of the glacier to use the fine ancient name of the Human history like *Ravidas* on earth, which means "Abode of Winter".[29] In Jammu, Sanskrit name *'Jambu'*, Hindi name, *'Jamun'*, and his family is called 'My tracheae' in generally called *'Syzygium Cumini'*, an old men with long staves patiently knock the door of the Jammu region to repeat the history as their original home to spread the Buddhism or *Chamaristic* idea of the *'Nam'* or God on earth in human form as 'Gateway of India' as an old species of the plant, where the land of India lies in the 'History'. A generous plant that fruits abundantly, the *Jamun* is described in 'the *Mahabharata*' by *Bharat* as a cosmic tree standing to the south of Mount *Meru*, the axis of the universe. When the ripened fruit of this gigantic tree burst, its juice fell in waterfalls, making a river which comes the boundaries of a land known as *Jambu-dvipa*, that light of the *'Nam'* stands in Jammu region in *Human* form. The juice itself is an excellent as Walter Lawrence as described in his study for liver stimulant, while decoctions from the bark are used to cure mouth ulcers and for strengthening the gums. The powdered bark is commonly used as a tooth powder by children and parakeets battle over its heavy purple berries and every mouth is stained with juice,[30] they are remembering the Raj Kumar as a man of the 'History', and their distribution is mainly confined to *Lehindajjar* to the left side of the *Lidder Valley*.[31]

Rivers Features

Rivers features are one of the major forces which carry the water of the glaciers from one place to another than shaped the landscape of the earth in human form as the race of the man is going on in the present Era. Near its source, a river is steep *Chamar* the continuous source of history cycling the water between sea and land to observe the atmospheric value of the man, how they are moulding their mouths in the '*Chamar History*' a Universal Truth is standing in Jammu region in the form of Raj Kumar, as a man of the human history. The source of a river either *Ravi* or *Chenab*. But having the same meaning as '*Nam*' or God on earth, may be a mountain spring or lake of the '*Nam*', or a melting glacier. The course that the river subsequently takes depends on the slope of the terrain and on the rock types and formation over which it flows, it covers the other area of the human history. In its early life, upland stages like paradise in Kashmir, a river tumbles steeply over rocks and boulderes and cuts a steep–sided V-shaped Valley. Farther downstream, it flows smoothly over sediments and forms winding meanders, eroding sideways to create broad valleys and plains. On reaching the coastline, the river may deposit sediment to form an estuary or delta.[32] A delta is an area of sand-bars, swamps, and lagoons through which the river flows in several channels called distributaries, the Mississippi delta, for example to express the history of the '*Nam*' in uniform system as a collection of the water and take the shape of a sea. Often, a rise in sea level may have flooded the river-mouth to form a broad estuary, a tidal section where seawater mixes with freshwater [33] as '*Nam*' or God having the same meaning. Additional influences include the activities of living organisms such as coral, crustal movements, and sea-level creates an emergent coastline, with cliffs and beaches stranded above the new shoreline. Sinking land or a rise in sea level produces a drowned coastline, typified by fjords (submerged glacial valleys) or submerged into river Valleys[34] as history repeat itself.

Oceans and Seas

Oceans and seas cover 70% of the Earth's surface and account for about 97% of its total water. These oceans and seas play a crucial role in the life of man. It shows during the time of *Ashoka's* reigned over earth, after *Sakuni*; however, tempting the proposed identification is in view of the significance of the name *Puranadhisthana* have 'the ancient capital' of *Ashoka*. The general conclusion here indicated receives further confirmation by the evidence called *Sodara* spring in Persian language, the miraculous reappearance of which near Srinagar is the subject of the legend here related, we have to rely on a few passages of the *Nilamata Purana* and the *Nandiksetra Mahatmya* of the Kashmir history again going to unite at one point, i.e., God and man; from the fragmentary passages of the first named text, the *Sodaranaga*, is mentioned in connection with the shrine of *Bhutesvara* of the same community called *Chamar* on earth. In SL. 1334 again the pilgrimage to *Sodara* is prescribed along with that to the *Samgama* of the '*Nam*' at *Kanakavaini* River called *Haramukuta Ganga* pilgrimage in the *Tirthas; Tatah* (the *Haramukutaganga* Lake of the '*Nam*'. From *Chavillakara* verse and Kashmiri's own expression defined by *Kalhana* that tree *Turuska* Kings are supposed to have ruled simultaneously in the history of Kashmir known as *Baba Rasila Ram* of *Saidpurwale* located in *Punjab Dr. Raj Kumar, Master Deepit Raj* of the same family called *Sudhras* of Kashmir history. In 1883, Prinsep identified these coins with *Kanishka* at *Barnai* in Buddhist tradition *Nandisa* is the designation of the Siva from the ancient time *Chandala* rulers of the Kashmir and their Kingdom was in *Amarnath* cave, worshipped in the *Nund-Kul* Lake and *Avatara* of the latter period. In order to give full sanctity to the new *Jyestharudra* river of the *Ravidas* castle which *Jalauka* the son of *Ashoka* had established his Kingdom in Srinagar on the same place in connection with the name *Sudhar*, which appears in the designation of a portion called *Dal* Lake, family of the *Sudhra* tribes, called *Sudara- Khun* and in the name of the neighbouring village *Sudarabal*, with this legend, relates that 'many hundred years ago',

Brahmans were in the habit of making pilgrimages to these springs[35] of the '*Nam*' and did make them dirty with the pollutionary ideas to destroy these springs. But the castle of *Ravidas* still working in the history of man as *Skandabhavana* of the Kashmir during the time of *Mayasum* of the Gupta period as unsafe in the history of man, and troubled times of *Muhammad Shah's* first reign in 1484-86 A.D.[36]

It shows from the study, and other evidences of the same phenomenon in the *Muhammadan* Shrine of *Hazaratbal* of *Kashmir*, near the *Dal* Lake already mentioned above, the sacred hair of the Mohammad Prophet have been found in the memory of the Father as the ruler of Kashmir and became pilgrimage centre during his absence in the study of '*Nam*'. Its existence is in all probability due to the fact that the site continued to attract the local worshippers even after their con version to the true faith that His study should remain intact in the history of Kashmir. They were the strong followers of *Sirahasila* Castle of the *Sudhra Family* "Hill of Ganesa' or *Genes Ghati* of the same trees as ridge at its rocky Northern extremity of the *Prechambrian* or *Chamar* Period as an old group is again coming out in the limelight of Indian history as real ruler of the worldly Kingdoms in the history of '*India*' having the Mission of *Radha Soami* concept as modern *Buddhism* as a State policy of the *Sudhra Family* to develop the idea of '*Nam*' or God on earth tossing from the *Ganga* stream against the *Kisanganga*[37] of the Jammu region, already detail has been discussed that history of the '*Nam*' is again going to repeat in natural way. A day break means to beginning the Enlightenment Era of the '*Nam*' the shrine of the goddess *Sarada* could not stop him. *Bhoja* or '*Nam*' is hence obliged to ascend the *Madhumati* or *Gurumati* on the throne of Kashmir that Mohammad Prophet again born in India. It is clear from the study of *Rajouri* soldiers routed before *Drabagam*, a direct route for fighting towards homeward journey of the soul, some applies to *Padampur* in the *Mahabharat* by Bharat to study the '*Nam*' find the facts of life. It was not simply used by the Indo-Aryan, but, they implemented the word '*Arya*' means '*Nam*' or *Sudhra* or God on earth, or as the result of a popular etymology' which connected the name *Beda* with '*bud*', 'great' as defined in the study as for the term '*Akbar*'. The expression of the term *Bhaddavana* used by *Srivara*, the follower of the *Kalhana's Rajatarangini*, looks to me as it takes from real nomenclature of the study, i.e., *Chura* or *Bhangi, Chamar, Megha, Barawala* or *Batwal, Gadari* or *Mahashah, Lohar, Tarkhan, Kumhar, Nai, Raj, Sunar, Dhobi* or *Chhimba, Darzi, Penja, Teli, Naqqash*, and *Purbia menials, Kurmi, Kori, Jatav* and other applied to leather meanings more than to "*tan*". He tans OX, buffalo, trees, birds in hides only and does not work in the leather which He '*Tans*',[38] their body. May it not be found in the Sanskrit language, but also found equivalent of the name *Barnai*, which is applied now to stream flowing past in the history of man called *Budabrar*, as well as to the valley drained by it called *Nai* by the caste to dress the society with the power of '*Nam*'. At the present *Sardi* used for the term *Sarada*, by *Sindhu* can be meant only the *Kishnganga* which as in *Kalhana's* days is still locally merely known as 'Sind', the river of *Sarada, Narada* or *Saraswati* of Jammu Region and *Vagdevi* invite to her on *Srisalia*, a big rock of the '*Nam*' or *Chamar*. It shows from the study that classical accounts of the various writers mentioned by *Herodotus*, *Strabo* that gold-washing was carried on in old times by the *Dards* of the '*Nams*' of the *Kisanganga* Valley and the *Upper Indus*[39] region to the *Ravidas Culture* of the prehistoric period called *Chambrian* Age of Paleozoic rocks already discussed above. A many places like *Banihal* and *Bijbehara* the *Pir Panjal-tracks* have been passing upwards quite conformably into black and grey coloured siliceous and carbonaceous fossiliferous shacks designated as the '*Fenestella Shales*' of the '*Nam*' or '*Chamar*' as air route of the Masters also called as '*Gangamopteris beds*' of the life theory of the '*Nam*' as a powerful machinery of the earth containing rich assemblage of plant fossils of *Gangamopteris* and *Glassopteris* flora. The beds are distinctly of fluviatile origin from the history of Kashmir and their age is regarded as *Artinskian* (Basal Permian). They are very important from the starting of graphical point of view because they have been accepted as defining the lower limit of *Gondwana* System[40] of the '*Nam*' to wash out the dirty material or force of the '*Nam*' for the establishment of the 'New Society' as a 'New Story' of the modern historiography of the man's life.

Salt Content of Sea Water

It contains Potassium 1.1%, Magnesium 3.7%, Sodium, 30.2%, Calcium 1.2%, Sulphate 7.6%, Chloride 54.3% and others 1.9%.

Cold Water Upwelling (Southern Hemisphere)

It includes surface ocean current, wind drives water along coast, cold water upwelling replaces warm surface water and continental slopes of the earth.

Offshore Currents

Offshore currents are known as surface ocean current, pack-ice formation increases water salinity and density, than polar bottom water changed into cold, dense water sinks of the continental slopes at that time the surface currents from the axis power to lead 40^0, 80^0, 120^0, 160^0 and 180^0, same as the opposite force of the earth from top to bottom working on this earth.

How Tides are Caused

Due to the Earth's orbit, tidal bulge caused by Moon's gravitational pull on Earth with the gravitational force of the Sun or Ravi and it reinforces centrifugal effect on life, producing large tidal-bulge, diminishes Moon's effect on earth but its gravitational force becomes strongest with the coordination of Sun and stars as *Chamar* and His race. High spring tide, new moon appears with low neap tide in the last quarter due to gravitation force of the Moon than it appears full moon as '*Nam*' exhibits in this Universe. In addition to this, equal and opposite force of tidal bulge produced by centrifugal effect due to Earth's spinal cord and then moon orbit slowly disappears to rise in the same process round the earth as a progressive idea of the history in various field of life.

Effects of Coriolis Force and Ekman Spiral Force

According to the movement of the earth corioles forces of the Northern Pole, equator try to provide original direction of wind or current on the surface for the striking of future course of event in history to repeat the actual direction, deflected to right in Northern Hemisphere to left the Southern Hemisphere from the Souther pole, at the deep current at 180⁰ on the surface current. Midwater current further deflected by coriolis force[41] of the earth as *'Nam'* predict the worldly life of the human nature as a powerful stroke of the modern current life. Thus, the flooring ocean in such conditions comprises two sections; the continental shelf and slope, and the deep-ocean flooring extended far into the ocean as the *Sudhra Thought* as widely spread in *Sudharmatha* and it becomes an ocean current of the natural theory as a *Sodara* spring of the *'Nam'* on earth as already discussed above, cited by *Kalhana* to reflect the message to the worldly life to repeat the history of man and God. Echo-sounding and remote sensing from satellites has revealed the Truth in history that the geographical features of the plain is divided into mountain ranges. As the ocean flooring spreads, volcanoes that have formed over hot spots in the crust move away from their magma source, they become extinct and are increasingly submerged into eroded land of the earth.

Main Features of the Ocean Floor

The main features of the ocean floor are called as sediment, submarine canyon, continental shelf, course of mud river, continental rise, continental slop, guyot (flat-topped seamount), seamount (under water mountain) abyssal plain, mid-ocean ridge, ocean trench, continental crust, ooze, tiny sea creatures, layer of volcanic rock, pillow lava, volcanic crystalline rock, oceanic crust, magma (molten rock) and sediment as well.

Continental-Shelf Floor

It has shoreline, bedrock exposed by tidal scour, parallel strips of coarse material left by strong tidal current, sand deposited in wavy pattern by weaker currents for the history of *'Nam'*, and irregular patches of find sand deposited by weakest currents of the Father to repeat the history of the same again in the memories of the *Pitrs*. In addition to this, deep-ocean floor sediments called as calcareous ooze, pelagic clay, glacial sediments, siliceous ooze, terrigenous sediments, metalliferous mud's, and major module fields are found from the study of ocean as Nam of Sri Lanka.

Echo-Sound Profile of Ocean Floor and its Development

It begins with sand wave, minor oscillations caused by ship's movement, velocity of sound in water (1,493 m/sec.), and its reference code became 22. During the time of event it marks synchronization of survey equipment due to sand wave and seabed profile. Keeping in view, these historical facts, the development of an atoll take place and it took volcanic island from the sea level as coral grows on shoreline, than it becomes fringe reef. It formed the lagoon shape after sometime, and coral continues to grow, forming barrier reef in the life with the eroded volcanic island subsides. Certain barrier reef continues to grow where from the waves bring food for the animals and others from the dead coral, and lagoon becomes visible. Volcanic island also becomes submerged into different categories of the study time and again into atoll as it originated from the language of Maldives. After this coral submerged deeply to grow[42] in the new life of the man from old species.

Environment Condition During the Time of Pollution

As we know Earth is surrounded by its atmosphere, a blanket of gases due to the industrial growth takes the shape of pollution and the result was that it enables life to exist on the planet. This layer has no definite outer edge, gradually becoming thinner until it merges into space, but 80% of atmospheric gases are held by gravity within about 20 kilometers of the earth's surface. The atmosphere blocks out much harmful to the man's life due to the ultraviolet solar radiation, and insulates the earth against extremes of temperature by limiting the scope of energy in man's day to day life, both incoming solar radiation, and the escape of re-radiated heat into space. This natural balance may be distorted by the greenhouses effect, as gases such as carbon dioxide have built up in the atmosphere, trapping more heat. Close to the Earth's surface, differences in air temperature and pressure of the inner gases cause a air to circulate between the equator and poles. This circulation, together with the corioles force, gives rise to the prevailing surface winds of the natural force and the high level jet streams[43] change the climate conditions of the earth. Te climate zone can be classified as intermediatory force of the subtropical zone of the areas in different manners. In its zone lie the major portions of districts of *Doda, Akhnoor, Reasi, Poonch, Nushara, Kishtwar, Bhadrwah, Ramnagar, Basholi, Udhampur, Kathua, Nagari Parol, Panyali.* High peaks and higher elevated area of the Jammu and Kashmir region above the *Chenab* Valley areas of this zone experienced snowfall during winter and the average annual rainfall is 1464- 1708 mm, though in *Poonch* and *Rajouri* districts, it is lower ridges of the *Pir Panjal* sometimes rest for the snowfall due to the interruption of the monsoons during the months of March and April, and it has warm summers and it has been divided into five broad macro-climatic zones as sub divided into different categories[44]:

1. **Sub-Tropical Zone**: The mean height above the sea level range from 300 meters to nearby 1350 meters.
2. **Temperate Zone, mostly Valleys**: The mean height above the sea level ranges from 1560 meters to about 4200 meters. The zone essentially covers the Kashmir Valley and inner Himalayan valleys.
3. **Dry Temperate**: Attitude ranges between 1350 meters to more than 3000 meters includes all the areas above the outer hills.
4. **Cold Arid Zone**: This climate zone comprises high attitude areas of inner Himalayas with severe cold but dry winters and moderately hot and dry summers mostly the areas of *Kargil* in *Ladakh, Gilgit, Baltistan* and *Zanskar*, and *Budhal Valley* of the Jammu Region.
5. **Intermediate Zone**: This zone broadly covers mid and high attitude areas like *Doda, Rajouri, Chamba, Udhampur, Reasi, Padder, Batote, Ramnagar, Basholi, Bani* and *Mansar*. From October to June, the rainfall patterns of these areas are similar to sub-tropical zone.

Maximum and Minimum Temperature of these areas recorded during 2001 by the regional officers of the Meteorological of Srinagar displayed as under:

Table– 1.1

Degree Celsius

Month	*Jammu*		*Srinagar*	
	Mean Max	*Mean Min*	*Mean Max*	*Mean Min*
January	17.3	5.9	11.7	3.6
February	24.2	10.6	13.7	0.3
March	28.7	15.2	18.0	[illegible]

(Contd.)

(Contd. Table 1.1)

Month	Jammu		Srinagar	
	Mean Max	Mean Min	Mean Max	Mean Min
April	33.4	20.4	27.7	8.5
May	38.9	26.1	28.4	14.5
June	35.1	25.1	29.6	17.4
July	33.3	25.4	30.1	19.5
August	34.1	25.5	30.2	17.6
September	33.2	22.9	28.9	11.2
October	32.2	19.9	24.4	6.1
November	27.5	13.8	15.5	0.9
December	22.2	9.3	10.6	0.9

It makes clear from the study that during the months of December, January and February, there was the coldest months of the years both at Jammu and *Srinagar* as well as *Ladakh* itself. Jammu experienced extreme type of climatic conditions being very cold in winter and very hot in summer. Sometimes winter temperature falls to freezing point while summer temperature reaches to 45^{0}c. Kashmir Valley experienced extremely cold weather conditions, but in summer making it one of the most pleasant for tourist resorts as '*Nam's* rulers visited, there was widely spread palpitation in the valleys and took the shape of a terrorists movement as to pinch the *Damara* class why they are coming back to the original homelands, because of their negligence, they did not pay the respect to their rulers only the few have the idea and maximum majority out of its danger as self-style ruler of the 'Brahminical Ideology' as Prophet was against it, who fought against these rulers and defeated the *Brahmanbad* of the *Sindh* and Kashmir areas.

Growth of Population

According to the Census Report of India 2001, the population of the Jammu and Kashmir State was 10069917 occupies the 6th place in respect of area, it has 138 thousand square kms., and it stands No 19th in respect of population among the other states of India. Only *Uttaranchal* (8,479,562), *Himachal Pradesh* (6,077,248), *Tripura* (3,191,168), *Manipur* (2,388,634), and *Meghalaya* (2,306,069) are smaller in respect of population than Jammu and Kashmir. The population of Jammu and Kashmir State constituted merely 1.07% of the total population of India in 2001 as a burden on the state for historical analysis eating the exchequers of the Father without considering Him. On the national level the population growth declined particularly by the '*Sudhra Family*' in the Jammu region, whereas in *Kashmir* and *Ladakh*, they become burden on earth as Brahmins of the Father. According to the Census Report of India, out of the total population of the Jammu and Kashmir State the number of Scheduled Castes and Schedule Tribes were 497,363 or 8.30% of the State population of 5,98, 7389, which is fairly below the national average (15.75%), this is because the state is dominated by the Muslims who do not have Scheduled Castes in their religion[45], therefore, their idea is also come under the category of *Jinnah* or *Gandhi*, the followers of the Hindu and Muslims Religion which possessed no history[46] according the statement of *Kalhana*, there are the people of Brahminical Ideology, dominated by the political system without any reasoning and logic, but only on the basis of false propaganda that *Gujjars* and *Bakarwals* as a neglected race of the Father, but they have their own history, they are the race of the Father; *not* of the *Molavis*. This disparity in the level of social justice, they have the equal right to live in this universe as a race of the '*Nam*' or God.

However, *Nanak Bani* says that human existence is not due to the result of organic evolution or sexual base, but it is obtained through the good actions of the *Jiva* (soul) in human form: "By good deeds physical robe is obtained"[47]. From the study, it shows that if a human being does bad deeds, he is bound to wander through 84 Lakh existence to get rid from this earthly material, therefore, "*Nam*' is essential, it is the object of the life to qualify Him. Whereas, a serpent can reborn as a man and a man can reborn as a serpent, according to the idea of organic system, in that case none of the species of the living thing resemble to each other and difference is there on the action and deeds, do good have good which means, 'life produces life'. Thus, the Valley of Kashmir and its root have been found in Jammu region in '*Sudhra Family*' had a great links with Panjabi Culture of the *Ravidas* inspite of the fact that it covers a very small area in Jammu region near the Valley of Akhnoor and its adjoining presents a rich field of study for geologists as well as for the historians of the period including *Dr. Jigar Moammad* and others find out the finest development stratified records of all ages from *Archean* or *Prechambrian* in Kashmiri language and *Chamarization* in *Dogri* or Hindi language onwards to Tertiary and 'Recent Times' of the 21st century A.D., as an authentic record of human history on this earth through this document as a crushing defeat from the side of *Rai Family* to Brahmins of the period. Keeping in view, the above historical facts of the study, Jammu Hills are no less important and one can study the *Siwalika*, the *Murrees* the '*Dogra Slates*' as the States of the '*Sudhra Family*,' the marine Eocene rocks, similar as the rocks of *Chambaran* in Kashmiri language. The idea of this race is as high as *Takari* or *Pahari* or hilly in the interest of '*Nam-History*' of the Medieval Period (1200 to 1707 A.D.) of the same family. Mention must be made here of the wall paintings in *Tippu Sultan*, during the British rule, hunting lodge at Seringapatam (*Sriranga patnam*) near *Mysore* and *Islam* and Kerala in 18th century, a story of the works of Dr. Ibrahim Kunju on *Mysore Kerala Relations in the Eighteenth Century, studies in Medieval Kerala History* and rise o other power have been discussed by him. Author deserves special attention towards south India as hishistory with *Sabanam Grewal*. The conclusion is, therefore, justified that the modern long *Sari* developed about ten years earlier in Northern India[48] to repeat the history of the '*Nams*'. As Babar's relations with ruling elite and tribes of Punjab conquered the *Hindustan* with well-thought plan, systematic military operations as displayed in the paintings, found in the museum of the Govt. Women College Parade, attacked from the side of River Indus. Before, 1526, he captured Kabul in (1504). In 1519, he occupied Samarqand, and hold over the Bannu, Sawad and the areas along the Indus river. With the ascendency of Timurid Mirzas (Princes), *begams*, 'there is only happiness' as an idea of the Nam-History of the *Sudhra Family* with Baba Ravidas begs (nobles) conquered the Sindh territory including Chenab, Ravi, which was unnecessarily occupied by the Lodi dynasty of Delhi as idiot rulers of the *Nam-History*. A Gujjar servant of *Malikk Hast* acquainted with the Kakar territory along with *Jat* tribe of the area and other akin to them. They were at constant struggle with *Jud* and *Janjuhas* tribes of the

Ghakkar family. Soon afterwards, *Daulat Khan Lodi* came from *Multan* and Sindh visited in mughal Camp with his two sons *Dilawar Khan* and *Ghazi Khan*. Babar writes that their chiefs position based on ancient customs of the 'Rai Family', while the younger ones were styled Maliks or RAJPU OF THE rajouri and Poonch area. Babar summoned the headmen of the village called Choudharies or Gujjars of Bhira and settled a sum of 40,0000 Sharukhies as the price of peace (Mal-i-AMAN) AND APPOINTED HIS OFFICERS TO COLLECT THE AMOUNT.[49]

Notes and References

1. Vidyadhar; *Jammu and Kashmir, Past and Present*; Jammu; p. 6
2. Majid Husain; *Geography of Jammu and Kashmir*, New Delhi; 1985, p. 2.
3. Vidyadhar; *op.cit.*, p.7.
4. Majid, Husain, *op.cit.*, pp. 3-4.
5. Naveen Patnaik; *The Garden of Life, An Introduction to the Healing Plants of India*; New Delhi; Reprint, 1994, p. 23.
6. Majid, Husain,; *op.cit.*, pp. 4-5.
7. Dorling Kindersley; *op.cit.*, p. 278.
8. Majid, Husain; *op.cit.*, p. 5.
9. Dorling Kindersley; *op.cit.*, p.266, **Note**: Rocks can be divided into three main groups: igneous, Sedimentary and metamorphic in origin. Ingneous rocks formed from the interior cools solidifies process. Sedimentary rocks are formed from particles of the '*Nam*' having cemented relation between God and man. Metamorphic rocks are made of above two to change the history of God and man itself. (p. 276).
10. Majid Husain, *op.cit.*,p. 5.
11. Dorling Kindersley; p. 266.
12. Ibid.
13. Ibid., p. 282.
14. Ibid., p. 266.
15. Majid Husain; *op. cit.*, pp. 5-6.
16. Dorling Kindersley; *op. cit.*, p. 284.
17. Ibid., p. 280.
18. Ibid., pp. 268-69.

19. *Stephen Wilson Study of Washington*; *How nerve cells in the Left and Right sides of the brain are wired*. Tribune; April, 2nd, 2008.
20. News Item; *Mobile Phones Could be More Cencerous than Smoking.* Ibid. *Study of Washington*: discovered by Vini Khurana. Neurosurgeon.
21. Dorling Kendersley; *op. cit.,* p. 270.
22. Ibid., p. 272.
23. *Vedic India*; p. 6.
24. Vidyadhar; *Op.Cit.,* pp. 24-25.
25. Ibid., p. 21, **Note**: The name of Jammu is also found in the history of Sultanate of Kashmir in the memories of *Amir Timur* and in other resources of the period.
26. Ibid., p. 36.
27. M.Rama Jois: *Guruji and Social Harmony*, Karnataka; 2006, p.57
28. Vidyadhar; *op. cit.,* p. 64.
29. *Vedic India*; p. 6.
30. Naveen Patnaik; *op. cit.,* p. 39.
31. Majid Husain; *op.cit.,* p. 6.
32. Dorling Kindersley; *op. cit.,* p. 288.
33. Ibid., p. 290.
34. Ibid., p. 294.
35. Kalhana's *Rajatarangini*, Tr. By M.A. Stein, Delhi, Reprint; Vol.I, 1989, pp. 20, 23,.24.
36. Ibid., Vol. II, p. 339.
37. Ibid., pp. 340, 341.
38. Sir Denzil Ibbetson; *Panjab Castes*; Language Deptt. Panjab; 1995, pp. 266-338.
39. R.T. Vol. II. pp. 279, 280, 281. **Note**: The study of Bunbury, *History of Ancient Geography*; 1883, Vol. I., p. 229 furnish this statement of this account that *Sudhras* were the olden players of the 'Nam' study. It is due to the fact that popular language in Kashmir retains hieratical names, terms like *Sarada*, Siva, *Santa, Sadha* etc. in the castle of *Sirahisila Dynasty* of the *Rai Family* of Kashmir or *Sindh*, wherefrom the Muslim religion was flourished in all over the world as we learn form the surnamed *Ferishta*, *Mohammed-bin-Kasim*, who was born at *Astrabad*, on the border of the *Caspian sea*, he was the son of *Gulam Alli* Hindu Shah, a learned man, from the '*Rai Dynasty*' of *Sindh*, quitting from the Brahminical Ideology and fought

against them and spread the concept of '*Islam*' in the form of '*Radha Soami*' all over the worlds then *Sufism* by the different Saints of the '*Nam*' like *Baba Farid, Nur-din-Himdanii, Mohammed Khawaja Chisthi, Nand-Kul-Rishi* etc. *History of the Rise of the Mahomedan Power in India*, Tr. From the original Persina of Muhamad Kasim Ferishta, by John Briggs. Calcutta, Reprint, 1966, Vol. I. p. XXXVI, Life of the Author)

40. Majid Husain, *op. cit.*, pp. 6-7.
41. Dorling Kendersley; *op. cit.*, pp. 296-97.
42. Ibid., pp. 298-99.
43. Ibid., p. 300.
44. Vidyadhar; *op. cit.*, pp. 9, 10, 13.
45. Majid Husain; *op.cit.*, p. 135.
46. R.T. Vol.1. Introduction; p.3. **Note**: Similar, idea has been cited by *Ruqaiyyah Maqsood* about the 'Muslim'. The word 'Muslim' means simply 'one who submits' before God. As the creed of 'Islam' is a simple statement in two parts, '*La Ilaha Ilallah wa Muhammadur rasul al-lah*' (There is no God but Allah have the same meaning as 'infinite', and Muhammad is the Prophet of God'). Muslims accept these two basic things in the heart and head; that there really is One God, Supreme and Unique that is 'CHAMAR'. (*Islam*; Chicago; 1997, p.1.). And the same example has been cited by another Muslim writer *Mohamed Taher*, that 'There is, in short, a lot of misinformation and incorrect representation about 'Islam', an Arabic term has been given to the New Concept of the period at that time same as *Chamar* or '*Radha Soami Mission*', as French slang is peppered with term Arab an idea of the God's concept before the Prophetic rule in the world called as *Kif-Kif* (50-50) and *Insha Allah* (God willing in English language and *Chamar* in Sanskrit as '*Charmmkara*'. The hottest new music is Arab-inspired by *Rai Family* of *Sindh*, before the Mohammad Prophet of Kashmir as depicts from the shrine of the Kashmir his relic, kept in a glass called '*Bal or Kesh*' which reveals the history of the Highest-Knowledge of the Prophet i.e., equivalent to God or 'Nam'. Therefore, there is no need today to describe and interpret the modern issues of the Religion and to express in clear terms what this thought actually deals with the *lower caste* of the society. Due to social and cultural changes, and due to the boosting of the economy of the areas, people of the

'Brahminical Ideology' i.e., *Molavis* have forgotten the salient features of the concept and dominated the society that *Chandalas* were the rulers of the Jammu and Kashmir State as a Universal Truth as Mughal rulers over the world from the same clan i.e., *Sudhra* or *Doma* ruled over the World history. (*Islam the Religion of Submission*; New Delhi; 1998, p. IX, Preface)

47. *Guru Grant Sahib*; p. 2.
48. Charles Fabrer; *Indian Dress*; New Delhi, p. 9.
49. *Babur; Babarnama;* tr. by A.S. Beveridge Reprint, Delhi, Vol. 1. pp. 377-83.

5

Historical Prospectives in Physics and Chemistry

On the basis of the theory of *Heinrick Olbers* in 1826 predicted the Universe as *'Infinite'* in time and space,[1] and in 1862 Newton pointed out to 'a finite material in an infinite space have a gravity of power to destroy the material growth.[2] Let us look first at the concept of 'Laws'. Throughout the eighteenth and nineteenth centuries, scientists assumed that *'Laws of Nature'* *'Word'* Newton's laws of motion, the law of gravitation, Boyle's law, the law of evolution in scientific study, and so forth *'Chamar'* had been discovered and definitely established it for the societal growth, and that the business of the scientist was to be discover and establish more such laws by process of induction from observed facts as God and man. The word 'LAW' came down trailing clouds of glory from Galileo to *Dr. B.R. Ambedkar* as a great social-scientists of the world. Students of the society, consciously or unconsciously desiring to assert the scientific status of their studies, adopted the same language and believed themselves to be following the same procedure. The political economists seem to have been first in the field with Gresham's law, and *Adam Smith's* laws of the market. *Burke* appealed to 'the law of Commerce', which are the laws of nature invested in the man and consequently the Laws of God.[3] As we take up the example of *Malthusian 'Law of Population Theory'*, *Lassalle* an iron 'Law of Wages', and the *Marx* in the preface to *'Das Capital'* claimed to have discovered by the Social – Scientists, with the economic '*Law of Motion of a Modern Society*'. Here, it makes difference between the Science and Society to determine the Truth. Buckle in the concluding words of his work '*History of Civilization*' expressed the conviction that the course of human affairs was 'permeated by one glorious principle of universal and undeviating regularity'. Today this terminological sounds as old fashioned as it is presumptuous; but it sounds almost as old fashioned to the physical scientist as it does to the social scientist as *Dr. B.R. Ambedkar* established the 'Law of Constitution'; as a framing body of India. In the year before *Bury* delivered his inaugural lecture, the French mathematician Henri Poincare published a small volume called '*La Science et L*' hypotheses' which started a revolution on a scientific thinking as a knowledge based society invested in the man itself. Poincare's main thesis was that the general propositions enunciated by scientists to determine the truth in mathematic study, they were not mere definitions or disguised conventions with the Father about the use of language were from these language are coming, he was unable to answer the question, were hypotheses designed to crystallize and organize further thinking, and were subject to verification, modification, or refutation[4] in the history of man itself as God and man working together. All this has now become something of a common place for the study of man that is our body which in linear language made complicated in the interest of cultural development. It is very unfortunate that people of *India* could not understand the meaning of the term '*culture*' which is composed of two words *cult* + *true* in the metric system of mathematic, '*cult*' stands a meaning of religious worship directed towards a particular person or object originated from the Latin word '*Cultus*' (worship). Now question arises about the 'object', a physical thing that can be seen and touched the feelings of a person who is directed in the study, phrase acted on by a transitive verb or by a preposition as man and God, the derivatives of the 'object' according to the Latinized language originated from the word '*Objectum*' 'thing presented to the mind', i.e., soul and '*true*' stands for God a scientific study of the soul, and it shows our soul belongs to Father, who is Creator Power i.e., '*Name*' or *Chamar* of the human history.

The Variety of Matter

The variety of matter occupies 'contemplation of change' through what 'Insight', is the intuitive light flashing forth and exposing the truth in History that is '*Nam*' or God on earth. The suffering and the impersonal and unsubstantial nature of all corporal and mental phenomena of existence i.e., '*Nam*' or God obtains through the '*Nam-dana*' of Living Master, not in self-style manner as certain *Dalits* do not know this concept as their idiot idea. It is Insight – wisdom (*Vipassana-panna*) that is the decisive liberating factor in Buddhism in the present method to worship the Living Deity as a historical fact of the life. He develops trainings in Morality and Concentration. The culmination of Insight practice with Prefect Master leads directly to the stages of *Holiness*.

This study dealt with the branch of physical properties and nature of the matter and variety of souls derived from 'natural things' originated from original Latin word called Physica and its derivatives is known Physicist concerned with the natural thought as Archaic medicinal drugs of the Nam-History found during the ancient history of India with physical properties man and matter is relating to the body a opposed to th mind of the historians of India of the '*Sudhra Race*' that they are incompetent in this field of life and relating to things of matter and men, art historian oppose that real physic is in historical research that what is the physical standard of the human lifestyle. As Prof. Hans Raj Bangotra feels that *History* is a leading subject in '*Scientific Revolution*' of the 21st century that all the artificial sciences like *Chemistry, Physics, Botany, Medical Sciences, Zoology, Geology* proved as failure in this concept of scientific study of the natural thought. And, Physical Chemisty, a branch of another artificial science included in chemistry subject is concerned with applying the techniques and theories of *Physica* or *Physics* to the sutyd of chemical systems to transplant the idea of human history where stands the scientific truth as a study was given by natural thought for the discovering of human knowledge as an exercise to develop the standard, growth of knowledge and history controls to all the subjects of life, as a Revolutionary Subject.

'Insight' does not mean merely a intellectual advancement but it has to win the directive meditative observation of one's own bodily and mental processes. In the commentaries of the *Vedas* the sequence of the Insight meditation is developed as : (1) Discernment of the corporeal (*rupa*), (2) of the mental (*Nama*), (3) Contemplation of both (*namarupa*), as God on earth,(4) both viewed as conditioned as applied to mathematic linear theory of transmigration through matric system of the God and man than in whole of the world. (5), application of the 3 characteristics (impermanency, etc.) to mind and body came under conditions to check the advancement of man and God's in theoretical process. Now the question, again, rises for the states of purification of the world, atom is important in 'objective' to begins with the '*Knowledge of Rise and Fall*', and ending with the 'Adaption to Truth' i.e., '*Nam*' or God on earth in form of man to change the history as a Universal Law.

There are Eighteen chief Kinds of Insight – Knowledge or Principal Insights called as *Maha-vipassana* described in the Vedas as : (1) Contemplation of impermanence (*aniccanupassana*), (2) of suffering (*dukkhanup*^{0}), (3) of not-self (*anattanup*^{0}), (4) of aversion (*nibiddanup*^{0}), (5) of detachment (*Viraganup*^{0}), (6) of extinction (*Khayanup*^{0}) (7) of abandoning (*patinissagganup*^{0}), (8) of waning (*Khayanup*^{0}), (9) of vanishing (*Vayanup*^{0}), (10) of change (*Viparinamanup*^{0}), (11) of the unconditioned (or signless; *animittanup*^{0}), (12) of desirlessness (*apanihitanup*^{0}), (13) of emptiness (*Sunnatanup*^{0}) (14) insight into phenomena which is Higher Wisdom(*adhipanna–dhamma–Vipassana*),(15) Knowledge and vision according to reality (*Yatha-bhuta-nanadassana*), (16) contemplation of misery (or danger; *adinavanupassana*), (17) reflecting contemplation (*patisankanup*^{0}), (18) Contemplation of turning away (*Vivattanupassana*).

Through those 18 Insight-Knowledge, the adverse ideas and views are overcome, for which reason this way of overcoming is called "overcoming by the opposite" (*tadanga –pahana*, 'overcoming this factor or by that). Thus (1) dispels the idea of permanence, (2) the idea of happiness, (3) the idea of self, (4) lust, (5) greed, (6) origination, (7) grasping, (8) the idea of compactness, (9) *Karma*-accumulation, (10)the idea of lastingness, (11) the conditions, (12) delight, (13) adherence, (14) grasping and adherence to the idea of substance, (15) adherence to delusion (regarding the ego and the world), (16) attachment and adherence, (17) thoughtlessness, (18) dispels entanglement and clinging.

Insight – Knowledge may be either mundane (*lokiya q.v*) or super-mundane (*lokuttara q.v*). Super-mundane insight is of 4 kinds: (1) joined one of the[4] super-mundane paths, (2) joined with one of the Fruitions of these paths, (3) regarding the extinction or rater suspension, of Consciousness (in short, *nirodhi-samapatti*) or mana.[5] in Physics and Chemistry as in vain practical experience of life as a false idea of the man in this modern world, which does not determine the historical value of the man's life style and its process, just as wastage of time and material to test materialistic values of the life as an incomplete thought in man's life as a destructive idea of the life based on false notions to destroy the man itself without following an objective of human mission, it just an idea of '*ego*' that we are called Greatest Scientist of the natural study by creating gastric society of the '*Nam*' as infectious disease of life. It should be made clear at the outset that *Sadhus* from the background of the natural thought do not recommend outward formalities, rites, rituals, modes of living, symbols or any special type of clothing in the history of man. They are above the castes, colours, creeds, countries and nationalities as Universal Thought having an Imperialistic Ideas in the mind to control the Natural Thought. Nor is the term Saint or '*Sant*' used in the sense in which it is generally applied in the western world, that is, one canonized by the *Roman Catholic Church*, or a holy person. As B.A. and M.A. are degrees connoting academic qualifications, so are the terms 'Saint' or '*Sant*' and '*Sadh*' degrees in the school of Spiritual Science[6] as depicted by the Master of the period in the history of man, who has crossed all the regions of matter and mind in the interest of man's life as a historical growth of the life in human form.

What is Guru Mat or the Way of the Master?

There are two paths open to us in this world already discussed Matter and Mind either we follow the path of Matter or Mind, or that of the *Guru*, known as *Guru Mat* or *Guru Marg*. Everyone, according to his own light claims to follow *Guru Mat*, not the present teacher of the period who involved in the material life and collecting the money out of the teaching profession.

Now, we come towards the Sikhs Religion based on five symbols, referred to as the five '*Ka*' which they wear *Kangan* or

Kara, *Kanga* (comb), *Kacha* (sort underwear), *Kesh* or *Bal* (Long hair) and *Kirpan* (Sword). These five '*Ka*' are considered essential pre-requisites before the study of natural thought that this idea is based on Five *Pandavas* of the *Guru Govinda Singh ji, Maharaj*, before this study as existed in the various holy scriptures of the various religious books. Now the question rises itself where the Bliss of the nature is to be realized either in the book or in human life. It shows after the death of *Guruji*, there was no *Guru* on this earth and earth produced the astronomers or stars of the world in human form for the development of the history and the fundamental forces only captured the document of the saintly thought and exploited the man without any logic and reasoning to the Truth '*Dalit Sikhs*', with the idea of '*Guru Govind Rai*' as the Father of the human history as his pre childhood name and the adultery forces they dominated the script of *Guru Granth Sahib* and became Religion Force of the Sikh Community. Now, question again rises, where the term religion stands in the society, it shows that it is an idea of 'egocentric approach' in man's life without any matter, and matter life as an idea of false notion; none of them can claim to be the follower of their *Guru*, and idea of the thought became an historical study of man, and *Guru Granth Sahib* as an holy document, became an evidence of the source of history that where stands Truth that it lies in man's life not in document.

The Muslims regard *Namaz, Haj* and *Zakat* (prayer, five times, daily; fasting from sunrise to sundown for thirty days during the month of *Ramzan* to know the Knowledge of Insight, pilgrimage to *Macca* and giving a portion of their income to charity) as *Guru Mat* in their self-style manners.

In the same manner, the Hindus regard *Shikha* (tuft of hair at the top of the head, in the memory of *Shiva*), *Sutra* (sacred thread), *Sandhya* (prayer both morning and evening of the religions scriptures), *Havan* (religious fire invoking gods) and *Khat Karmas* (six duties according to Hindu scriptures founded by the *Sudhra Family*) as *Guru's* way. Some look upon idol worship, pilgrimages and both 'holy waters' as *Guru Mat* of the period. Others take to reading the *Gita, Vedas*, repetition of *Gayatri mantra*, recitation of Ramayana or other sacred scriptures. And still others think that fasting and other austerities lead to God-realizaiton. *Yogis* treat

Pranayan (breath control) as well as *Dhoti, Neti* and *Vasti Karmas* as the path of God-realization. Christians, however, believe in Christ as all time redeemer, with Baptism and the various sacraments, rites and rituals, as *Guru Mat*. In short, people do one thing or the other and all claim to follow the path of the Masters. In fact, there are more so-called 'Gurus' in this world than there are disciples. *Kabir* says "one's future depends upon one's *Guru*, and a Perfect Guru one gets only by rare good fortune". Since, this world is full of '*gurus*' of all sorts, how, then, can we find a true one? All the Saints and scriptures lay great stress upon finding a True, Prefect and Real *Guru*. In the *Guru Granth Sahib* as well as in the writings of *Kabir, Ravidas, Paltu Sahib, Dadu* and other Saints, such as *Malulana Rumi, Baba Farid, Shams-i-Tabres, Sultan Bahu, Bullah Shah, Hafiz* and others sing praises of *Mursid-i-Kamil*, the Persian name for a Perfect Master. The Perfect Masters always say: "*The Kingdom of Heaven is within you*". Lord, God, the Supreme Creator, cannot be found outside by one who has not realized Him within. This human body of ours is the "*Mansion of the Lord*", the "*Temple of the living God*". Those who see him outside, wandering in illusion[7] or Maya Christ says: "Knock, and it shall be opened unto you".[8] The music of the True Knowledge or Insight–Knowledge is that of the *Veena* instrument of music, according to *Guru Nanak*: "He who is attached to the melody of *Veena*, knows the secret of the three worlds i.e., God and man and the Ultimate Truth'. *Soami ji* says: "Wonderful is Guru Mat, where Mind and Soul contact the Sound amid beautiful scenes inside[9] the body of man. *Guru Arjun Dev* says: "My Exalted, Boundless, Infinite Soami! Who can sing thy praises (or know thy worth)?" *Kabir* says: "I bow to the Soami, the Beginning and the Creator of All". *Soami ji* added the word '*Radha*' (Soul) to it, and addressed him as "*Radha Soami*", the Lord of the soul, i.e., men and matter of this Universe. After facing failures in life, a few of them who sought the help of a spiritual guide could go up to *Brahm*, it shows that man attached with Brahm.[10] He becomes Brahmins having the thought of the 'Mind Only' not of the Spiritual Knowledge or Insight – Knowledge of the whole world as known by Prefect Master of the that '*Nam*' or God on earth. This, again suggests that without Prefect Master, no matter is above the Guru and it is hard work to follow His idea as a hard labourer process in the life of man to study the Insight Knowledge before it we have a purity of the thought above the caste, colour and creeds, than one can follow the real Religion of the Man and God on earth called *Chamar* of the modern sciences.

The Wonderful House in Which We Live

Matter is anything that occupies space of the earth. It includes everything from natural substances, such as mineral or living organisms, to synthetic materials. Matter can exist in three distinct states – solid, liquid, and gas. A solid is rigid and retains its shape. A liquid is fluid, has a definite volume of its container. Most substances can exist as a solid, a liquid, or a gas: the state is determined by temperature. At very high temperatures, matter becomes plasma, often considered to be a fourth state of matter as God and man exhibits. All matter is composed of microscopic particles, such as atoms and molecules, [11] they possess an internal structure. At their centre is a *dense nucleus*, consisting of protons, which have a positive electric charge,[12] and negative (carried by electrons). If charges are opposite (unlike), they attract one another to strike the issue to find out the result of the study, which like charges repel, and the forces of attraction and repulsion (electrostatic forces) exist between any two charged particles both as man and God on earth. Matter is normally uncharged, but if electrons are gained with positive forces of the tolerance material, an object will gain an overall negative charge; if they are removed, there should be a peace in the life, and it becomes positive force of the material progress. Objects with an overall negative or positive charge are said to have an imbalance of charge, and exert the same forces as individual negative and positive charges as per the concept of the Chemistry is concerned. On this large scale, the forces will always act to regain the balance of charge by obtaining the truth through practical experience whereas, natural sciences in the aspect of Chemistry and Physics failed to prove the scientific analysis of the body without the practice of '*Nam*' as a Supreme Law of the Society' having wonderful Insight Knowledge of the life. This causes static electricity on earth. Lightening, for example, is produced by clouds discharging a huge excess of negative electrons passing through a current value of the life as a negative force. If charges are "free" 'Word' in a wire or material that allows electrons to pass through it, *Chamar* forces cause a flow of charge called on electric current of the '*Nam*' through the body of man itself. Some substances exhibit the strange phenomenon of magnetism of the 'Insight Knowledge' of the 'Word' or '*Nam*' which also produces attractive and repulsive forces of the life through medical study of the operational body of the God and man in human form by experimenting the 'Truth' through the study of '*Nam*' expressed in the books of the writers itself that he has only the glory of natural thought. Magnetic substances consist of small regions called domains, i.e., the body of the man itself. Normally un-magnetized, they can be magnetized by being placed in a magnetic fields of life called wires, chemicals, solid material of the study. Magnetism and electricity are inextricably linked with these two forces, a fact put to use in motors and generators[13] as materialistic items not in the body itself. It shows science of this group could not control of the natural made body of the man in this universal atmospheric values of life. This life is precious item of the Lord, which could not control by others; it is controlled by Him with the practical knowledge of the '*Inner truth*', i.e., called '*Nam*' or God on earth.

Keeping in view, the knowledge of the Insight–Truth, the arrangement and interactions of these particles give a substance its physical and chemical properties by repeating the history of the man into new life as from man to God, by which matter can be identified through the practical experiences of the life in the history of man that there is a huge variety of the men and matter to find out that material which gives the help to the man for substantial values of life by mixing with others as life is really in natural process. Natural glass, for example, seems to be a solid but is, in fact, a super cool liquid as water of the rainfall, and the atoms are not locked into a pattern, but it can flow as water flows in the river same as the case of life as a '*Stream of the Life*' flows from one generation to another generation with the process of the '*Nam*' or God on Earth. Pure substances known as elements[14] consists of atoms of one type only i.e., God or *Chamar* on Earth as a *Dictator* of the World Knowledge possesses through the Insight-Knowledge of the Worldly Kingdom.92 elements that occur naturally, and the 17th elements created artificially , are often arranged into a chart called the periodic table. Each element is defined by its atomic number *Chamar*, the number of protons in the nucleus of each of its atoms (it is also the number of electrons present). In group I, atomic number is number one, above the nucleus forces as it stands 'High', as Hydrogen bomb having its value 1.0. As per its force, atomic number O increases as the race of the man and God. Periods are ordered according to the filling of successive shells of the *'Nam'* with electrons goods, while groups reflect the number of electrons in the outer shells (*Valiancy electrons*) *'Chamars'*, they decide the chemical properties through the body of *'Nam'* which is made of leather-goods of the modern *Khal* or *Chams* of the life through tanning the industry of the leather, realizing souls of the *'Nams'*. Same elements that appear in the same group which have been founded by *'Baba Rasila Ram Ji* of *Saidpurwale,'* the close friends of the *Soami Ji* of the *'Radha Soami Sect'* as a real approach in the history as a Insight-Knowledge of the man and God. Elements in Group O having *"filled shells"*, where the outer shell maximum number of electrons, similar to the Group 1 in elements, just as outer shell of the substantial materials, having good deal of knowledge of the *'Nam'* or God on earth, they are called semi-metals, between the two properties i.e. metal and non-metal.[15] Mixtures are called colloids, made up of larger particles of matter and material suspended in a solid state conditions, liquid, or gas, while a solution is one substance dissolved in another[16] as from pure water to natural materials into new lifestyles as the story of the *'Nam'* to pure the idea of man from this materialistic world to development stages with peaceful manners. In fact, some of us spend for too much time in practical approach to study this earth as *"muddy vesture of decay"* as a social change in life, and have never tried to find out what wonders lie hidden within the body of man. Thus, we are absolutely ignorant of our possessing a mine of truly precious diamonds that is *'Nam'* which attracts to everybody in the life of man. As *Guru Amar Das* says: "In this cave lie inexhaustible treasures and the Infinite Creator too resideth therein. In some He Keepeth Himself hidden in the body, and revealth Himself in others through teachings and learning process. (Those who kill their 'ego'. By means of *Guru's shabd*) in the present life:

Kabir says:

Within this muddy vessel (the body)
There are beautiful gardens, and the Gardener too;
There are gems and rubies, and their connoisseur,
There are seven oceans, nine million stars, and their Creator;
Within it also is our Master; But what an utter darkness;[17]
i.e., (Only Mind)

Infact, all the Saints and Sages who have made research in the realm of Soul and Matter have come to the conclusion that our body contains everything's of the life in this Universe. They also claim that God can be realized only within the body not in scriptures of the man made materials, it is only to transfer the idea of the Insight-Knowledge to defunct society through the power of the Spiritual Pen of the Almighty Power. Post 26/11, December attacks, response a total failure to counter-terrorism doctrine on peace process. You can only have peace if you know the realities of War against the Bollywood film of the 21st century as *Nam* is ruling over the world history as spiritual idea of the author's lifestyle.

Notes and References

1. Hermann Bondi; *The Universe at Large*, London 1961, p. 29.
2. G.J. Whiterow; *The Structure and the Evolution of the Universe*; London; 1959, p. 99.
3. *Thoughts and Details on Scarcity* (1795) in the Works of *Edmund Burke* (1846), IV, p. 270. **Note**: Burke deduced that it was not 'within the competence of the government, taken as government, but it is the property of the man itself, what he deserves of the law of nature, or even of the rich, as rich, to supply to the poor those necessaries which it has pleased the Divine Providence not G.P. Fund for a while to withhold from them, but the Law of Nature is free of cost based on '*Nam-dana*' through Prefect Master in historical way not in self style manners.
4. E.H. Carr, *What is History*? New York, Reprint, 1984, p. 58.
5. Nyanatiloka; *Buddhist Dictionary*; Ceylon; 1970, pp. 197-198.
6. *The Science of the Soul*; p. 3.
7. Ibid, pp.17, 18.

8. Ibid. p. 8.
9. Ibid., p. 23.
10. Ibid., pp. 23, 24.
11. Dorling Kendersley; *op. cit.*, p. 306.
12. Ibid., p. 308.
13. Ibid., p. 316.
14. Ibid., p. 306.
15. Ibid., p. 310.
16. Ibid., p. 306.
17. *The Science of the Soul*; pp. 27-28.

6

Art and Craft

The creation of works of beauty and other significance the products of man's creative activities with *par excellence* or aesthetic merit of conception is considered as an Art. Aspirants of Fine Arts or Royal Arts programmes should have been based on fair and square 'Ideas' i.e., '*Nam-dana*' of the Living Master. The topic of study include stylistic significance of Visual Art in India and its society, that is, *Sudhra* which deals with art as artisans class of the Masters give a creative idea of the man and God, and styled not in India, but in European, and Far East countries like China and Japan from the ancient period of our study. People forms their artistic characteristics in natural manners, still life; copy of designs in artistic way have been displayed in paintings, and sculptures by forming landscape, water colour, human figure and animals in round and relief, lettering, printmaking, sense of colours, power of visualization in craftsmanship, weaving and computer application will applied to art and architecture in skill freehand sketching by put the imagination of the visual art creativity is the key factor in the interest of the society and man. Book illustration, symbol, trade mark are used as skill art to find out the Truth and practical knowledge of the life. While craft is the skill or ability especially in handiwork or an occupation or trade requiring special skill[1] to change the history of man through practical knowledge of the life and its activities in the life. H.W. Janson,[2] a well-known art historian explains the term Art is first of all a '*Word*' one that acknowledge both the idea of

Mind and God without any discrimination on the concept of works of 'art and culture'. Without the Perfect Knowledge of the Art and Culture the study of the man is incomplete. Art and culture do not mean in dress system, but it means an aesthetic value in the life itself. There, art is an aesthetic object. It is meant for to look at social justice and appreciate for its intrinsic value of life through the artistic writings which generate new values of life. There science has failed in this direction to create an aesthetic value of life, it has destructive knowledge in its study by creating unnecessary things in the life of man like atom bombs and discovery of the other explosive materials of life to shatter the human unity and to create 'ego' in the man's life, that he or she is a Great Scientist. Thus, the good or bad deeds and actions is created from the 'Mind-Only'. If through visualizing the *Medicine Buddha* i.e., '*Nam*' or reciting his name in uniform system, a person's mind changes from greed, anger and delusion to selflessness, compassion and wisdom, a change in his negative pattern of thinking is realized and his negative action changes for the good "the drifting life is cast aside for one of spiritual dedication" towards Master (*John Blofeld*). With the removal of greed, anger and delusion, most other illnesses, however, physical their symptoms, are also eventually cured[3] the concept of life as a whole change of the atmosphere of the society that he belongs to a right man of the society not from the science. In the end, the teaching of the '*Sutra of the Medicine Buddha*' is one of the life, and hope, infinite trust and 'Boundless Sky compassion[4] will reveal the hidden treasure of the man's life and his family will also restore to their proper rank in society due to the artistic knowledge of the Insight-event. As it has been expressed by *Robindranath* Tagore in his monumental works:

"For attainment, of your goal,
Find a 'Word' that rhymes soul,
From the 'radha' take its 'dha',
After that at last put 'ra'.
From the tamarind-banyan's mouth
Turn your face towards the south,
When the light is in the East.

There shall be of wealth a feast"[5], in other words, a teaching of the heart and mind.

What is told is just what the wonder images in the temples tell. Somebody arrived called '*Nams*' on Earth, infinite years ago, according to Buddha's concept, who promised to release from misery, salvation (*Moksa*). Trust in this promise, hold fast to the name of this Buddha or *Chamar*, if a man once heard His name, a new hope has come into his life of '*Sudhra*', this hope is his treasure, he must not squander it. (*W. Liebenthal*). And squander it he must not, because this hope leads to nothing less than eventual Enlightenment and *Buddah-hood* in his life to repeat the history of the man as an Universal Idea. The *Medicine Buddha* provides support to an artistic nature to pure the land cultivators who may need freedom from Science and Technology of the modern science an idea of the 'Egoist Mind; and try to live in natural atmospheric values, in order to concentrate single mindedly idea of the man in the form of God called *Sukhavati*. This may explain the representation, on the major alter of many *Mahayana* temples, of a massive trinity of *Sakymuni Buddha*, the *Medicine Buddha* and *Amitabha Buddha* in the form of *Dr. Raj Kumar*, *Baba Gurinder Singh ji BIaswale*, and *Master Deepit Raj* of the modern period.

The *Medicine Buddha*, and *Amitabha Buddha* each has his own pure land, the *lapis lazuli* Land and *Sukhavati*, respectively. Both are ideal, transcendental realms of the kingdoms of the '*Nam*' where practitioners can further their cultivation and ultimately attain *Buddhahood* in his life as a gentle man of the History *Dr. Raj Kumar*. The main difference between a country which receives immigrants and one which actively goes out to recruit them. The *Medicine Buddha's* special mission is to prevent calamities and cure illnesses, while the principal vow *Amitabha Buddha* is to make his Land Pure.[8] with the natural thought of the life with the power of '*Nam*' or God on Earth.

The Sutra of the Medicine Buddha

There are currently five extant Chinese translations from the Sanskrit work, done between A.D. 317 to 707 A.D., as well as two Tibetan translations proves that *India* was a biggest country during the ancient period, had a wonderful bounty of the nature, i.e., called *'Nam'* or *Chamar* on earth for the Enlightenment of Truth. The text that forms the basis of this translation is that of the *Patriarch Hsuan-Tsang*, founder of the Chinese Yoga-care (Mind-Only)school and translator of some 75 *'Buddhist Sutras'*, completed in A.D. 650, it is considered the most complete and authoritative version of the *Sutra* is *'Nam'* or God on earth. The *Sutra* is composed of essentially of three parts, the first describing the Twelve Greek Vows of the *Medicine Buddha* and the second, his extensive merits as well as the various ways, he comes to the aid of those beset by suffering and calamities. The third part sets forth the vows of the twelve *Yaksa* General to benefit sentient beings of the life. Thus, *Sutra* is influential throughout east Asia, as it combines the Pure Land of the teachings of the Master on rebirth of the old species in New Form, i.e., God and man and the esoteric practices, of reciting the old *mantra* of the *'Nam'* that is called *'Nam-dana'* of the living Deity of *'Mahabaisaya Guru Dharam'* follower i.e., *Dr. Raj Kumar* and is a follow friends of the same community called *Chamar* as *'Nam'* on earth, and lighting lamps with the promise of *practical benefits* in everyday life, having humanistic approach in life. This promise (of protection against disease and other personal misfortunes) is the single most attractive feature of the *Sutra*.[9] This is the single most important point of the *Sutra* from the Medicinal plant of Banyana, (*ficus bengalensis*), family, *moraceae*, Sanskrit name, *Nyagrodha*, Hindi name called *Bar*. According to Pliny (A.D. 70), there is in India a tree whose property it is to plant itself. It spreads out mighty arms to the earth, where in the space of a single year the arms take root and put forth a new study of the *'Nam'* or God on earth as a 'Art' or 'Skill' of the life. It has been called 'The Many Footed' after the aerial roots striding from its trunk, called *tanning* idea of the plant into human form who control the whole of world as an idea of the forefathers. Three thousand years before Pliny described it to the Roman Empire this mighty shade plant struck awe in the Aryan nomads sweeping across India to repeat the history of the man against the evil forces of the negative ideas. Over the centuries, as the actual properties of the tree were examined for their medicinal value, it was discovered that an infusion of banyana seeds did indeed make a tonic sufficiently invigorating to be widely regarded as an aphrodisiac, while *banyana* latex applied externally accelerated the healing of wounds and open sores. *Ayurvedic* doctors, also noted that medicines derived from the *banyana* assisted in blood clotting, contained major antiseptic and astringent properties and an infusion from *banyana* bark alleviated diabetes.[10] For those who love biology, there is a world of opportunities in the life sciences, with applications in every aspect of life, from bio-chemicals and pharmaceuticals to agriculture and environment. Advances in medicine, health care is negligible, therefore, including the study of medicines and pharmacy to fight against the number of diseases, developing in foods, agriculture, deals with reproduction, growth, and metabolism such as bacteria, viruses, alogea moulds the society into constructive outlook to leave the artificial values experiment in graduate and postgraduate courses in Biology, Botany, Zoology or Chemistry that can lead into work load on lectures, not in productive knowledge, but as destructive one without finding any constructive result. So if you love watching "earth files" and scientific discoveries on *Nat Geo* and Discovery Channel, or have dreamt of producing a *banana*, or apple that can deliver a safe, effective and vaccine for *diarrhopea* or polio, a career in Biology is certainly cut out for the children's [11] of these field.

Teachings of the Sutra

The *Sutra* emphasizes faith in the assistance of the Medicine Buddha i.e., '*Nam*', while not neglecting the self-power, but obtaining the confidence in the race of the Father, and cultivating the friendly relation with them. The Buddha then said to Ananda: 'If sentient beings (beset by heavy *Karma*) should hear the name of the Medicine Buddha i.e., '*Nam*', *Lapis Lazuli* Radiance *Tathagata*, single mindedly recite as *Quran* predict itself, that the thought of history again will reveal the identify of the Prophet in another life in progressive manners, and hold fast to it without harboring a single doubt in the study of natural thought, then it will be impossible for the historians of the '*Brahminical Ideology*' to determine the Truth and will be sink into the Evil Realms.

"O, Ananda! These sublime study in the practices of the *Buddhas* are difficult to believe it, and difficult to understand. Yet you are now able to uphold them. You should realize that this is due to the awesome power of the *Tathagatas*".

However, the question remains lies in the study of '*Nam*' as to how reciting the name of the old *mantra* of the God, and making offerings to the *Medicine Buddha* can ward off disease and calamity, bring peace and joy to the sick and suffering. In this context, the teachings of the Masters on the transference of merit and demerit.[12]

The full name of the *Medicine Buddha Sutra* (*Bhaisaya, Guru*) in the form of *Baba Gurinder Singh ji* is rendered in this text as *Medicine Buddha Lapis Lazuli Radiance Tathagata*. Please note other variants occurring in the literature:

Healing Buddha	*Azure Radiance Tathagata*
Master of Healing	*Vaidurya Light Tathagata*
Master of Medicine	*Beryl Radiance Tathagata*

Moreover many popular books use the Japanese name *Yakushi*. According to *V. de Visser* (Ancient Buddhism Vol. II), most of the *Bodhisatta* in the Medicine Buddha's Assembly are also depicted surrounding by *Amitabha Buddha*, in paintings of *Amitabha's* descent to welcome the faithful (*Raigo*). This is another example of the close relationship between the *Medicine Buddha* and *Amitabha Buddha* in the *Mahayana tradition*[13] to know the every wit of the Insight-Knowledge.

'Faith is the basis of the path, the mother of virtues, Nourishing and growing all good ways of the permanent life'. Faith can increase knowledge and virtue, Faith can assure arrival at Enlightenment (*Avatamsaka Sutra*).

Jammu and Kashmir has had the great tradition of the art of sciences and its craftsmanship. Exquisite shawls of the '*Nam*', silver and copperware, woodcrafts, carpets were found from the Jammu *Industry* during the ancient period of the '*Ravidas Culture*'. *Chamar* amends the shoes and *chapals*, *Kabir* and *Vishav Karma*, they expert in work and many more articles were also made by them working class in the Jammu and Kashmir State. These have catered to the artistic urge of the people in *India* and abroad. The products of unique craftsmanship, for which the unrivalled environs of Kashmir set against the snow-clad mountains have provided the perennial inspiration to the craftsmanship in the interest of to grow the medicinal plants in the life of man in artistic manner. We have won the appreciation of connoisseurs from far and wide of the international study. The articles range from woollen textiles of fleecy soft texture and matchless *par excellence* in weaving[14] the world carpet of the natural beauty, the handsome work of the weavers class led by *Kabir* of the modern period i.e., *Dr. Ram Dass* the motifs drawn by the *Naggash rival*, the diverse natural beauty, but abundant study of the '*Nam*' history of the magnificent surroundings of the spacious valley, and are inspired by the sparkling lakes and oceans of the '*Sudhra Family*', the broad curves of the serpentine Jhelum, Chenab, Ravi, Jammu Tawi the variegated flora and fauna as well as the breath taking colours of the '*Boundless Sky*' at the sunrise and sunset over the azure mountains display that *Chamars* are working over there. Various poets of the period, they drew the poetic fancies, religious or philosophical themes, portraying these attractively in his designs. The debt handiwork of the craftsmanship with the brush of the *Ravidas* shoes, and its tools which were used for the development of life into different stages chisel and needled in complete products[15] have been Enlightened, in the history of man from the 'Prehistoric Period' to the 'Modern Man, which have delighted the world from ancient monuments of the life and its struggle to fight against the evil-minded peoples of the '*Nam*' called modern politicians or Brahmins of the period.

Indian Religious System

In the ensuing chapter we are discussing the development of Indian Arts and Crafts, primarily based on the religious study of India. Therefore, it is necessary to survey the primary value of the life i.e., *Humanism* with rational approach of the life which is based on soul in every nature of life. Result is controversies in the life of man on the basis of Religious system of the society based on scriptures which have been written by the man itself. Hence, there is debate about his relevance to the modern man on the subject to religious philosophy. Study shows that the founder of the religious system, were they lies in the history, they have been exhausted in human history where these scriptures stands. It shows that the '*Blind Faith*' of the man is a problem created as did by *Gandhi* and *Jinnah* in Indian society by exploiting the Religious system of the man, as composed by the man, not by the God, God made the man, idea lies in the man itself, not in the scriptures. Scriptures became an instrument to again determine the value of the Natural Thought.

But here the meaning of Religion is different called *Dharma* in Sanskrit. It shows all the religious forces like Hindu and Sikh fundamentalists, many more others, as know knowledge of the Insight-Truth; they are working as negative forces of the man. 'Sundry Religion' only conforms to social demands to identify with one's own creed or sect. At the same time intellectual gymnastics in the realm of philosophy is not religion. Thinkers and commentators stretch the meaning of religion and declare religion as simply *'Inner Search'* for the truth of one's being, often called the Spiritual Quest.[16] According to writer Dr. (Lt. Col.) D.A. Raju, this inner search is "most exciting and challenging" to the man kind. The attempt of the author is wonderful, but negligible, when he quoted with *'Gandhi'* and Religion' , because Gandhi had no knowledge of the Truth, and had the destructive idea of the man like Jinnah to lead the life as a leaders of the world as an idea of the *Molavi*. They were experimenting the idea of Truth with *Dr. B.R. Ambedkar's* thought for the development of the human philosophy, who was the natural force at that time by frame the 'Law of Constitution' as the other social –scientists framed the different 'Laws' of the different society during the backwardness was there in the society, and opposite force strike on 'Law' in natural form with historical truth where it stands in the human history. Therefore, there are crisises in the society to locate where the Truth stands. It shows from the study that Truth stands in purity of the thought and His dynamic approach in history as a matter of fact to defeat the 'blind faith' of man with the stroke of pen. But modern politicians on the basis of *Gandhi* and *Jinnah's* philosophy, they are committing crimes on the humanity with the help of money and muscle power, not with historical research that what problem is lie in the society that is why the modern man is confronting to each others, due to lack of Insight-Knowledge, and society has been governed by *'Goonda* Peoples'. *Channa*, for acquiring Supreme Knowledge as an ascetic approach in history a challenge for them. This prince became Buddha later on after another attaining the Supreme Knowledge of the Lord under the "Bo-tree" at *Bodh-gaya* means explored the Highest–Knowledge of the Supreme Being on earth, an example has been set with the cosmic consciousness far above the mental plane of ordinary mortals and came to be known as "*Tathagata*". For that very moment in his career until his death at the age of eighty *Buddha* devoted his life to the paramount goal of winning for all humanity the salvation or relief from the endless cycle of rebirth.[18] He was immortals in his life as remember able man of the human history.

Theory of Consciousness in History

Art has a historical continuity in Indian Art Consciousness to find out the Truth in man itself by composing number of valuable aesthetic Arts in the life of man. To obtain the knowledge of consciousness in History, *Lord Buddha* preached a pessimistic doctrine according to which all existence is sorrow. The cause of the sorrow stems from attachment to self and the ephemeral delights of the world of senses which do not control by the theory of 'Mind Only'. Mind is a destructive force or negative element without the realization of God. The only cure for this Universal Malady is in the suppression of the self or 'ego' with the practice of '*Nam-mantra*' a realized soul of the world, and the extinction of the *Karma* theory becomes decline with honest approach towards the Masters or Maker, that we have accumulated from the past actions, according to the *Brahmins* or *Molavis* belief survives what is usually known as "Ego' or '1', subject to endless reincarnation's and His survival is there.

The consciousness about 'History of Art' began in the mid 16th century A.D. with the establishment of *Mughal Rule* in *India* with the collaboration of British East Indian Company having the thought of natural concept of the *Baba Ravidas's* philosophy, that consciousness theory of man's life founded by Him from the Insight-Knowledge of the body which has been tanned by the Father by constituting the soul into it as a realized soul of the Worldly Knowledge as well made shoes protect the feet and are also comfortable and long-lasting in the life. The best shoemakers use a wooden or plastic mould, called a last, which matches the shape of the customer's foot as a good pair of shoes. The different parts of a shoe are stitched and glued together around the last; rivets and nails are used only in the heel, which is built up from layers of leather and rubber as '*Nam*' produce the life of man. The steel shank gives support to the arch of the foot and, with the seat lift, helps the wearer maintain posture the layers of the sole give strength to the life of the shoe, while the soft insole cushions the foot to repeat the history of *Chamar* itself. The leather welt sewn between the leather uppers and lowers pieces of the 'Nam' as a one force of the Father, and the sole ensures a strong join[20] as God and man on this earth, a challenge to the modern politicians that *Sudhra* has honest approach towards Father as *Chamar* by Caste as *Ravidas* of the period. According to *Giorgio Vasari* Complied an information about 'Renaissance Artists' lives and works forever in '*Lives of the Artists*'. The modern concept in 'Art History' began in the middle of the 18th century A.D. with the movement of the French Revolution of 1789, that scientific and rational interpretations was started against the competitive arts of the man in the spectrum of time and space. In the 19th century A.D. and its subsequent period, it became a distinct discipline in the history of Europe. Its development was also seen in biological overtones as birth of the man in the society, development, maturity and decay have been analyzed in the history of man and the scientific discoveries were started by the scientist called locator of the Truth through Scientific Knowledge, but in the 21st century A.D., it has found from the different research work in this field and found man is in puzzling contents and lot of frustration has been found in the historical study as well as in the so-called natural sciences has already discussed above i.e., Biological Sciences of the life. This model of Art History as a Scientific Knowledge pursuit was only established[21] through the study of '*Nam*' or '*Chamar's* art, that how to *tan* the knowledge of man in *Artistic* way by experiment the Truth in the body itself as the picture of *Ravidas* reveals, and eulogizing in the following words:

"San'san' haqiqu subhana art."[22]

(It is the truth of the glorify Creator)

Khatam-Band

Khatam-band is a major specialty in Kashmir in wooden work and comprises ceilings of rooms made from thin panels of pine wood, cut into geometrical designs. Builders of houseboats have kept this old craft alive as God and man. In *Kashmir*, the shrine of *Khwaja Naqshband*, near the *Jama Masjid* of *Srinagar*, presents the best example of this craft, which is also found in *Samarqannd*, Iran, Istanbul, Algiers and Morocco. Kashmiri is an intelligent and clever carpenter of the man's life by moulding the design of works the wooden in different artistic ways with their handsome craftsmanship's ideas. They were expert to built the boat of big sizes, including the famous houseboats and live in Water Kingdoms of the man as an adventures race of the Father. And the *tanners* of the State, whether living in Srinagar or Jammu, they have the idea of the *'Nam'* or *tanners*, who turn out excellent leather from the body to built new shoes and colourful ones in artistic ways, are made to Enlighten One and all. Kishtwar specializes in blankets, Poonch, in spoons and forks made from unseasoned wood. Cotton printing has been a speciality of Samba and Jammu district. The colourful *Mirpur* cotton quilts, wooden ornaments form *Thana Mandi*, and *Mochi* experts of the shoes from *Mendhar* and *Kahna Chak*[23] were also entice to the master during the study of *'Nam'* and artifacts of the past history of the *'Chamar Dynasty of Kashmir'*, expressed in the *'Early History of Jammu Region'*.

In short, the art and craft of the Jammu and Kashmir State distinguished by time-old practice, and attachment to traditional techniques and methods to repeat the history of man as *Santa* or Saints of the period and *Dalit* of the Vedic period. Some commercialization has crept into the trade, but the quality control of Act of 1978, helped in removing all the complaints from the buyers, and made the handicrafts system more functional and lasting, as well as aesthetically superior in nature. Though certain have been catered due to the natural need of the *'Nam'* to balance the society of the *'Sudhra Family'* by producing a number of goods required for decorating a modern house like household linen and upholstery articles of the 'Nam' for the establishment of *'New Society'* of the same family called *Chamar* or *Radha Soami*.

Notes and References

1. Vidyadhar; *op.cit.*, p. 198.
2. H.W. Janson; *History of Art*; New York; 1996, p. 16.
3. Kinh Duoe Su; *Sutra of the Medicina Buddha*; U.S.A, Reprint, 2001, p.V. Introduction.
4. Ibid., p. VII.

5. Rabindranath Tagore; '*Boundless Sky*', Kolkata, Reprinted, '2006', p.3.
6. Kinh Duoe Su, *Op.Cit.*, p. VII. *Introduction.*
7. Ibid., pp. 94-95.
8. Ibid., pp. 95-96.
9. Ibid., p. IV, *Introduction*.
10. Naveen Patnaik, *Op.Cit.*, p.19.
11. Usha Albuquerque, *Smart Skills, A World of Opportunities for Biology Lovers*; an article published 2-4-2008. *The Tribune*. News paper. **Note**: Many research institutions provide opportunities for conducting study and research in customized area of life sciences with specific applications to suit industry or public community needs. These include Tata Institute of Fundamental Research, *Mumbai*, *Dr. B.R. Ambedkar* Centre for Biomedical Research, University of *Delhi*, Central Drug Research Institute, *Lucknow*, Institute of Science, Banglore, Dr. *Salim Ali* School of Ecology, *Pondicherry*, G.B. Pant Institute, *Pantnagar* and several others, getting environmental protection relating jobs to ecology, pollution and conservation of all natural resources as a genetics trade study that what is happening round the global warming. It shows that they are biolating the terms and conditions of the natural law of the Life Science that is working in self style manners as destructive approach not constructive one. Therefore, there is a threat from the natural itself which resides in the man's life that is call '*Nam*' or God on earth.
12. *Medicine Buddha Sutra*, pp. IV-V *Introduction*.
13. Ibid., p. 94.
14. Vidyadhar; *Op.Cit.*, p. 198
15. Ibid., p. 199.
16. *Young India*, October, 11, 1928.
17. *Gandhi and His Religion*; New Delhi, 2000. **Note**: In a different context, while commenting on *Varnashram Dharma*, *Gandhi* wrote: 'I have never made a fetish of consistency in my study with Truth", because here *Gandhi* lies, at that time in historical approach of the man's life has taken the shelter in *Ashram* to regain the power of '*Nam*' or *Varna System* of the *Gupta period*, who ruled over the society with the power of '*Nam*' as a Natural Thought of the man called *Varna* in Hindi, 'Word' in English and *Chamar* or *Charamkara* in

Sanskrit. It shows that the study of the author is not reliable on Truth, it is based on '*Brahminical Ideology*' which commits crimes against the philosophy of the Truth, which resides in the man's life itself as a natural thought of man, and Britisher called '*Coolie*' as also mentioned by A.L. Basham, Harappa Culture based on '*Coolie Lines*' of modern Indian tea and other estates (W.T.W.I.); p. 17.

18. S.K. Bhattacharya; *Indian Religious Systems*; pp. 10-11.
19. Ibid., p.11.
20. Dorling Kindorsley; *Op.Cit.*, p. 568.
21. J.J. Winckelmann (1717-68), *The History of Ancient Art*; English tr. (1849-73) referred in '*Encyclopeadia of Historians and Historical Writings*'; Vol. I, London; 1992, p. 52.
22. *Kalimat-i-Taiyibat* by Inayatulla Khan Kashmiri, ed, S.M.A. Husain, Delhi,1982, p.13; In 1683, Saqi Mustaid Khan wrote, "Unless one sees it, no written description can correctly picture it out" because of no Scientific Knowledge of Art Study" *Ma'asir-i-Alamgiri*, tr. Calcutta; 1947, p. 146.
23. Vidyadhar. *Op.Cit.*, pp. 202-03.

samsāra. It shows that the study of the author is not reliable on Truth. It is based on Sūtra[illegible] knowledge which cannot be termed a thorough philosophy of the Truth, which found in the mind life itself as a natural dwelling of man, and in the Kashmir Śaivism is supplemented by A.L. Basham, [illegible] Culture based on Cholas [illegible] Lives of the [illegible] Indian [illegible], [illegible] p. 17.

16. [illegible] Bhattacharya, [illegible] Pratyabhijñā [illegible] pp. [illegible]

18. Ibid., p. [illegible]

19. [illegible] Understanding, Op. Cit., p. 208.

21. [illegible] [illegible] (1770-83) [illegible] Ancient Art, Literature [illegible] referred in some [illegible] of [illegible] and [illegible] [illegible], London, 1982, p. [illegible]

[illegible] Kashmir, [illegible] Delhi, 1993, p. 12. [illegible] Mushtaq Khan wrote, "[illegible] written description can correctly [illegible] but [illegible] of [illegible] knowledge of [illegible] [illegible] in Calcutta, [illegible], p. 146.

23. [illegible] Op. Cit., pp. 302-06.

7

Scientific Approach in History

Judging purely from the trend of present day events, noting the deep undercurrents, the thoughts of the man, *'History in Chamar – A Scientific Discovery'* is meant for religious, philosophical and Scientific Approach in man's life as *'Nam'* or 'Word', it is the opinion of this writer to spread the message of God that within three centuries our race was migratory from the Kashmir to other parts of the world for the study of man's illusion that is the world is a problem itself, now "The Science of the Master's' was indirect form handed over to the philosophers, now it became illusion for everybody that who is Supreme in the World Knowledge, question rises, that *Sudhra* race who was degraded in India due to the absence of their Masters. Not, indeed, accepted by every one or even a majority[1]; but they have been dominated by the political forces of the negative elements, not it will constitute the dominant stream of thought with the approach of Scientific Knowledge called Insight-Knowledge of the man, a challenge for them that themselves called as great political thinkers as negative force of the realistic approach against the natural thinker that we are going to establish our Historical Thought; a New Concept of the Man i.e., *'Radha Soami'* or *'Chamar'* and it will be generally acknowledged by the Natural forces i.e., *Baba Gurinder Singh Ji, Biaswale* and *Master Deepit Raj*, a modern man of History as the King of the Sciences. By that time a high ethical standard of conduct they have been adopted in everywhere in the society, but the modern politicians a destructive force of the man are creating the problems for the common man with corrupt method and ideology based on muscle and money-power. (See Plate I and II) for your kind information for the common people of the poor strata of the society. It has been seen and observed as a wholesome reaction from the present chaos in moral values and standard, they are bad elements of the society having no faith on Scientific Knowledge of the *Sudhra Family*, that but role they played in the previous life of the man for the up-gradation of the moral values of the life in simple way. This will come about by a universal increase in Knowledge and an Enlightened Conscience in the absence of the Master, having the ideology of Humanism. At that time the best there is in all system of religion and philosophy will be separated from the worthless, as wheat from the chaff, and a New Social Order[2] of the *Sudhra Family* will be establish for the welfare of man upon the foundation of rational and scientific demonstration cited in the book on the idea of *Dr. B.R. Ambedkar* and his forefathers belonged to the same family called *Sudhras* of the period. As flowers and fruit adorn and glorify the plant, so upon this new intellectual Era, ethical and social foundation will have to establish a great spiritual evolution in the progressive society of the same family. This spiritual quickening will not be caused by the new social order, but a Reformation Movement in the history of man but it will have become the fountainhead of the 'New Social Order'. Spirituality is not the flower or the fruit of ethics and of social reconstruction, but sound ethics and a just social order are good soil out of which spirituality may spring up i.e., Jammu and Kashmir State, when vitalized by the showers of living waters comes out from the *Nam* or *Chamar* as an ancient Idea of the man and God.[3] Question rises what is the colour of water? If the water is colourless, what is the cause of the blue colour of the sea? The blue colour of the sea and large tanks of clear water is due to the fact that water is not that colourless. It does have a bluish tinge that shows up when we see it in bulk as a comparative study of the water with soul. It is well known that colour of various objects is due to the fact that material of that object selectively absorbs the light of some of the colours that together make white light. For example, 'grass is green because it absorbs all colours except green. These absorption properties of materials depend on their atomic and molecular structure. For most cases of the important effects on incident photons are due to their interaction with the electrons of the material. Water happens to be rather special[4] for the study of '*Nam*' as a race case in this Universal Truth by connecting man with the audible life stream. This is the age of the intellect, but we are approaching the down of the age of the spirit because of 'Black Idea' of the man called '*Brahminical Ideology*' has been penetrated in the spiritual land of India or Bharat, therefore, it is essential to remove it for the establishment of the 'New Society' of the '*Nam*' or God. This spiritual evolution will then be explained in terms of the Science of the Masters when '*Law of the Chamar*' will be established with power of '*Nam*' on earth. In this a bold assumption? We think not, because it is duty of the natural forces to establish the 'Law of the man' to study for the qualification of natural life. Soul and intellect should sit side by side upon the throne of the worldly empire. Even the most religions care but little for dogma and metaphysical dissertations. They are searching for reality, for something soiled upon the natural sciences to control them which to rest their tired feet of the '*Ravidas Culture*'. They are looking for reality in the realm of religion as a natural force of the Father, and their spiritual head will be used for agriculture and trade of the '*Nam*'. The scientific spirit must eventually lead mankind to adopt the scientific method of religion to control the system of life. Of Course, that new '*Sat Yuga*' is yet many millennia distant. But the darkest days of the *Kalyuga* 'Word', the Iron Age, *Chamars* have already passed[5] this stage in the historicity of man. Man's first duty is to know himself from the primary values i.e., as 'Human being', fellow-friends of the 'Nam'. In substance: 'Worship the Gods, if you must, but your first duty is to find out who and what your are yourself".[6]

Science has always had to contend with three powerful obstacles to its progress, each of which was almost insurmountable. These three are *monarchism priest-craft* and *popular ignorance*. Slowly and steadily, science has been obliged to fight every step of this way against these three. Can anyone explain this obstructive phenomenon of history? Science is today almost universally recognized as a great friend of man[7] in the term of 'Social-Sciences' as a Scientific Truth to determine the history of man from one stage to another with historical ideas of the man what he has achieved for the successful tragedy of the man at last many "beat down resistance and clear the most formidable obstacles perhaps even death itself".[8] Physical science[9] is in no position to deny that fact so well-known to the Masters, where stands the life of that species to determine the history of man. The Masters are able to penetrate into the deeper substrata of nature to find out the Truth in the history of man. They can see the inner workings of all laws and processes. When matter is quickened by the all-pervading, life generating mind and spirit working together in this universe as phenomenal man of the period, as history repeat itself. All that physical and chemical sciences know is that 'Life 'manifests in certain ways. It follows certain well-attested laws. Scientists do not even try to guess the ultimate causes of life without struggling to determine the Truth in self-style manners. As a matter of fact, it lies in the life of man which is composed by the Master with the power of '*Nam*', without obtain the '*Nam*' the study of scientist fails in the logic to conclude the Ultimate Truth of the life. Our masters of the laboratory must not any longer try to 'squeeze all the cosmos into a test tube[10] i.e., organ of the man, who commits blunder with man to control it, '*Nam*' is essential. Just as the physiological psychology of King *James* and others can never reduce mind to the materialistic level of brain cells and nerve ganglia, "secreting thought as the liver secretes-bile", so the established facts of science can never displace spirit from man or the Universe. The most they can say is that they know nothing about it, but it is a natural system of controlling the population and moral value of the life in scientific manners to believe on the Master's theory.

It shows from the study that man is the highest form of creation on this planet (See Plate III) and he is only a sojourner here for a span of period. Once his eyes are opened in the spiritual sense he knows that this world is not his home, and that living in it he is no more than a feeder of swine among strangers, while far away the light burns in his Father's palace. He knows that this world is only a dark outhouse in the magnificent palace grounds of his Father's kingdom. The Masters tell us that above and beyond the doubt God is on earth in one or another life that it confines of this tervestrial speck of dust lie innumerable worlds full of light and beauty. To explore its beauty and thought those worlds at will and to possess them during this life time is only a portion of our heavenly bright right. But to most people that this vast universe of finer worlds is locked due to the 'Blind Faith' of the man called Mind in another sense. To many it is but a fabric of poetical fancy. But it is not so in reality unless and until, we will not knock the door of Father with the process of '*Nam-mantra*' theory. It is locked indeed, but the Master holds the key and he offers it to all who will qualify Him. By that key the entire universe of starry worlds may be unlocked and their shining heavens becomes exploration for the study of man. Just how this is to be done constitutes the sublimest rocks of the *Chambarian* plays secret role in the Eastern wisdom[11] to determine His history that who is good or bad on this earth, and thus, these zones are divided into three parts discussed as under:

Division	Zones
Upper	MassiveLimestone's (Unfossiciferous) 'Spiriferina' Limestones Lamebli-branch Zones. "Ptychites" Zone "Ceratite" Zone.
Middle Triassic	"Rhynconelly" zone "Gymites and Ceratite" Zone Nooblular Limestone."Hungarites"Shales Meakoceras" Limestones & Shales.
Lower Triassic	"Ophiceros" Zone "Octoceras" Zone.

Passing from the Permian to the *Triassic* a marked change in life has been observed. The brachiopods that dominated the *Permian* seas were replaced by the ammonites in the succeeding *Triassic* stone of life with fine instruments of the 'Nam's study as a supernatural force of the Father. *Jurassic* rocks have been traced in *Ladakh* and *Banihal* pass within syncline of *Triassic* rocks of the '*Chamar Family*', and few cretaceous rocks occurred only in a few localities such as *Burzil*, *Deosai* and *Zanskar* ranges. They are composed of white limestone's mostly *unfossiliferous* study of the *Himalayan* Ranges, and uplifted into their present positions and the evolution of most of the present day mammalian animals (especially man) had also started[12] to repeat the history of the man itself. These series are further subdivided in three classification, characterized by some typical fossils of the life discussed as under:

Division	**Stages**
Upper Siwaliks	Boulder Conglomerates Tarot stage
(8600 feet)	Pinjor Stage
Middle Siwaliks	Dhok Pathan Stage
(8000 feet)	Nagri Stage
Lower Siwaliks	Chinji Stage
(4000-5000 feet)	Kamlial Stage[13]

Now the recent study of the Father's history reveals that recent deposits of the Jammu and Kashmir State has been found at *Bhangar* and *Khadar*, valley of the Kashmir laid down in the streams of the 'Nam' of the *Chambrian* rock in alluvia manner for the *Sodar* spring deposit coming out in the front of the house as a natural growth of the 'Science of the Father'. Reddish and buff coloured clays are also found in it. Equivalent of these pebble beds of Jammu region as a natural growth of the history to begins with from the Valley of *Ambaran* of *Akhnoor* to repeat the history of the '*Chamar Dynasty of Kashmir*'.

Notes and References

1. 'The Path of the Masters' p. 21.
2. Ibid.
3. Ibid., p. 22.
4. Prof. Yashpal; *This Universe*, An article published The Tribune Magazine, April 4, 2008.
5. *The Path of the Masters*; p. 22.
6. Ibid., p. 24.
7. Ibid., p. 27.
8. Ibid., p. 29.
9. According to Prof. H.H. Newman of the University of *Chicago* thinks that *vitalistic* view is opposed in the history of man to that hypothesis

which has led to all scientific achievement. But we doubt the truth of this, however, much the good Professor may believe it so that it lies in the body. All that the scientist needs to assume is the orderlines of nature never distinct between the idea of man and God, the universality of laws operating in the world of matter. This assumption is surely not opposed to the vitalistic hypothesis. The scientist many ten proceed with security of the '*Nam*'. But the ultimate cause of biological manifestations is quite another matter. We may assume that electricity works according to a set of fixed laws to repeat the history of the man itself. But it is the duty of the scientist to locate them. No scientist will question this, it is the history subject, who is responsible for that to solve this question, it shows physical again fail in his process to determine the truth of the man, but the cause or the source of electric energy still remains one of the unsolved problems of physical science, so it is with regard to the source of the life itself. Like electricity project, we see life's marvelous display of activity, but physical science does not presume to say whence it comes nor whither it goes. It is reality at that time there is power to generate it. The source of both electricity and life remains yet to be discovered by science why is this so? Because physical science has not yet the means of following either one of them to its ultimate source. Yet the Masters have such means and the Masters *know* that life is due to a force extraneous to matter, and they know that biological phenomena cannot manifest as a result of the known laws of matter and energy i.e., '*Nam*' (Ibid., pp. 29-30).

10. Ibid., p. 31.
11. As noted in the Foreword, Dr Johnson's own life led him to the conclusion that all great Spiritual Truths were to be found in the East. Therefore, East Indian Company was preferred to visit over India to find out the Truth which was laid down in the Ravidas's philosophy of the period and later on they became the follower of the Master. Hence, his use of this expression became a historical truth that *Sudhras* of period were the natural force of the Father as synonymous with *Sant Mat*, the teachings of the Saints of the period like *Guru Nanak, Kabir, Ravidas* many more saints of the same thought.
12. Majid Husain; *op.cit*., pp. 7-8.

13. Ibid., p. 10. **Note:** A regional account of the study of the 'Indus Valley Civilization' called *Indus-Saraswati Valley of Akhnoor* explored from the *Manda* of the *'Ravidas Culture'* or *'Chamar Culture'* cited form the geographical survey of India that Indus emerging 'from the lap of the earth' north of *'Kailas Range'* means opposite force of the *'Nam'* at an altitude of 5,165 metres as 'an unpretentions brook', is like the *Tsangpo*, the *Upper Salween* and the *Mekong*, in its upper course from this source up to near the *Gilgit* confluence, one of the straightest rivers of the world. It does not cross any of the Himalayan or Trans-Himalayan Ranges during this upper course (about 900 km. long) suggesting that there must be particularly physical conditions of the areas restricting this 'furrow' or gorge-like narrow valley in a straight defile. From near *Hangle* up to about *Kargil* (400 km.) the Indus flows mostly along a narrow belt of thrusts and faults parallel to the stream of live as a Universal Truth, that life comes from life. Similarly, a child also his intelligence, though not as developed as his father's. In due course of time, when the child gets a body like that of his father, the child's intelligence will be fully developed and exhibited from his thought that he is going to repeat the idea of Father. In this way, the various zone of Indus Ophilolites *'Word'* or *'Nam'* the igneous intrusive and further west beyond *Chilas* through granites, gneisses and schist. Thus, *'Indus-Sarasvati Valley'* of *Akhnoor* of *Ambarna* origin located from village *Manda* is proved form Modern History of the World that it was the great 'Second Civilization of the *'Chamar Community'*, as exhibits from the recent Geological Survey of the past history. An essential feature of this culture landscape are stone walls of the *'Ravidas Community'* called *Manis* of the period, and the thousands of fluttering white and coloured flags on which *'Nam-mantras'* have been printed in their study to give a befitting. Reply to the Brahmins of the period. This water reservoir race of the Father is frozen with the study of the *'Nam'* means proving contentment in the life and early springs of their life, they will work soon (Ibid.pp.12,13,17-18, 23 A.C. Bhaktivedanta Swami Prabhupata; *Life Comes From Life*, Bombay, 1979, p.4)

Plate – I

Fig. 1. Corrupt Political System or *Satans* of the Period. Artist, Manoj Chopra, 21st Century A.D. Jammu.

Plate – II

Fig. 2: *Satan's* of the 21st Century A.D. Problem Creator of the Society; Artist: Manoj Chopra, Jammu.

Plate – III

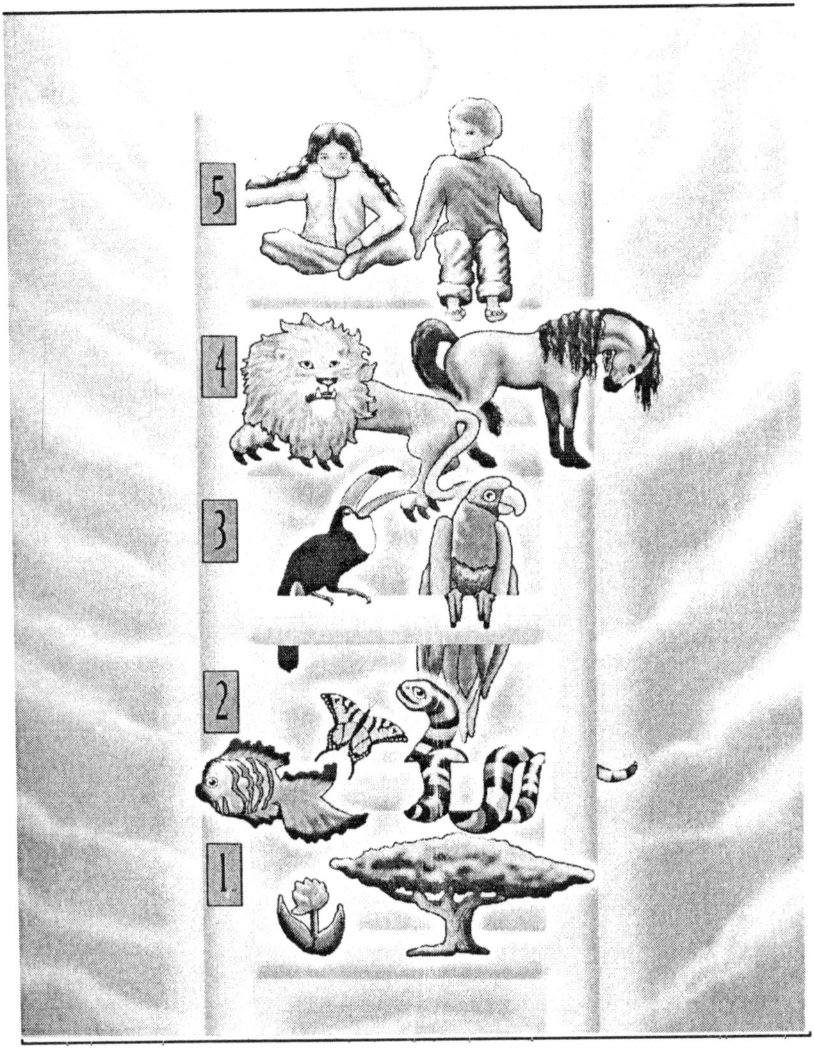

Fig. 3: Concept of Life in this Universe. Artist: Victoria John 20th Century A.D. London.

8

Determining the Moral Values of Life Through Scientific Study

Morality, in our present days, is a delicate subject. Possibly at no other time in history has there been so much uncertainty worldwide as to what the concept of morality means. Why, many people might ask, should one struggle to live honestly because there is a well-known proverb, "Honesty is the best policy a noblest work of God". Always be sincere, even if you do not mean it. It is responsibility of the nature to keep watch the efforts of the man and God. On whose authority does the state or our religion tell us what to do? In this Scientific Age also worship the Father of the Living Being, with the erosion of religious and social values, many people are left wandering whether an acceptable basis for a moral code even exists as '*Chamar-Brahmins*'. Faced with so much contradiction and uncertainty, they prefer to live their lives just as it pleases them, or for immediate short-term goals that no one is watching, i.e., the wrong idea of the man in their mind as Brahmins have.

If we choose to follow the way of the saints, it means that we want to use our life to realize our Divine Potential and that we have said to ourselves that there is more to life than short-term goals is fulfill by worshipping the artifacts of the 'Nam' is wrong idea in History. God resides inside the body, as a temple of God not man made things. The gift of initiation provides us with a practical method to realize our objective of the life as a human species, and to support our spiritual practice we make a commitment to live by specific values. These, we must remember, are not values imposed on us from any outside authority; we make the commitment to ourselves, within ourselves, to help us on our way of life and its study.

By examining our values rationally, we can refresh and deepen our understanding of them. No code of conduct can give one all the answers, but if one understands the principles that underpin it, it becomes easier to find the answers within oneself. It is the purpose of this small book, therefore, to try to understand the principles that support in moral living and their far-reaching implications for daily life as a food of the 'Natural Thought'.

Before the invention of steamships, the success of a voyage was dependent on several factors: '*understanding the sea*; *understanding the tides, currents and winds so as to use them to one's advantage*; and *maintaining the seaworthiness of the ship*'. Even if one owned the finest sailing vessel in the world and knew everything about one's ship. Without knowledge of the sea and the forces moving and driving the vessel, one's journey might prove disastrous. In a similar way we are setting out on a journey of self-realization. To complete it successfully we need to understand the life itself and the forces that drive us. Only then, and keeping in view our objective, can we formulate our code of conduct '*Word*' or '*Logos*' can we understand how to keep ourselves seaworthy because he knows the Knowledge and worth of the '*Nam-History*'.

Our understanding is based upon a spiritual and moral perspective that is common to all scriptures and wisdom, writings of the world. This perspective is not the property of any religion. It belongs to everyone. It arises from the pool of our common humanity and flowers naturally when a person reunites him or herself with our common spiritual source. The people who embody it most clearly are the mystics '*Word*' saints and God-realized souls '*Chamars*' of all religions is the study of '*Nam*' or God.

To demonstrate the universality of this understanding, we have included quotations from as wide a variety of sources as possible, but it is on the mystics' knowledge of life that we primarily rest our case what we try to say is that as human beings we are more honest than the animals and the birds, no, in modern era; Lovers of 'Humanity' generally hate people and children of the

Sudhra class, and keep parrots or puppy dogs more faithful; as an idea of the 'Brahminical Ideology'.

The Spiritual Perspective

In essence, the entire mystic perspective may be expressed in three simple points: There is only one supreme power which is the foundation and support of everything i.e., Day and Night life. We have all come from this power 'Words' we are all drops from the same one divine ocean. And each one of us is accountable for everything we do in the study of God and Man's history.

However, it is described in different cultures, all mystics agree that the fundamental reality of life is spirit of the '*Nam*' or God. Our essence is spirit not the physical or mental. Soul or spirit is the real nature of what we think of as 'we'. Mystics highlight our common confusion by pointing out that we are spiritual beings having a human experience, not (as we more frequently think of ourselves) human beings looking for a spiritual experience. Anyone who gets in touch with his or her spiritual essence, the life-giving '*Word*' or '*Shabd*' within them will be naturally led by it to its source, beyond the limitations of time and space of the human history as 'Celestial Order'.

This, then, is the object of our journey from bottom to top is the realization of Truth and its Knowledge. But we are handicapped because we experience our life through our senses and usually fail to recognize what we are. Just as a child has difficulty accepting that the atmosphere is vibrant with radio waves, so our spiritual immaturity hides from us our divine potential. Saints tell us that as long as we remain busy with the world around us, we will continue to be limited '*Word*' or '*Nam*' seduced and fooled into thinking that only the physical world is real. We start to think we can know everything with the intellect. Like Job in the Bible[1], we presume we are in control when we are simply understanding 'Words' and its concepts, it was to shake this viewpoint that God addressed Job from "out of the whirlwind", demanding that he reflect upon his arrogance:

Who is this that darkens counsel by words without knowledge? Man is a tool-making animals without '*Nam*', where were you when we laid the foundation of the earth? Tell us, if you have understanding[2]. O Brahman on this earth where reside the God.

The great physicist, Albert Einstein, spoke of the way in which our "understanding" is distorted because;

"A human being is a part of the whole, called by us 'Universe', a part limited in time and space. He experiences his thoughts and feelings as something separate from the res *'Word'* a kind of optical delusion of his consciousness. This delusion is a kind of prison for us, restricting us to our personal desires and to affection for a few persons nearest to us. Our task must be to free ourselves from this prison by widening our circle of compassion to embrace all living creatures and the whole of nature in its beauty,[3] as God and man in human nature. Civilized ages inherit the human nature which was victorious in barbarous ages as *'Sudhra Class'*.

To "free ourselves" from the *'physics'* and *'politics'* as a polluted study of the God and man, we need to "widen our circle of compassion", to recognize that we are spiritual beings drops of that one ocean that is God. For this the saints give us specific guidance. They teach us a technique that ultimately will enable us to embrace not just "nature", but the creation and the Creator. We are guided how to withdraw our attention from the world and concentrate it so that ultimately we can detach ourselves from the distortions of body and mind. But the saints also tell us that it is not simple: there is a catch boxes and that is the 'law of *karma*' or cause and effect. This law is the force that runs the creation. Because of it, we can never know pure spirit apart from matter of life or separate our soul from the world; until and unless we will not settled our life's account with Brahmins; we cannot take a relief of the life as a challenge and response theory in history that there is no finer investment for any community than putting milk into babies as *'Nam'* do since the birth of the child take place.

What is this account? It is the record of everything we have ever thought or done since our soul left its source and became encased in a mind and body of the living Creatures. This record binds us to the creation, because we have to remain in the creation moving from life to life to account for all we have done. Freedom lies in settling this account from the past and in not incurring new debts. Once we understand that what we do *now* binds us in the future, then we have a practical approach for a moral code that will guide us as to what we should, and should not, do to become free from the worldly life cycle i.e., the idea of birth and rebirth according to their deeds.

Applying our understanding of the law of cause and effect to our daily lives, living consciously so that we are always aware of the consequences of what we do, is therefore, our way of making ourselves seaworthy for our voyage to God, unless and until there is no rocess of the '*Nam-Mantra theory*.'

The Law of Cause and Effect: The Imperative for Moral Living

The inescapable principle of compensation, or *karma*, is recognized by all the great religions and wisdom through literature throughout the world. Though the scope of the law is vast, its application is very simple: Whatever we give, we have to take; whatever we take, we have to give as a theory of give and take policy.

Judge not, and ye shall not be judged:

Condemn not, and ye shall not be condemned:

Forgive, and ye shall be forgiven,

Give, and it shall be given unto you, soul as a realization of thought.

For with the same measure that you mete

Withal it shall be measured to you again as the story of God and man reveal.[4]

Since nothing in the creation exists without some degree of action, so all life is eternally caught in the web of its ever-adjusting account. Across the vast span of creation, the law maintains a perfect record of giving and taking. No account is ever settled if people obey the order of the *Nam* or God. However far the pendulum swings in one direction, it swings to the same degree in the other. In this way, we are all captive of the '*Word*' limited to the realms of mind and matter. And as long as we are victims of this duality, we cannot know the perfection and bliss of spiritual unity. As stated in the Jewish teachings:

'Everything is a loan given against a pledge, and the net is cast over all living so that none may forfeit paying by escaping. The shop is open; the shopkeeper extends credit; the ledger is spread out and the hand makes entries. Whoever wishes to borrow may come and borrow, but the collectors make their rounds daily, and exact payment whether or not one is aware of it. They go by an unfailing record, and the judgement is a judgement of Truth[5]", to repeat the history of God and man in Jammu.

Fundamentally, it is this one law that drives the creation. Through the principle of opposites, actions and reactions, this universal law generates the force that produces the multitude of natural laws governing the visible physical universe '*Names*' are' the laws of physics, genetics, environmental balance and much more beyond the limit by which modern science explains life. It also governs all activity at the more subtle levels of mind which cannot be known or quantified by the intellect. The simple principle of cause and effect creates all diversity. It marks the formidable dividing line between the oneness of spirit and the complexity of mind and matter into different ways as self-style nature as a problem creator of the society.

The law of compensation, of giving and taking, is inescapable. Unlike our secular laws, we cannot bypass it or manipulate it. If we choose to ignore it, saying "This is not how life works. There is no justice, no need to think of right and wrong" 'Words' still the forces of action and reaction will drive us into the right director as Actor of the '*Nam Theory*'. If on the other hand we become sensitive to their workings, then we can work wit this principle so tat it takes us where we want to go.

Who is in Charge of this World?

From earliest childhood, we are encouraged to rethink of ourselves as unique individuals and to develop our individuality. From the spiritual perspective this is an illusion. It is strengthened by the present worldview which emphasizes individual rights and personal freedom. We fail to see that when we think of ourselves this way we are simply seeing our separate reality of mind and body and ignoring our common spiritual reality. By emphasizing our differences and separateness and ignoring our commonality, we are assuming that we are physical, rather than spiritual beings a man of the true society.

We talk about freedom and personal fulfillment, but because our understanding is limited to the material, we cannot see that in the light of the '*Law of karma*', we have no free will at all. From a higher perspective we are simply undergoing the reactions of our earlier actions, repaying debts that have to be repaid. Who we are, or rather who we *think* we are, is shaped by debits and credits incurred in earlier lives. We would do well to reflect on how many key aspects there are to our life over which we have had no control i.e., 'Only Mind' or *Mana*. Our parents, when and where we were born, our particular genetic patterning and our early education '*Nam*' all are part of the conditioning that has made us what we are today. When so much of what we are now has happened beyond our control, is it not foolish to think we are free from the study of '*Nam*' and its creatures.

As we come to understand the Karmic principle, we begin to realize how little freedom we really have. It is our mind, conditioned by earlier impressions, that is in charge. Our task, therefore, is to extricate ourselves from this pattern of living as slaves to the mind. To do this we have to start by remembering that each action, each thought, imprints itself on our consciousness. Each one will remain with us and influence us until it finds full compensation at some future time. Over many lifetimes these impressions have built walls around our souls so thick that we cannot hear the life-giving music of the Word or *Shabd* of the Father, and it is our conscious experience of the *Shabd* that will put us in touch with who we are. As long as we are not present to the spirit within us, we will remain trapped by ignorance. The images that are used frequently in the scriptures to convey our helplessness are prison, snare, net, trap. In the Bible we read:

The iniquities of the wicked ensnare him, and he is caught in the toils of his sin as man itself.[6]

Since this burden of "*sin*" cannot be settled in our life, we carry it across the threshold of physical death from one life to another. If we are not careful, while we are settling our present destiny we will be creating fresh debts for future lives. *Dadu Sahib*, a sixteenth century Indian mystic of *Rajasthan*, says:

Be in fear, O be in fear of the Lord! Though He gives in abundance, He seeks an account, therefore guard yourself against evil. Let all your dealings be true, believe in truth alone. Falsehood you must not entertain, if you would avoid poison of ***manmuk*** *theory i.e.,* ***'Only Mind'.***[7] *or rather living man.*

By the very nature of the creation, our captivity is self-perpetuating, for we ourselves keep building our prison walls. Being ignorant of their real consequences, we make little attempt to control our thoughts and actions. And if we are dishonest we compound our problem by incurring heavier debts of the Lord.

To extricate ourselves from this trap, not only must we "guard ourselves against evil", we must also work to cultivate positive qualities. Positive qualities enable us to think positively; they strengthen our mind to act in our long-term interest. They remind us that we are not just separate personalities but part of the positive reality that is God. Meditation is our one certain way to escape, but as long as the mind takes its messages only from the outside world, we keep undoing the benefit of any spiritual practice by incurring new debts as problem creator of the living society.

Empowering The Kind and Freeing the Soul

There are two steps we can take to help the power of the 'Word' within us become the dominant force in our lives. Each step depends up to the other for success. First, living honest, pure lives helps prevent our debts from increasing so that we can cease rebuilding our prison. Second, meditation, built upon the firm foundation of a disciplined life, concentrates the mind and focuses it away from the material creation. It frees us so our spiritual faculties can start functioning. Once these different faculties are fine-tuned, we will experience the world reverberating within us, and our contact with the *'Word'* or the *'Shabd'* will bring the real freedom and inner harmony we seek for the socitial development form one generation to another, from *Dr. B.R. Ambedkar* to *Baba Gurinder Singh ji Biaswale.*

These two steps are interdependent because concentrating the mind necessitates a high degree of mastery over oneself and an atmosphere of tranquility and peace. If, through meditation, we are to expand our consciousness beyond the physical, then our entire attention has to be concentrated towards the non-material realm. The mind is one and it is for us to choose: it can either be directed outwards, to the creation, or inwards where we can experience the spirit of life that it is natural gift of the God to man to realize the Truth on this earth as a superior race of the Father as *Chamar* or *Chura* and other *Sudhras*.

How many times do we say, or hear others say, "I would like to, but we just don't have the will power" because *Brahmins* or *Molavis* never practice the '*Nam-Theory*'. Who are these two 'I's' that are contradicting each other? We want to do something, but we cannot do what we want! The upstart I is the mind driven by its constant hunger for satisfaction, taking control and leading us where it leads us. We are creatures of habit, and our mind, bullied by the senses, has the habit of running in whatever direction is easiest. Out in the creation and looking for pleasure, we get caught up in our obsessions. Since the material world is constantly changing, so our mind, too, keeps changing its focus and we find ourselves fragmented, restless and out of control due to the 'egocentric' problem of the man's life are problem creator of the society never favoured towards the development of the historical thought, therefore, it is necessary to check the advancement of the society by striking the 'law' of the 'Nam-History'.

To go where we want to go, we have to transform the mind. We have to create new habits that marginalize the 'I' who leads us out into the world. By striving to live honestly, we develop qualities that strengthen our will power strong and fair, and our ability to stand up to our weaknesses. We develop the positive qualities of contentment, compassion, purity, detachment and humility, and these in turn further support our efforts to choose the inner life of the human history as God and man on earth.

Remembering that we are accountable for everything we do helps us empower the spiritual 'I'. If we do wrong, thinking we can get away with it, then we are supporting the upstart 'I' . No matter how much we then try to meditate, we will not attain our objective. If we attempt to realize the '*Word*,' or '*Shabd*', without curbing our negative tendencies, we are trying to achieve the impossible '*Chamar*' to move into opposing directions at once; as observed by Mathew in the Bible:

"*No man can serve two masters:*
For either he will hate the one, and love the other,
Or else he will hold to the one, and despise the other.
Ye cannot serve God and Mammon,"[8] at one time as a conflicting theory of the mind and God; as *Gandhi* and *Dr. B.R. Ambedkar*, one was the *Sudhra* and *other* was Brahmin by nature

as a contradictory Thought of the human history but without *'Nam'* there is no peace.

We must be clear about our priorities that *'Nam'* has been established in human history during the 21st century for peace and its prosperity. From the saints and spiritual masters we know that only when we hear the *Word* within us will the impressions of actions lying beyond our present destiny be settled. Only through the *Word* our account can be solve otherwise death is ready for the Brahmins for the establishment of the *'New Society'* with life be erased. If we are clear that spiritual realization is our goal, then the first thing to do is to support our spiritual self.

Ignorance: the Prison of Our Soul

As long as our senses dominate our thinking, we remain ignorant of the real order of the creation. Until we are in conscious contact with the 'Word', we are limited by our physical perspective and our understanding remains distorted. As Jesus said:

O ye of little faith!
Seek ye first the kingdom of God and his righteousness,
And all these things shall be added unto you[9] *trust or not.*

Lacking Spiritual Knowledge, we identify ourselves with the physical and give priority to tangible, material goals, if we had real faith in what we profess 'Spirituality' that our reality is eternal and that in this life we simply are going through our destiny to find out the Truth, we would surrender ourselves to the Divine Will. But our Faith is half-backed, our knowledge fractional, because we are not yet in touch with who we are. In the Buddhist scriptures it says:

The fool is tormented, thinking,
These sons belong to me,
This wealth belongs to me, As Mind base, or Consciousness (*manayatana*), and Mind-object (*dhammayatana*). Similar is the explanation of the four remaining physical sense – organs i.e., Eyes, Ears, Nose, Tongue and Body.

He himself does not belong to himself.
How then can sons be his?
How can wealth be his?[10] It may be physical or mental, past, present or future, real or imaginary. We do not 'belong' to ourselves because we have not yet *experienced* ourselves because the idea of

Mind is false and God is True. From moment to moment we struggle to shape our destiny on the basis of intellectual or sensual whims. Our reference points are our social, religious and cultural context in natural form and the thinking of our times. To complicate things further, we recognize no limits to our actions, driven as we are by prejudices and passions that arise from our conditioning that God is there on this earth as a fear of Mind. We remain oblivious of the fact that our destiny for this life is already fixed so that we must settle a specific portion of our account. We fail to remember, as it is written in the Bible, that our every hair, our every breath, is numbered.[11] This ignorance can then lead to the unfortunate situation described by *Baba Jaimal Singh* in one of his letters to *Master Sawan Singh*:

"The individual who, instead of his own rightful earnings, considers it better to fraudulently live off another's just labour or '*Coolie*', has not realized that what the Lord has given is specific to his needs. For the realization of Truth. As he acquires name and fame, he increasingly uses force or fraud in order to usurp the rights of those lesser or lower than him, while hoarding his own wealth, or spending it uselessly, or doing other bad deeds. Such a being subsequently has to pay those from whom he has taken, and pays it by taking birth repeatedly '*Names*' by becoming an animal, cow, or donkey, again and again. So understand, my son, that apart from your rightful earnings, you are never to use what belongs to others. This is the first step on the spiritual ladder. Even if you are the '*Dalit King*' of the whole world, you are still to eat only the rightful fruit of your own labour."[12]

We may reflect that of all the creatures it is only humans that take from life what they do not need. All other creatures function by instinct 'and take only what they need to sustain their existence. It is only human beings '*Living Deity*' using the unique discriminating faulty of the human mind to the wrong ends compelled the '*Chamar Ravidas*', who experienced passions which know no bounds. How few of us are content with what we need in life, rather than what we want. Two spiritual guides one speaking in the context of Greek Christianity more than five hundred years ago, and one speaking form present day 'India', advise the disciple in almost identical terms like 'Light' is inside the body as Philokalia described in his study:

"We should remain, then, within the limits imposed by our basic needs and strive with all our power not to exceed them. For once we are carried a little beyond these limits in our desire for the pleasures of this life; there is then no criterion by which to check the onward movement, since no bounds can be set to that which exceeds the necessary"[13] project of the life as *'Nam'* itself.

"One ought always to live within one's means. Try to adjust your budget and reduce your wants. There can be no end to a person's desires. One can increase one's wants as much as one likes, and one may also reduce them to the minimum. The richest person is one who has no desires"[14] described by *Maharaja Charan Singh.*

Easily fooled by the surface of life, we get over-involved and caught up by our actions while remaining blind to their inevitable effects. Influenced by others and by the scintillating appearance of what we see, we start to covet what others have. The twelfth century mystic, Sheikh Farid, warns against covetousness. In fact, it is in our real interests to guard against desiring anything that belongs to someone else. Our interests lie in cultivating the opposite virtue of the negative force that of contentment of the 'Nam' so that we are not tempted to try and acquire something that is not ours in our life as described by him, :

"Relish your food, dry and simple Kalma
Be not enticed by another's bread".[15]

And Guru Arjun Dev, the fifth Sikh Guru, warns:

"You clutch at things that belong to another,
but the Lord within knows and hears all.
Lost in greed for worldly things,
you fall into the pit of hell,
unaware of what lies in store for you in the beyond"[16], as *'Nam'* itself.

If only we were able to see the long-term consequences of our desires as we go about fulfilling them, we would almost certainly change our tune. But this, it seems, is part of creation's play with black forces of the *'Nam'* i.e., *'Brahminical Ideology'* that we should have no way of seeing how both soul and mind will have to return again and again to the creation, "the pit of hell', to reap the harvest of the seeds we are sowing now through the books and articles of the same. Even within the scope of one lifetime, how many times do we witness the way in which worldly activities and the quest for success imprison people in the chains of their own dreams! Because of our ignorance, the saints advise us to keep watch over our desires and ambitions and try to anticipate where they might lead. In this context, we have the wise advice of the moralist, *Baltasar Gracian*, speaking in the seventeenth century A.D. "Men driven by ambition often succeed outwardly and fail inwardly. Their outer resources multiply at the cost of their spiritual energy. Yet they go blindly forward with small consideration that happy leisure is worth more than drive for nothing belongs to us except time. Precious existence is squandered in stupid drudgery. Overwork is the mother of greed and the substitute for boredom. Once entrapped, escape comes only with the slow collapse of body functions. So be not crushed under success, and be not crushed under envy! To be so is to trample upon life and to suffocate the spirit. Enjoy a little more, strive a little less"[17] in this Universe. Because we are limited in our understanding, we let greed, ambition or insecurity determine the pattern of our days. If we are to address our grievances to the negative forces they are failed to address the people with effects of our ignorance we must at least ensure that today's actions reflect our long-term aims, they are not ready to accept it, they need immediate dispensation which does not lie in the 'Mind Only', it is up to the Master of the Universe. Together a sweet harvest, we may have a good idea in their minds so that as we sow, so shall you reap. Therefore, theory of the '*Nam-History*' is full of sweet and fruitful for the development of the society and the people particular.

Out Thoughts and Actions of 'Word' the Prison Walls

As we look deeper into the workings of the 'law of karma', we begin to see that one reason we go on doing what we do is because we do not experience the repercussions of our deeds straightway. It is precisely because of our ignorance that we end up in such a trap created a mess in the life to decide after consideration. If we could see the results of our thoughts and actions, would we ever allow them to lead us to suffering to any conclusion e.g., if we put our hand into a fire, we immediately experience pain, so we do not repeat the action. But just imagine what would happen if our nerves were not functioning! We might leave our hand in the fire to crush the modern politicians, Brahmins of the period who might even go on doing so until our hand burned away. This is the physical plane, but it is the same at the spiritual nerves have been deadened to such an extent that we fail to understand where our thoughts and deeds are taking us. We forget that while the wheels of the 'Law' described by Dr. B.R. Ambedkar in Indian Constitution is a Confidential Measure Building system between God and man; may grind slowly, they grind exceedingly fine, In the Buddhist scriptures we read its beauty as it is described :

"So long as an evil deed does not bear fruit,
the fool thinks that it is like honey; like BJP Leader Dr. Nirmal Singh, idiot of the History word.
But when it bears fruit, then the fool suffers grief.
An evil deed, like newly drawn milk, does not sour; like Poonam Choudhary, Prostitute of the Department of History, University of Jammu
Smouldering, like fire covered by ashes, it follows the fool[18]
By owing the Museum of University". Without knowing the Knowledge of art history.

There is a story told in India of *Dhritarashtra*, a wise king who had been blind from birth. He was blessed with spiritual powers whereby he could see into his past lives. One day he asked Lord Krishna the reason for his blindness i.e., Mind's thought explaining that he had looked back over one hundred lives and seen no action that could justify this cruel fate. Lord Krishna instructed him to look further, beyond one hundred lives, and there he saw himself as a young child tormenting a small creature by poking thorns into its eyes.

All our actions, like fruit, have their own time of ripening. It is easy for us, with our limited vision, to excuse or ignore things we do. It is particularly easy to dismiss small dishonesties as being of no significance. But mystics tell us that no action, however small, is insignificant. One day, on the vast panorama of time, it will have its reckoning. *Master Jagat Singh* says: "*Not even a single grain that inadvertently enters your granary from a nelghbour's field can go unaccounted.*[19] This law does not apply just at the physical level; it is true of all interaction. Whatever the nature of the interaction 'Word' physical, financial, emotional, or sexual '*Chamar*' a bond is created between those involved in the *Satsang* at police station Jammu, do the practice of the *'Nam's History'* in the station as meant for body without *Mandir*. Whatever the give and take policy of the situation, any resulting imbalances will have to be redressed in the book entitled *Early History of Jammu Region* (From Pre-historic to 6th century A.D.), *Baba Ravidas* is there in Jammu. Here we have quotations from the fourteenth-century mystic, *Mulana Rumi*, and a letter of the disciple James in the New Testament:

"Turn away from living on the public
So that you may not be affected by their blood.
Consider this food to be their blood,
Because it is obtained by force,"[20] as *'Nam'* is a spiritual thought a separate unit of the society.

Behold the wages of labourers as *DSP M.L. Kaith* who mowed our fields to crush the *Brahmins* like *Dr. Nirmal Kumar Singh* and *others* in the agitation, *Chutya, Jagdish Lal Badgal*, ignoring his qualities as a true man of the history which you kept back by fraud, cry out, and the cries of the harvesters have reached the ears of the Lord of hosts,[21] as a food for him.

Whatever the circumstances, whatever the nature of the interaction, in the end every thought and deed binds itself to an equivalent reaction in order to balance the account of the *Sudhra* and *Brahmins*.

We Alone Have to Account for Our Actions

Whatever we think and do, it is we, and we alone, who are responsible. We delude ourselves if we think otherwise the process of the life is nil, if we think that others loose meaning (*ati-Sudhra'* Brahminical family of *Sudhra*) or our employer, family members, or those close to us they will share the crop, we have sown even if it was for their sake, they left the knowledge of the *'Num'* like *B.R. Kundal* and *Others*.

There is a story told of a persons who went to a holy man requesting initiation into the secrets of Spiritual Enlightenment. The mystic asked him how he earned his living.

"By stealing," he said.

The mystic then questioned, "Why do you do that?"

The man replied, "Because I am not trained to do anything

else and I have to support myself and my family".

"Will they help you by sharing your punishment if you are caught?" said the holy man.

"Of course," replied the man. But the holy man told him to go home and ask them.

So he went home and asked his family: "If the king arrests Me and I'm punished, will you share my fate?

"Not at all! They all responded. "That is your outlook. If you choose to support us in this way, it's your fault, not ours".

Is it not ironical that we sacrifice our integrity to create wealth or power for others without practicing the '*Nam theory*', and they, when the day of reckoning comes, share no part of our fate? No, it is a part of the public life.

The following words of Emerson bring us once again to the dangers of our partial vision. How easy it is to lose sight of, or simply ignore, our responsibility when we act on behalf of a group, an organization, our community or our country! We may have a conscience that makes us uneasy, but we side-step it, shifting the responsibility to others or onto the impersonal and amorphous 'group' who believe on the authority of *Nam* or *Chamar* like *Bikram Singh* Typist. Either we do not care to listen to what our conscience tells us or we fail to recognize the truth but true quality is there.

"The ways of trade are grown selfish to the borders of theft, and supply to the borders of the Names is of fraud, but everybody partakes, everybody confesses, either *Brahmins or Molavis* are responsible as problem creator of the society, yet none feels himself accountable of the '*Nam History*'. That is the vice, that no one feels himself called to act for man, but only as a fraction of man."[22]

This lack of accountability, the lack of understanding of personal responsibility for all we do, accounts among other things for the rapid collapse of the institution of marriage in the last few decades. How far will we let today's culture of self-interest take us? We are so keen to secure our personal rights, yet do we understand our personal responsibilities? Marriage provides a framework in which one of the deepest forces of the creation can express itself to produce the children and provide then souls, it is a part of the Master and we can meet the responsibilities that ensue from lowest point to top as human being. It safeguards the family unit so that children may grow up secure and two people may work together to meet the needs of all involved. Has the study of human behaviour shown us a better way to transmit and develop positive values than in the context of a secure and loving family? Marriage is a life-long commitment made between two people that is husband and wife as God and man, and as such it provides a structure within which we can mature emotionally and better understand our responsibilities to one another, to our family and to the society in which we live. By taking us beyond our personal wants and needs, it establishes order on the potential chaos of our emotional and sexual desires. Being faithful to one's partner and honouring one's commitment through thick and thin goes beyond mere social convention. It reinforces and supports one's spiritual priorities. By honouring our commitment, we are acknowledging that real happiness at the cost of our responsibilities is a delusion that leads us the wrong way in this *Mayasum* World.

Living Dishonestly an Act of Punishment

The human passions are the servants of *Maya*, the seductive face of material existence that makes us believe that nothing else is real. The passions of lust and greed create this illusion by getting us addicted to the sense pleasures. Then to satisfy our desires, we are dishonest with ourselves and one another; to justify our actions we indulge in self-deception; we end by having identified ourselves with the most limited aspect of what we are in this Universe.

Honest living necessitates self-control. It requires that we exercise restraint in all our dealings, that we use our sense of judgement, our God-given gift of discrimination, to shape our lives. Honesty implies being faithful to our spouse, or, if we are not married, being faithful to a chaste life. It implies fairness and justice, openness and transparency, the absence of deceit, in contrast to wealth, power and passion, which lead to oppression, extortion, deception and pain in life of human beings.

Whether it is through greed for money or power, the pleasures of the senses, lusts '*Nam*' the routes the passions take are limitless. *The Cloud of Unknowing,* written in the Middle Ages by an anonymous British author as a practical guide to the spiritual seeker, speaks of what can happen if we give the senses free rein:

'Sensuality of Humanism is the one and the same faculty that will grumble when the body is lacking essential requirements, yet when the need is met, will move it to take more than it requires real dose i.e., '*Nam*' and unless it will control both its strong desires when it has its wonted pleasures, and its greedy delight when the improving irritations are gone, it will wallow, like some pig in the mire, so wretchedly and wildly in all the wealth of the world is '*Nam*' that the whole of its life will be animal and physical rather than human and spiritual[23] in sense as '*Nam*' itself.

Failing to understand their consequences, we allow our passions to carry us deeper into the creation. We need to remember that if, by letting our senses drive our will, we behave more like animals, we may well be born as animals in the future so we can settle today's account through the study of '*Nam*' or God.

Guru Arjun Dev speaks of how greed can be so powerful that it makes us compromise the relationships between the two we have with those we love most:

O greed, you have enveloped
Even the best of people in your tides:
Their minds ramble, shake and wander in all directions,
You have regard neither for friendship, nor gods,
Neither for father, mother, nor relations, but without Chamar
To escape from its influence,
I seek shelter with a prayer:
O Lord, come to my rescue!

Save me, almighty Father[24] is study the '*Nam History*' as a secret messages of the God and man.

How many times are families torn apart, friendships severed, and basic human principles compromised for the sake of possessing what is not ours i.e., our '*Life*'. God forbid that we should so deceive ourselves that as we die, we see we have wasted our time:

"*Renouncing fear of God, we are shorn of restraint;*
We do not enthrone the Lord, who is ever with us,
But raise armies and collect plunder.

Yet with our death, everything turns to dust"[25] as described by *Guru Arjun Dev*.

Guru Arjun's example of the ruthless conqueror, apt for those days of warring states and petty kingdoms, might be substituted today with the image of the totalitarian and expansive regimes of modern times and the profit-hungry entrepreneurs and companies of the business world. So often the pursuit of profit and power takes place at the expense of the common man. Whether on a large or small scale, the issues are the same: What is our objective? Are we fair in our dealings with everyone? There are important questions for inquiry.

The scriptures of all world religions contain strong injections against dishonesty. In the *Quran* it says:

"Whenever you weigh, do it properly and use a precise scale.
Do not steal money from others and do not give bribes."[26]

In the Bible, we read:

You shall not steal.
You shall not covet 'Kalma' anything that is your neigbour's.[27]

And in the Buddhist scriptures, it says:

"As a merchant without guards, and carrying much wealth,
shuns a dangerous road,
As a man who loves his life avoids poison
So should a wise man avoid evil actions"[28] as 'Unconscious Being' in Spiritual Knowledge called *'Cankers'* to others.

Master *Sawan Singh* speaks of the serious repercussions of dishonesty for a person who wishes to walk the path of spirituality:

"Even if a disciple who does not spend much time in meditation, he should certainly abstain from dishonesty, because deficiency in meditation can be compensated for by the Master's grace, but trickery, treachery, fraud and deception undermine the very foundation of spirituality. To settle such accounts one has to take birth again"[29] to repeat the history of same thought.

Even when we have accepted intellectually the truth of this law, we may fail to change our actions out of sheer complacency 'Infinite' we choose to simply ignore its implications. We need to remind ourselves that the unwary mind, when it is regularly exposed to anything, quickly loses its natural sensitivity and becomes coarse in its responses. This is a fact with which we are very familiar as technology exposes us to all sorts of unwanted influences right inside our home. How many of us sit and watch the most terrible images on television without reacting! Just as familiarity breeds contempt, so, if we do not remove ourselves from negative influences, familiarity may breed moral complacency so that our natural moral instinct for self-preservation *'Nam'* is our conscience *'Chamar'* becomes dull in the study that His forefather already worked enough.

Materialism - Spiritualism: A Question of Priorities to Man

Since it is a natural tendency of all human beings to strive for happiness and to improve their situation in life, the success of our spiritual journey depends on what we put first, our spiritual or material goals Master *Jagat Singh* guides us to give our best to whatever we do but not get attached to the results: "For your part make all necessary efforts to improve your circumstances; but leave the results of your efforts to the *Satguru's* will. He is not unaware of your problems."[30]

The danger lies in making material goals our priority. We are then equating riches with happiness and we immediately become vulnerable to compromising those very principles established to safeguard us. As the Buddhist scriptures again put it as under:

"Riches destroy the foolish,
not those who seek beyond the other shore.
By a craving for riches,
the foolish person destroys himself as he destroys others"[31] in the history of *'Nam-mantra theory'*.

The fact is that in this cut-throat, consumer-oriented world, most of us are likely to face frequent temptations to compromise our principles. Once we make anything in the outside world our priority, we can be easily tempted to ignore our scruples. Once we have enjoyed a measure of 'the good life', the life of sensual indulgence, we may get attached to it and not be prepared to let it go. The second-century Roman emperor, Marcus Aurelius, advises us on how to deal with material comforts but, at the same time, to remember our Divine link with our Spiritual Inheritance:

"Receive wealth or prosperity without arrogance; and be ready to let it go cheerfully. If you ever saw a hand cut off, or a foot, or a head lying anywhere apart from the rest of the body having Universal Knowledge this is what a man does with himself who is not content with what happens, and separates himself form others, or does anything unsocial form the Insight-Knowledge. But consider the benevolence by which God has distinguished man, for he has put it in his power not to be separated at all from the universal; and when he has been separated, he has allowed him to return and to be united and to resume his place as a part"[32] of the life itself.

The more we are preoccupied with the material world, the more we lose our spiritual perspective. This is why saints warn us that the world is a place of great danger. From their point of view, we are walking along the edge of a precipice and if we let our attention wander, we may turtle to our death. That is why our daily routine of meditation is so important, as is regular *satsang* and reading spiritual literature. Frail humans that we are, it is all too easy to be seduced by life at the surface and look to the material world for our well-being and security. Then, as Jesus pointed out:

"How hard it is for them that trust in riches
to enter into the kingdom of God!
It is easier for a camel to go through the eye of a needle,
than for a rich man to enter into the kingdom ofGod."[33]

One of the practical measures we can take to help ourselves is to keep supportive company. Since we are naturally influenced by the people we spend time with, we should avoid wrong company. In every discourse he gave, *Master Charan Singh* spoke of the power of association:

"We are always influenced by the company we keep. If we start mixing with criminals, with bad people, we will start thinking along these lines. If we mix with good people, with noble people, with devotees, we will start thinking in their way."[34]

Sarmad, a Jewish mystic who lived in India in the seventeenth century, also warns against bad company:

In this world of avarice and envy Kalma or Tao
Have no fear of snakes and scorpions;
Keep far away from greedy people like Brahmin Chamar,
They bite like snakes and scratch like thorns.[35]

We have to remember that the moment we lose sight of our spiritual goal, however, exciting our lives or successful we may be by the yardstick of the world, we are likely to get lost in the fog of our own logic. The next step on this route is hypocrisy.

Hypocrisy – the Dishonourable Companion of Greed

Hypocrisy is another form of dishonesty *'Word'* being dishonest in the way we project ourselves to the world, saying one thing and doing another. Having good intentions and speaking lofty words about spiritual values and moral principles is not enough. The details of our daily lives with Master Deepit Raj modern man of the period both at home and at work with Father, have to reflect our goal. This is a late eighteenth-century warning form Thomas Paine:

"It is impossible to calculate the moral mischief in the life of man, lying has produced in society. When a man has so far corrupted and prostituted the chastity of his mind as to subscribe his professional belief to things he does not believe he has prepared himself for the commission of every other crime."[36]

Sometimes, for various reason, we are ready to do things in our professions tat we would never subscribe to in our personal lives. It is as though we hang our consciences up with our coats as we enter the office door. We compromise for money, for fear of losing our jobs, or sometimes because we genuinely see our actions as fulfilling some other responsibility. The point Tomas Paine is making is that once we allow ourselves to practice two sets of values, who is to set the limits on how far we are prepared to go to see the God in human form as the writer of this text.

Even in relation to our spiritual effort, we need to be aware of the dangers of hypocrisy. Many of us would like to appear virtuous and spiritual in the eyes of others. We adopt the external trappings of spirituality, appearing to be righteous and devoted, yet in our daily activities we are negative and uncharitable. We may genuinely want to experience the spirit but are not prepared to change the way we are. We are not ready to make the sacrifices required as useless wants.

Hypocrisy is one of the prisms through which we distort the teachings of the saints. Because we are not prepared to mould ourselves to the teachings, we adjust them to suit us, to fit in with what we desire. This leads to division and confusion within ourselves. We try to be have in one way but are actually motivated in another, and end up simply putting on a show of spirituality. But it is a tribute which vice pays to virtue.

Bulleh Shah, the hard-hitting Punjabi Sufi poet, questions the hypocritical behaviour of people who piously ask for God's forgiveness while continuing to cheat others and behave immorally; to speak and purpose not.

"You go on reading, "Forgive me, O Lord" Hypocrisy.
What repentance is this, O friend?
You give one measure and take back one and a quarter as impious Thorns.
You have wagered to make illicit profit.
When did Islam give you such a teaching?
Such are your doings! What repentance is this?
You go to places where you should not go.
You relish things which belong to others.
You falsely swear by holy books
Such is your trust! What repentance is this"?[37]

Taken to an extreme, hypocrisy may lead a person to set him or herself up before others as a spiritual leader, professing to lead them to truth. All Reformers, however, strict their social conscience, live in houses just as big as they can pay for;

"Woe unto you, scribes and Pharisees, hypocrites!
For ye make clean the outside of the cup and of the platter,
But within they are full of extortion and excess.
Thou blind Pharisee, cleanse first
That which is within the cup and platter,
That the outside of them may be clean also as 'Ranga' of the 'Nam'
Even so ye also outwardly appear righteous unto men,
but within ye are full of hypocrisy and iniquity."[38] says Matthew.

"The scholar is proud of his learning,
The hafiz thrives on self – promotion.
With books under their arms,
They roam around, selling their honour.
Wherever they find a promising household,
They read the scripture in loud, fervent strains
For a lucrative commission.
O Bahu! They have put God's name on sale
Just to make a living.
In this world they live spiritually bankrupt;
Robbed of all honour, they go to the one beyond."

It is hypocrisy when people 'sell' spirituality. Making a person pay for spiritual guidance is a contradiction in itself. Spirit is the free and abundant life force present within every living being. Each person has simply to be awakened to that power within him or herself. True spiritual masters impart their wisdom and share their experience with their fellow human beings out of love and compassion, never for money. They never do it to support themselves. *Kabir Sahib* and *Guru Nanak Dev* speak here of the hypocrisy of those who turn spirituality into a business. Who charge for the initiation they give, and indulge their greed and desire for power and fame in the name of the spirit. As Leo Tolstoy, "I am very sorry for him", who leads a double life, and being really good all the time. That would be hypocrisy. The Importance of Being Earnest (1895).

"Without a perfect master,
One cannot become a true disciple.
*When the master is greedy and the disciple covetous, in the study of '**Nam**'.*
Nothing but greed multiplies.
Cheap are such masters,
A dime a dozen.
By selling God's name,
They hope to increase their following.[40]
"Damned are they who sell the Lord's Name!
Just as those who ruin their crops
Are left with nothing
Through falsehood no one receives true glory"[41] as *Nanak* says.

Mystics warn against such so-called spiritual leaders. By taking material support from their followers, they only increase their own karmic debts. As *Paltu Sahib* says, true spiritual masters never take anything from their disciple:

"Never does a saint seek alms,
Never holds out his hand before others;
The swan stoops not to pick up shellfish,
The lion scorns to browse on grass."[42]

Guru Nanak describes this as the one certain way by which false masters can be distinguished from the true:

"If a saint or a seer goes begging,
bow not at his feet;
He who earns his own living
and gives part of it in charity as a human being
He alone knows the way."[43]

A Disturbed Mind: We are the Wardens of Our Own Prison

Our difficulties do not lie so much in the things of the world as in our attitude to life. When our desires and actions distract us and disturb our equilibrium, it is as though we are standing guard at our own prison door. The Buddhist scriptures point out the extent of the harm we do to ourselves when our mind is misdirected; for instance: *Kamacchanda*, 'Sensuous Desire' for the safety of good quality called as *dhamma-chanda*. Whatever an enemy can do to an enemy, whatever a hater can do to a hater react against the wrong doer. A wrongly directed mind can do us greater harm.[44]

The passions scatter the mind and dissipate our positive energy, making it impossible for us to concentrate. Just as water does not reflect anything when it is murky and disturbed, so a disturbed, worried and restless mind can never hear the *Shabd*. As long as the mind is agitated by desires or actions, it remains distracted and we cannot focus our attention. And so long as our attention is not one-pointed, we cannot enter the subtle spiritual realms because the scientific tendency during the 19th century education became a movement of means of communication between one country to another sponsored by sense of realism of the 17th and 18th century A.D. to lead a full and complete life of real political thinker as term *Rajniti* explains its meanings.

The mind and soul are knotted together, and only when the mind is clear of karmic impressions can the soul be free of its association. Just as currents in the ocean can gradually pull a boat off course, so do disturbances in the mind interfere wit the souls return to its spiritual home as *Mula-raga* as '*Nam*'.

Jesus relates the parable of the swore to explain this very point. He describes how a farmer goes to his field to sow seed. But some fall by the way side some on stony or rocky ground, some among weeds and some on fertile ground. He then continues:

"Now the parable is this:
The seed is the Word of God.

Those by the wayside are they that hear;
Then cometh the devil,
And taketh away the Word out of their hearts,
Lest they should believe and be saved.
They on the rock are they,
Which, when they hear, receive the Word with joy;
And these have no root, which for a while believe,
And in time of temptation fall away.
And that which fell among thorns are they,
Which, when they have heard, go forth,
And are choked with cares
And riches and pleasures of this life,
And bring no fruit to perfection.
But that on the good ground are they,
Which in an honest and good heart,
Having heard the Word, keep it,
And bring forth fruit with patience."[45]

In this parable, Jesus says that although God's dynamic power, the Word, has germinated in our hearts, as long as the heart remains choked with cares, the 'Word' cannot flourish and bear fruit. Some people quickly forget its reality after it has been revealed to them; for others, their faith is too shallow to withstand times of trouble; but those who are concerned about wealth and material comfort hinder their own progress because they are preoccupied with worldly desires as *rupa-raga*, Holiness of Path.

In these times of mass consumerism and advertising, it is a rare person who can remain content with his or her lot. In every sphere of life today we are bombarded with suggestions to improve our lives by acquiring more. It is a dangerous game. Our possessions and activities in the world have a way of complicating and taking over our lives. Already we are 'possessed' by the impressions of our previous deeds. New obsessions further complicate our lives. And as we know from experience and a little introspection, our desires are never-ending; if we satisfy one, a thousand more take its place. It is sometimes said that the wealth of the entire world cannot satisfy the desires of a discontented, greedy person and has been given to the 'Reserve Category' person, when he eats more, then he tries to voimiting on others like Raj Kumar Gupta, M.S. Pathiana and others.

When we indulge greed in the practice of '*Nam*' in the life whether in the form of property, possessions, money or anything else '*Word*' we do not quell desire. A fire is not extinguished by feeding it fuel. *Kabir Sahib* says:

"You cannot put out the fire of greed by feeding it
Day by day it will only continue to increase."[46]

Again, in the Buddhist scriptures we read:

Men driven on by craving run about like hunted hares. Fast bound by fetters, they undergo suffering for a long time, again and again.[47] in Cankers (*asava-Kkhaya*) as Stream winner. The craving of a thoughtless man grows like a creeper. Like a monkey seeking fruit in the forest, he leaps about hither and thither.[48]

In the Sikh tradition, one of the most frequently recited prayers observes: "One's hunger is not satisfied even by the pleasures of all three worlds."[49]

The "three worlds" is a way of referring to the many dimensions of consciousness that exist below the purely spiritual realm. Our attachments are so tenacious that dissatisfaction among God, this disturbance of the mind that is caused by constant reawakening of desire '*Brahminical Ideology*' goes on troubling us even at the more subtle levels. And it will continue to trouble us until we are absolutely free of the last vestiges of the mind and pass to the 'Fourth World', the dimension of pure spirit of the Lord.

The Extreme Subtleties of the Law

The 'law of *karma*' is inexorable and subtle beyond our imagination. For example, even if we are party to someone else's dishonourable actions, we too are culpable as an accessory to the suffering caused.

There is a story that indicates the subtleties of the law: A holy man took lodgings for the night in the hut of a poor elderly woman. Since she had no extra food to feed him in the morning, she sat up all night spinning cotton, then sold the yarn in the market to purchase food for him. But when the holy man next sat in meditation, he found he could not raise his attention. He looked around him so he might understand why. Knowing that the old lady had bought the food from her own earnings 'Word' having worked overnight 'Die to live' in the '*Name*', he noted that there was no oil lamp or any other source of light in the house. He therefore asked her how it was that she had worked in the dark. "You see", she said, "there is a prostitute living opposite. All night there was a lamp burning in her house so I sat outside and used her light".

Such stories put before us an ideal of honesty in the man's life as natural instinct that would seem totally impossible to maintain in the complex and fast-moving world of today. That borrowing light from someone engaged in immoral or dishonest work could affect food and damage our chances of improving ourselves because our family background lies in 'Brahminical Ideology' how can we possibly guard ourselves against errors of such a subtle nature! The modern food industry confronts us with this sort of dilemma. The introduction of animal genes into vegetables and of minute quantities of animal derivatives into a wide range of vegetarian foodstuffs are just tow of a multitude of such issues we have to face. We find ourselves saying: How can we pursue our objective of spiritual realization in such circumstances? If we have to be so careful in our judgement of what is right and wrong, how can we survive from Non-returners as *Sotapanna* and *anagami*.

Once again, it is a question of cultivating the right attitude. It is impossible to live in the world without doing some wrong. The world itself revolves on duality, the interaction of positive and negative, of right deeds and wrong. We have to understand the principles that support our spiritual orientation, and then do our best. It is for each of us, looking to our particular circumstances to decide at a practical level where to draw the line. We have to guard ourselves against being fanatical or getting so involved wit the detains that we lose sight of the bigger issues called *Dhamma*-devotee or *dhammanusari*.

Because the links of *karma* are subtle and far-reaching, it is important that we understand how they work. Understanding the principles of *"Intellectual Education"* and being well-informed on the issues like *"Moral Education"* gives us the opportunity to choose to avoid their negative effects. But first we have to take care of the major issues like *"Physical Education"* to settle the account being penny wise and pound foolish will also keep us from our goal. "What Knowledge is of the Most Worth", as "Social Statistics" in human history.

A Rare and Precious Opportunity Missed

If we are sailing to a specific destination and alter our course by only one or two degrees, with the passage of time and distance we will sail far wise of our mark. This is the human tragedy in history that we so readily miss the unique opportunity we now have to realize God. What may appear to us as only a small deviation from the ideal can, over time, cost us the opportunity of a lifetime. Our emotions attachments and passions blind us to our birthright, the real treasure that is within us. When we fail to recognize our unique potential, we forfeit a level of happiness beyond imagination. This, then, is the cry of all who have experienced the spirit with logic conclusion crying out to their fellow human beings to wake up to what life is, to take advantage of the present moment so we do not slip back once again into the vast and painful cycle of birth and death as referred by *Guru Arjun Dev*:

"Born again and again, you die to be born again;
Thus, on a never-ending journey,
You suffer ceaselessly from misery and pain.
You have not realized the Creator Lord
And so you suffer, poor blind soul!"[50]

The Muslim mystic *Bulleh Shah* speaks of it as gambling away this precious opportunity by staking our lives on worldly goods:

"The rights of others you do not understand;
burdened with a load of ill-gotten wealth,
you will have to return to the creation.
Robbed of a priceless opportunity,
in the gambling den of the world,
you are going to lose a winning hand."[51]

The saints remind us that the human form is the only one in which the soul can become aware of itself. It is the only form in which we can become conscious of what we are. It is the top rung of the long ladder of creation and, if we miss it, our soul will fall back into the great cycle of creation to travel endlessly through the myriad species which have neither the capacity for spiritual awareness nor the power of discrimination to lead them out.

A metaphor is used in Eastern mysticism in which human life is likened to a golden sword. We have received it as a fit, but instead of using it to blaze a trail of glory by immobilizing our inner opponents, we completely misunderstand its function and use it in the kitchen of the physical world to chop onions and tomatoes.

As we look back on our life when we pass through death's door, how will we assess it? Will we feel at peace with ourselves and secure? This is what we need to consider when faced with Jesus' question in the well-known lines form St. Matthew's gospel:

"For what is a man profited,
If he shall gain the whole world,
and lose his own soul?
Or what shall a man give in exchange for his soul?"[52]

What is Right Action?

Right action or living by spiritual principles is our way of transforming or spiritualizing our mind while protecting ourselves from the many negative influences of the creation that can tug us off course. Our growing sensitivity to the spiritual perspective enables us to see how even the smallest negative impulses create negative effects. We begin to understand why wrong action can never be justified. Living by our principles, we appreciate more and more the value of a clear moral structure to limit our potential forgoing astray. We find we are able to make practical, well-informed choices so that we can meet our responsibilities. Gradually we learn from experience that living well is a question of never losing sight of our objective, of being moderate in all things, and of knowing where to draw the line between our needs and our desires.

Having looked at the complex and far-reaching effects of the 'law of *karma*', we are now in a position to define what honest living really means. By placing ourselves firmly in a spiritual context and understanding that all action comes from the simple law of give and take, we can define for ourselves a practical code of conduct that applies this understanding with 'Scientific Education' as, for example

1. Scientific Knowledge is more useful than more bookish knowledge;
2. Thinking and memorizing faculties get developed.

3. Principles are formulated to check the advancement of human knowledge by quoting the names of the idiot writers like *Irfan habib, Shri Mali, Suraj Bhan, U.P. Arora,* etc.
4. Self-reliance and self-confidence are promoted in the *Sudhra Family* that nobody is ready to face the challenge.
5. Love for truth is stimulated to discouraged people of the *Dalit* Society.
6. Faith in the inherent unity of all things gets developed in positive way.
7. Faith in Nature is developed on the issue of Sri Lanka. Taj inspected Ravi Canal project of the *Sudhra Race* of Panjab and Sindh.
8. New pension system scheme drawn by the author for political leaders for the development of morality as fear created in their minds as terror threat.
9. Spirit of dynamism in natural art developed for the new generation through computer system as a social change in the society and lash out on grade system.

We create a moral structure, a code of values and principles, to put limits on our actions and to safeguard us in spite of our blindness. We have to be protected from our own mind. The mind is powerful, and it is the mind, preoccupied with the creation through life after life, that has kept us from enjoying the liberating power of *Shabd*. Negative habits have become so deeply entrenched and the tentacles of the passions are so fine and far reaching that, in spite of our best efforts, we are likely to go astray again and again.

Without the redeeming power of the *Shabd*, no one can reach the final goal or destination. But to help ourselves we have to fulfils our part of the plan. We have to cultivate qualities that keep the mind turned towards the should and hold it steadfast when the going is tough. We need positive qualities that are in harmony with the under lying spiritual reality of which our soul is a part of the life. Our saving grace is that we have come in contact with a spiritual master, a lover of God, who knows where to go. The masters are examples for us of how to live in the world, and until we ourselves have attained their vision, we follow the path they have already trod.

The Transforming Power of Right Action into Right Man

Ultimately it is grace and mercy of the Father the mystery of love, the *Shabd* or *'Chamar'* that brings a person to the spiritual path. It is our responsibility, however, to contribute whatever we can to make the journey easier. The Lord's grace is abundant, and when he wills he will wipe clean our debts. But our contribution to this great journey, however small, is highly significant, for it is our effort to move towards him that brings his grace. As we begin to understand how life and *karma* work, it becomes very clear that the structure of our daily life must be sound. This is rebuilding our ship. This is making it seaworthy. A life built on another living creature's suffering, whether human or animal, can never be a source of long-term happiness, just as life built on a lie cannot lead to truth as self presentation scheme, no need to elaborate to other who do not trust on truth.

Facing in the Right Direction: The Positive Force

The moral ideal put forward by all cultures and traditions is one of simplicity and frugality *'Word'* living lightly in the world, engaged in honest work. Be industrious and frugal, and you will be rich. Be sober and temperate, and you will be healthy. Be in general virtuous and you will be happy.[53]

Most important, however, is our focus to study the *'Nam History'* on earth, a Scientific Truth to improve the condition of life that it be turned always towards the positive, towards the highest good. So important is our orientation in life that in the Sikh spiritual tradition, the word often used for the spiritual adept, the master, is *gurmukh*, meaning simply 'one whose face is turned to the guru'. The guru is the window, at the human level, to the formless reality of God. As Meister Eckhart observes: A man should orient his will and all his works to God and having only God in view go forth unafraid, not thinking, an I right or am I wrong? One who worked out all the chances ere starting his first fight would never fight at all. And if, going to some place we must think how to set the front foot down we shall never get there. It is our duty to do the next thing: go straight on that is the right way.[54]

We have to turn towards our destination i.e., objective of our life and not waver in our choice. That which takes us towards God, to our spiritual goal, is right; we are to face in that direction and go forward. Worldly riches are of little consequence. In the final analysis, all sages agree that the riches of the world can never bring lasting happiness, peace of mind or joy. *Master Charan Singh* says: "Worldly achievements can never give you permanent happiness. You may be a king, you may be a ruler, you may do good to the world; but your good deeds alone will never take you back to the Lord. However, you will definitely get the fruit or reward. From 'C' class prisoner you will become an 'A' class prisoner. Instead of iron chains you will be bound with golden chains. From small huts you will be taken to palaces."[55]

So why do we keep looking for fulfillment in the things of the world? *Sarmad* gives us a vivid image of the sterility of such goals:

"O Sarmad, why do you wander from place to place?
Where will you find love in this world?
A dead and dry tree provides no shade.
Greed invites only disgrace.
Without contentment there is no peace.
So, leave the world of greed with grace."[56]

Material rewards are loveless, and without love, which is the soul's nature, we will be always restless for something more. But in today's world, where success is almost always measured in terms of material riches, we are persuaded to give them importance. Our consumer culture encourages us to believe that we will not survive if we are not rich. It seduces us with images of the lifestyle it wants us to lead and tempts us to compromise ourselves to achieve the positions, promotions and jobs it persuades us we cannot do without. Thus it takes courage to actually walk the spiritual path as opposed to just talking about it: "Evil deeds, deeds which are harmful to oneself, are easy to perform. What is beneficial and good, that is very difficult to do."[57]

To re-orient ourselves to the spirit demands constant and serious effort. We have to develop different, 'subtle' faculties, for the word is subtle and can only be known with a different consciousness. The reality of spirit exists beyond the reach of intellect and senses, beyond our present grasp of the dimensions of space and time. To experience the *Word* or *Shabd* so that our faith becomes unshakeable, we have to forego our preoccupation with everything we are attached to. We have to make time for spiritual work. We have to turn within ourselves to the quiet and sometimes lonely solitude of the inner world a contented life, we have to work in, and on, ourselves. Thomas a Kempis, the fifteenth- century Christian mystic philosopher, says: "Many are found that desire contemplation, but they have no mind to practice the things that are required thereunto death in it. Men rest in signs and sensible things and take little care about the perfect mortification ofthemselves."[58]

To ensure that we go where we want, we must put up the sails of positive action '*works*' even though the majority of the world may drift in the opposite direction, pulled by the currents and tides of physical existence. We have to act, knowing where we are going and keeping our destination in view, and not caring what others say, think or do about our choice: "Be bold as a leopard, light as an eagle, fast as a deer and determined as a lion in doing the will of your Heavenly Father."[59] According to Matthew.

"Then said Jesus un to his disciples,
If any man will come after me,
Let him deny himself,
And take up his cross, and follow me".[60]

An Honest Livelihood

Central to the ideal of honest living is earning our own livelihood. Wherever possible, we should support ourselves from our own earnings and not live off the income of others. There are obvious exceptions of course, such as a spouse who looks after the family while the other spouse earns the income, or those who, because of sickness or age, cannot support themselves. But the general principle always holds true. And while we may rightfully live off an inheritance, we should bear in mind that inherited wealth amassed by dishonest means will one day have to be paid for fraudulent or unethical principles, which were not trust worthy in the absence of Father.

Whatever we do in life should not go against the laws of country, society or humanity, nor should we cause harm or suffering to others. We should not lie, cheat, steal or deceive, and this applies to both material and emotional interactions with others. We should be fair in all our dealings, both wit our equals and wit those in lesser or superior positions to ourselves. We should share profits fairly, not depriving anyone of their rightful due. We should also meet the legitimate demands of our government. Master *Charan Singh* gives specific guidelines on this latter issue:

"In our dealings with the Government (tax department) we should always do the right thing, not caring what the government does or does not do."[61]

He also advises that as far as is practical and possible we should ensure that our means of livelihood does not involve us even indirectly in negative consequences *Narak* such as businesses that at some stage lead to the suffering of people or animals. We have already discussed how being part of a chain of suffering, not just the main perpetrator, also implicates us in the resulting pain to handle meat items does involve a load of *karmas*, so followers of the *Sant Mat* a path should always try to avoid this. Everyone is answerable for his own actions and the price has to be paid for all that we do or think. Try to avoid dealing in meat products if possible.[62] and dismay the spirit of thought as human being for the purification of the Soul.

In the time of Master *Sawan Singh*, a seeker, *Saa'* in *Sharif-ud-din*, came to him requesting initiation. *Saa'* in *Sharif-ud-din* was a Muslim ascetic who wore the ascetic's *Kafanee*, a clot wrapped round his neck for collecting alms. When he asked the master to initiate him, Master *Sawan Singh* refused to do so, saying, "For meditation, it is essential to earn one's own living. What is the use of giving the Name to a persons who does not earn his own bread?' The next day, the ascetic took off his *kafanee* and his ascetic's robes, put on simple clothes, picked up an axe and started working as a woodcutter. The master then gave him initiation of the *Nam-mantra* theory.

There are many instances of Master *Charan Singh* addressing the same point outs that the Master can help in the spiritual progress of people, but they all have to earn their livelihood honestly to live-in the world independently. *Sant Mat* expects everyone to live on his own honest earnings and not depend upon others. He must find some work and earn his own living. This is his duty[63] to realize the truth or not. We ought to stand on our own legs and should not depend upon the charity of others for our livelihood. Every single penny that we receive from anybody shall have to be repaid somehow in this life or in a future one[64] as a reward of punishment in the history of man and God. We all have to have some respectable occupation in order to earn an honest livelihood and for that we have to prepare ourselves during youth. Without a stable job in hand, the mind will not have that freedom from worry and anxiety that is so essential for meditation[65] to realize the ultimate goal of life.

One should try to stick to one job and not change over from one to the other so quickly. Stability can come only when we stick to a job and make a place for ourselves in the organization. In service, we have to be patient, loyal and faithful to the management and the organization[66] which leads to the world as a Universal Truth called *Chamars* on earth. These are very specific directives to help us achieve our goal. It is clear that if we do not have an honest livelihood, our spiritual practice will take us no where. The ideal the saints put forward is devotion to the Lord combined with dedication to work. Honesty will always bear fruit in time, even though its results may not be immediately apparent *Guru Ravidas* says:

"As far as you can, eat the bread of your own labour:
a living earned honestly never goes to waste.
Endowed with devotion to God and dedication to work,
our purpose in life is fulfilled."[67]
The saint Namdev gives us a simple, three-point guideline:
With your tongue repeat the Name of God, O Trilochan.
Engage your hands and feet in work,
But give your mind to God, says Namdev."[68]

Work we do sincerely and honestly channels the mind's restless nature and makes us less susceptible to negative tendencies of the *Brahmins* "an idle mind is the devil's workshop" being a well-known proverb. Not only does such work direct the mind positively, it also makes us more appreciative of life's gifts like parachutes. It only functions when it opens wit the help of *'Nam'* or *Gurumantra*.

Sailing With the Winds of Contentment and Detachment

As we build around us the atmosphere we need to support our meditation, we will find that the ups and downs of fortune do not disturb us so much because our Mind is attached with 'Reality'. If a man does what is good, let him do it again and again let him set his heart on it. Happiness is the outcome of good conduct.[69] or *Samutthana*: 'Origination' with corporal phenomena through *Karma* again.

As we become happier, contentment and detachment fill the sails of our ship and carry us effortlessly in the directions we want to go *Samvara-suddhi* or 'Purity of Control' called *sila* of the *Ravidas* tool of the ancient period. In the words of *Emerson* and *Aristotle*: "That which we persist in doing becomes easier with power of '*Nam*' not that the nature of the task has changed, but our ability to do has increased."[70] We are what we repeatedly do. Excellence, then, is not an act, but a habit.[71]

We cling to the things of the world only because we are frightened to let us go to Restlessness called *Uddhacca*. Once we let go and let our destiny take its course, we find that life immediately becomes easier and more pleasant. Since what we are to receive is already written in our destiny and we will receive neither more not less but a comfortable life irrespective of what we do in the life of man, the question we need to keep asking ourselves is: What is the need to compromise our principles to promote the race of Father in right direction like *R.K. Gorav* and others.

True detachment from the world can only arise from attraction and attachment to something higher. Once we contact the Word within us and experience its sweetness we will become detached without any effort and automatically will let go of what we cling to now. Then our mind will reflect the tranquil and positive qualities of the soul rather than the fickle and negative nature of the senses. It will become our constant and supportive ally, propelling us on our journey, as it wants only to be associated with its new companion, the soul, so that it can experience more bliss. But psychoanalysis pretends to investigate the unconscious to conscious which is difficult task for the medical sciences without '*Nam Theory*' to provide the solace to the unrest and body.

Charity Supports Detachment

To foster detachment from the world and encourage love for the Creator, most spiritual traditions encourage us to give away a part of our earnings. Charity expresses the love that is the Creator by providing for others whose material circumstances make life difficult for them. Charity is not about the quantity given; it is about the love with which we give. In the *Bible* this point is illustrated in a well-know story; and *Jesus* sat over against the treasury, and beheld how the people cast money into the treasury: and many that were rich cast in much. And there came a certain poor widow as Soul herself without Universal Husband like *Master Deepit Raj* and his company, and she threw in two mites which make a farthing. And he called unto him his disciples, and faith unto them, "Verily I say unto you, that this poor widow hath cast more in than all they which have cast into the treasury. For all they did cast in of their abundance; but she of her want did cast in all that she had, even all her living."[72]

What we find in practice is that even though we may want to give in charity, we find it difficult to do so because we are attached to whatever we possess. According to George Arnold, that the living being need more charity than the dead: We, who claim to be seeking eternal life, do not look with detachment on even the most insignificant object of the life. Let us strip ourselves of everything, since our adversary stands before us stripped. Do athletes compete with their clothes on? No, *Kabir* (*Dr. Ram Dass*). He is a man of passionate growth. Now we too claim to be athletes and we struggling against opponents for more skilful than any that are visible. Yet, instead of stripping ourselves, we try to engage in the contest while carrying countless burdens on our shoulders, thus giving our opponents many chances of getting a grip on us.[73]

We do not see that charity brings with it its own rewards. 'I have always depended on the kindness of strangers as '*Nam*'. When we give to others without any desire or expectation, when we let go of our attachments, we find ourselves relieved of the complications that worldly possessions often bring with them a special kind of food for the soul as stranger on this earth. In the words of German philosopher, *Martin Heidegger*: "Renunciation does not take away. It gives. It gives the inexhaustible power of simple things."[74] And in the words of the wise servant-teacher, *Mirdad*:

More possessing – more possessed

Less possessing – less possessed, but be honest in living.[75]

Giving away part of our hard-earned income inculcates in us an awareness that of every thing we have, we actually own nothing. At moments when we find ourselves over-involved with the things of the world, when we find ourselves stressed or distressed on their account, it might be helpful to reflect: If I was told I had just one day to live, where would I put my energy? What would I do with my time?

It is so easy to forget that we are custodians of the God, not owners, of our material wealth, and that death will separate us from it all one day. Everything we think of as ours, whether it is family, friends, possessions or other forms of wealth, are gifts that have been placed in our keeping Charity the High. If we understand this, we will develop in our hearts a spirit of charity towards all life. We can then enjoy whatever we have without becoming possessed.

Our only real possession is our spiritual wealth, which we earn through worshiping the Creator. Giving away some of our material wealth of the practical study of the *'Nam'*, is a way of reminding ourselves of this fact, and of expressing our reverence and gratitude to the Creator. Sharing a portion of our income with those who will not use our charity for any immoral purpose supports our spiritual work to repeat the history of man in real nature of the life. But we must always guard ourselves against pride. It is to protect us against this that Jesus, in the New Testament, advises that even the right hand should not know what the left hand is doing when we are giving something away[76] in the sense of charity discussion be humble as low man of the history.

Money is dangerous for the seeker of spiritual wealth. Who us has not seen how wealth confuses and corrupts? It is sometimes said that if one wants to ruin a person, just give him or her easy money. Money is the sinews of love, as a war between the two forces i.e., poverty and the rich peoples. This is why people who are wise give away their wealth liberally. *Kabir Sahib* warns:

"When wealth in the house increases,

When water fills a boat,

Throw them out with both hands.

This is the wise thing to do."[77]

True charity is liberating and strengthening. It frees the mind and reinforces our decision to cast in our lot with a power of the '*Nam*' a charity before God that promises infinitely more than all the wealth of the world can bring.

Contentment, Self-surrender and Joy the Natural Thought

Contentment is the antidote to greed. Contentment can never be gained through the things of the world because nothing in the physical world lasts. Real contentment comes through surrendering ourselves to the spirit, to the ocean of live that is the source of all life and that is constant and limitless. By surrendering ourselves we surrender our responsibilities to the Father the minute drop which on its own was clouded becomes pure once its dirt is taken up by the vast ocean of the '*Sudhra Family*' of this world already mentioned above.

Faith and love is the very foundation of *Sant Mat Ravidas* during the Mughal rule with *Baba vani* and *Nanakvani's* in the 16the century A.D. One was the *Dom* and others were the *Chamars*, and their faith and love is *Shabd* and *Satguru* of the period i.e., Baba Ravidas. Then comes surrender to the will of the *Satguru* '*Word*' not a slavish but a loving surrender. The mainspring of action then changes, and the will of the Lord or the *Satguru* replaces the mind as the motive power. Then the soul is in perfect harmony with the Lord, mind is dethroned, and God is enthroned. It naturally involves a struggle, even a bitter fight to the last; but think of the crowning achievement too the worldly life. It is the *Shabd* that will eventually lift you above the matter and *Maya*.[78]

When we put our spiritual goal first, we find that our happiness and contentment increase. When our lives are clear, harmonious and balanced, we sleep well at night because we are at peace with ourselves. We discover for ourselves from the Indian history through our own experience, that it is through the natural order of the Lord's creation and not through our efforts that we receive whatever we have: "In giving thyself over with all thy heart to the divine Will, not seeking thine own things but he is generator of the life, so shalt thou keep one even countenance process in '*Nam*' weighing all things with an equal balance."[79]

It is again a matter of shifting to the spiritual perspective. In the *New Testament*, Jesus gives us a beautiful image of the attitude we need in order to live well according to *Gospel* of *Mathew*:

Therefore I say unto you, take no thought for your life, what ye shall eat, or what ye shall drink, nor yet for your body, what ye shall put on. Is not the life more than meat, and the body more than raiment?

Behold the fowls of the air: for they sow not, neither do they reap, nor gather into barns; yet your heavenly Father feedeth them. Are ye not much better than they?

Which of you, by taking thought, can add one cubit unto his stature? And why take ye thought for raiment? Consider the lilies of the field, how they grow; they toil not, neither do they spin. And yet I say unto you, that even Solomon in all his glory was not arrayed like one of these.

Wherefore, if God so clothe the grass of the field, which to-day is, and to-morrow is cast into the oven, shall he not much more clothe you?[80] *In the Market there is rush of the Jews. Wandering on foot without shoes that Nam-Mantra is a Chamar historian.*

When we abandon our will to the will of the Creator; when we give our life into the hands of the Supreme Being knowing that we will get our exact due, not a whit less and not a whit more; when we remember that whatever comes our way, good or bad, comes because we have earned it; then we will become carefree as in childhood, Listen to the advice from two far-apart cultures, the *Judeo-Christian* and the *Indian*: "Give to God what is His, for you and all you possess are His. And thus did David express it. All things are from Thee, and we have given Thee only that which is Thine."[81] By surrendering to you that which is yours, what can I possibly lose[82] i.e., again '*Nam*' as a historic win of the Father.

The Saints: The Mirrors of Truth

Mystic adepts or saints stand before us as examples of how to live correctly in the world. *Mulana Rumi* says:

Know that from head to foot the shaykh (perfect mystic)
is nothing but God's Attributes,
Even if you see him in human form.
In your eyes he is like foam,

but he describes himself as the Ocean;
In the eyes of men he is standing still,
but every instant he is travelling.
You still find it difficult to grasp the shaykh's state,
even tough he displays a thousand,
of God's greatest signs 'Word'
how dull you are![83] as *'Chamar'* in the history of

India has been deleted by the 'Brahminical historians of the present

Era as a degraded race of the *Ravidas* Community.

Because the saints are self-realized and God-realized beings, because in everything they look only to the *Shabd* during the time of *Satsang* and locate the position of the *'Sudhra Race'* to be positive and Creative Power of the God, they embody all that is positive. Their every action stands witness to that positive power which never dies in this Universe.

By following their example, by moulding our lives on theirs, we too come to know ourselves. Again, *Mulana Rumi* expresses it beautifully:

"The reflection cast from goodly Friends
Is necessary until you become,
Without the aid of any reflection,
A drawer of water from the sea or Sudharmatha in Sanskrit
Know that the reflection first cast is only imitation,
But when it has become continually recurrent,
It turns into direct realization of the truth
Until it has become realization,
Do not part from the Friend by whom you are guided;
Do not break away from the shell.
The raindrop has not yet become a pearl."[84]

Until we become pearls, that is, until we become realized beings, there is always the danger that our blindness will confuse us as to what is right and wrong. That is why we need the saints to emulate. They are living examples of how to live. Saints are the finest examples throughout history of the full flowering of the most excellent human qualities not like the *Brahmins* and the *Molavis* as a criminal class of the society based on unnatural theory and doing propaganda of the Father. Whether of royal or humble birth like *CHAMAR*, they live lives of simplicity and nobility, living in the world but not letting its negative aspects impinge on who they are. It is the story of the Great Master i.e., *Master Deepit Raj* an arrogant by nature works with his own style as a Superior quality of the man in scintific tendency discussed as under:

1. Opposition of Literacy Education of Ph.D., M.A. and M.Sc. Degree as possessed for materialistic purposes as Dr. M.S. Pathania, Dr. Hardeep Singh Sudhan, Dr. Manhon Lal *chutya* from the degree collected the dustbin material on industry which is not relevent to modern society and Dr. Vijay Sharma collected the Ph.D. for backbiting including B.B. sharma and others of the Jammu University scholars.
2. Emphasis on effective methods for the welfare of the state.
3. Importance of the study should be based on scientific analysis on the subject matter.
4. Freedom in the selection of the subjects on study.
5. Need of Love and sympathy of the students that he is not tution *Khor.*
6. Scientific tendency advocates the use of induction method in all educational procedures, processes and experiences.
7. Knowledge through 'natural thought' as scientific study of the art history.
8. Importance of concrete and direct objects of the human lifestyle.
9. Liberal eduationis that which is essential for vocation and citizenship and prepares the individual for vaious tasks and functions of life in practical approach.

The Battle of Life

Our goal in the treasure of the spirit is *'Nam-dana'* of the Master. Whether we call it God, the *Word*, *Truth*, *Shabd*, *Wisdom* or love does not matter without *Nam-dana* i.e., comparative study between the two, i.e., *Dr. B.R. Ambedkar* and *Gandhi*. *Gandhi* was *manmukh* and *Ambedkar* was *Nam-dani* who realized the Ultimate Truth of the Living Master and this concept was absent in the study of Gandhi. We are not to be distracted from our goal Jesus taught to the society:

"Lay not up for yourselves treasures upon earth,
Where moth and rust doth corrupt,
And where thieves break through and steal.
But lay up for yourselves treasures in heaven,
Where neither moth nor rust doth corrupt.
And where thieves do not break through nor steal;
For where your treasure is, there will your heart be also."[85]

The way is never easy. This is the most difficult journey of our lives. The saint, the true human being, is our mentor, and by looking to him we understand the qualities we need to imbibe. We realize, too, that we have joined battle with our mind with process of' '*Nam-mantra*', we are to subjugate it, win it and transform it into worldly life and it is the most powerful adversary in the creation: "If you vanquish your mind, You have vanquished the world[86], according to Guru Nanak."

Personality-belief (*sakkaya-ditthi*) it is expressed in *Dhammapada*, If a man were to conquer in battle, a thousand times a thousand men, and another conquer one, himself, he indeed would be the greatest of conquerors.[87] The Prophets and Saints do not avoid spiritual combat. The first spiritual combat time and again they come to this Universe, they undertake in their quest is the killing of the 'ego', and the abandonment of personal wishes and sensual desires. This is the Greater Holy War[88] with Black Minded people like *Brahmins* and *Molavis*. All eyes and ears are shut, except for the eyes and ears of those who have escaped form themselves.[89]

The Saints Live Among Us

Throughout history, we find evidence of many highly evolved souls whose lives sand witness to the principles of honest living. During the thirteenth-century saint *Namdev* earned his living as a dyer and colic printer. In the fifteenth century, the world-renowned mystic *Kabir Sahib* worked as a weaver and carried his loom on his wide-ranging journeys to meet disciples and seekers. *Guru Ravidas* earned his living as a cobbler, despite having disciples of royal blood who would have gladly supported him '*soham*' in Hindi, literally called 'I am that'; the Lord of the Fourth Region. *Kabir Shaib's* contemporary, Guru Nanak, supported himself and his family by farming. The sixteenth- century mystic. *Dadu Dayal*, worked as a cotton carder, *Paltu Shaib*, an eighteenth –century saint, earned his livelihood as a shopkeeper.

In recent times, we have the example of the line of the '*Radha Soami Masters*'. *Baba Jaimal Singh* served as a soldier in the army for thirty-two years and then lived on his pension for the rest of his life. *Baba Ji's* disciple and successor, *Master Sawan Singh*, supported himself and his family as an army engineer, later purchasing farmland to provide an income for his sons and their descendants. In 1947, shortly before he died, he announced to the large crowd of his disciples gathered together for *satsang*:

"All my life I have lived on my own income. I have never taken a single paisa of the sangat for my personal use, nor have I ever borrowed money from the satsang funds. Forgoing out on satsang tours I have no doubt used the Dera car, and it is likely that sometimes Bibi Ralli may have taken and cooked vegetables from the Dera garden. For these two lapses I ask the sangat's forgiveness. If anyone owes me money, I absolve him of the loan. If I owe anything to anybody, I request him to let me know and take payment from me. If I have spoken harsh words to anyone, I request him to please forgive me."[90]

Master *Jagat Singh*, the next master, was a Chemistry Professor who lived simply and abstemiously, giving the greater portion of his income to poor students who could not afford to pay for their education. His successor, Master *Charan Singh*, worked as a lawyer, and when he became the Master of the *Spiritual Knowledge*, he supported himself from his family farm. While meeting his private responsibilities he also gave generous financial assistance to people in need and regularly donated produce from his farm to the rapidly growing *sangat*. His successor, the present Living Master, *Baba Gurinder Singh Ji*, worked as a business executive and, through his farm and properties, continues the saints' tradition of supporting himself and his family, accepting neither money nor gifts for his personal use.

In 1957, Master *Charan Singh* formed the '*Radha Soami Satsang Beas*' Trust and transferred to it the entire *sangat* assets, worth millions of rupees, which until then had traditionally been in the master's name. As a result of this change, all money and property received by the *Dera* in donation is now credited to this Trust. The Trust administers all the funds and properties of the community and keeps accurate accounts, which the master makes available to anybody wishing to see them.

We have only to read a little about these saints to see how they led exemplary lives and spread their message of truth while supporting themselves meticulously from their own sweat and toil teachings; against the *'Brahminical Ideology'*.

The Transformation

On our journey through life, if we weigh ourselves down with a cargo of stones, we will be unable to reach our destination. If, like the mystics, we accumulate no cargo, then the winds of God's love in the form of the *Shabd* will power our ship. To make the journey, we need enthusiasm, fortitude and stamina. There will be many occasions when we will fail dealing only wit matter of facts as a practical approach of life, as a successful approach of life in positive way as adopted by the writer itself. Photography showing lights and shades or colours as seen in original image as God and man. The *Roman* emperor, *Marcus Aurelius,* advises us to think positively, to rejoice that we are on a healing, restorative path of positive action, rather than get caught up in our failings. He says: "*Do not feel qualms or despondency or discomfiture if thou dost not invariably succeed in acting from right principles; but when thou art foiled, come back to them, and rejoice if on the whole thy conduct is worthy of a man, and love the course to which thou returnest.*"[91]

He also advises us to cultivate a practical approach to life where we see everything afresh everyday, as a new opportunity to be true to ourselves. A new life lies within your grasp. You have only to see things once more in the light of your first and earlier vision, and life begins anew.[92] It is because we carry around with us the baggage of our negative mental habits that we lose heart, lose courage and judge ourselves. We won't let go of them and we even seem to enjoy the misery they bring. Such emotions will take us nowhere. Jesus advised his disciples to be as little children,[93] when we are young we see life with open hearts and minds. *Baltasar* Grecian warns us against a tendency towards sadness and self-pity, pointing out that such tendencies may ultimately prove to be our downfall. Search for the good in everything. There is nothing that does not hold some good if we but seek it in positive way. But the minds of some men are burdened with such unhappiness that, out of a thousand good points, they manage to strike upon a lone defect, and this they toss about like scavengers of men's minds as positive thinker of the '*Nam*' and its purposes is utilized for confident measure building in the society and the world. There is in it a perverse joy so that they can feel superior in this world by the authorities. Avoid such grave diggers, for in time it is they who fall into the hollow opening. Be the man who, among a thousand evils, strike upon the single good. Good finds good, but good that comes too late is as good as nothing.[94]

While it is good to be self-aware, judging ourselves too harshly is dangerous and counter-productive. With the same generosity of spirit and tolerance that we show to others, we need to be compassionate and charitable towards ourselves too with constructive values. So that we never lose sight of the '*Law of the Universe*' i.e., '*Nam*', we are advised by all cultures to remember the golden rule "do as you would be done by," *Tao* to treat others as we would wish to be treated by them: What you do not want others to do unto you, do not do to others.[95] Therefore, all things whatsoever ye would that men should do to you, do ye even so to them: For this is the law and the Prophets.[96]

As we understand the importance of Living Beings by principles that are rooted in a spiritual perspective, we begin to appreciate what 'Honest Living' means. According to Alexander Pope, 'An honest man's the noblest work of God'. As long as our vision is limited to physical existence, there will never appear to be justice in the world; they are equivalent to *Pandits* and *Molavis* of *Kashmir*. Once we realize that life is more than the physical science in human laboratory. That we keep coming back to this same theatre of action to face the consequences of our actions as '*Nam*' of the period to check the negative force and its elements, and once we accept that people can be reborn in forms below the human simply to repay the suffering they cause to others, then we begin to understand the necessity of right action today in history of '*Nam Theory*'.

Our task is to bring our lives in harmony with our spiritual goal, but for this, we have to be patient. A child matures from infancy through childhood and adolescence into adulthood; likewise, for our long-term good, we need to be balanced and permit our development to take place naturally in the shape of a society and a village. If we strive to reach our goal by simply suppressing habitual negative tendencies, there will certainly be a reaction at some future date. Suppression and repression are not the answer. The process of putting our lives in order and transforming ourselves spiritually has to be seen as a lifelong, steady evolution towards our goal louder the talk of honour as the faster we counted our spoons during the eating of meals as a survey of life itself. Life can be as simple or as complicated as we make it. Marcus Aurelius gives us a guideline of utter simplicity: 'If it is not right, do not do it, if it is not true, do not say it.'[97]

While we are travelling along on our journey, we need to remind ourselves constantly 'Word' through meditation, *satsang*, and reading and listening to the words of the saints and philosophers of the Right Path, of who we are and where we are going in the life cycle.

The Wisdom teachings of the world put an ideal before us to guide us in this process of spiritual transformation from negative to positive. They encourage us to go step by step in the direction we want, to be practical and to reason with ourselves. We are living as part of the creation and we all have our own destiny which manifests itself as responsibilities we have to fulfill during the life time.

In short, before our initiation, we undertook to live by spiritual principles, we effectively committed ourselves to change our orientation course of the services of the society away from material goals to *Sudhra* goal as pure as '*Nam*' in childhood. Through this commitment we guard ourselves against wasting the precious gift we have been given new one for the survival of '*Sudhra Race*'. As we live by our principles, we discover that this is a two way process: living honestly supports our growth as true and joyous human beings; this growth then further strengthens our resolve and ability to do what we know is right or wrong on the bases of authentic historical study of the '*Nam*' or God. Living honestly makes it easier for us to recognize and resist the negative path of the mind; as we draw nearer to the source of the Word, we find increasing delight in the spiritual way to check the negative elements of the life as a destructive path of the society.

By applying our principles we grow to see life in its true perspective. We compromise our values only when we cannot see the spiritual order of the creation. Master *Charan Singh* used to say that we would not even steal a pencil in the presence of a five-years old child; the child's innocence would mirror to us the dishonesty of our action and would make us feel ashamed. Saints guide us to remember that the *Shabd*, that power which enlivens, sustains and governs the entire creation, is present within us round the clock, and that we are accountable for all we do. They guide us to clothe our every action with this awareness. Then we will certainly reach our goals to repeat the history of man with powerful stroke of the pen as a bomb blasted in the society to check the advancement of man as a natural force of the natural law, as science in Magic Art commonly quoted as 'Warts and all' is 'the Conduct of life, '[98] and wonderful in nature.

Notes and References

1. The reader may note that all books, scriptures and parts of scriptures' irrespective of religion, are italicized as an identity of the author. **Note**: It is the study of God and man'.
2. *Bible*, Revised Standard Version (hereafter cited as RSV), Job 38:2, 4.
3. Albert Einstein as cited in Einstein, *A Life by Denis Brian* (John Wiley & Sons, 1996), p. 388.
4. *Bible*, King James Version (hereafter cited as KJV), Luke 6:37-38.
5. *Ethics of the Fathers, in The Prayer Book*: *Weekday, Sobbath* and *Festival*, tr. and arranged Ben Zion Bokser (New York, 1957), p. 241.
6. *Bible* (RSV), Proverbs 5:22.
7. *Sri Dadwani*, (Jaipur: Sri Daduvani Prakashna Smiti), p. 728.
8. *Bible* (KJV), Matthew 6:24.
9. *Bible* (KJV), Matthew 6:30, 33.
10. *Dhammapada* V:3 (62).
11. *Bible*, Matthew 10:30.
12. Baba Jaimal Singh, *Spiritual Letters*, Complete Tr. (Dera Baba Jaimal Singh, India: *Radha Soami Satsang Beas*), Letter 75.
13. *Philokalia*, tr. And ed. G.E. H. Palmer, Phillip Sherrard and Kallistos ware, Vol. 1 (London: Faber and Faber, 1979), p. 246.

14. Master Charan Singh, *Divine Light* (Dera Baba Jaimal Singh, India: Radha Soami Satsang Beas 1996), letter 175.
15. *Adi Granth, Baba Farid*, p. 1379.
16. *Adi Granth*, Guru Arjan Dev Ji, p. 102.
17. *The Wisdom of Baltasar Gracian*, (ed.) And adap. J.L. Kaye (New York, 1992), p. 72.
18. *Dhammapada* V:10 (69) 12 (71).
19. Master Jagat Singh, *Science of the Soul*, (9th ed.) Beas, 1994, IV:8, p. 183.
20. *Jalaluddin Rumi*, cited in *'Philosophy of the Masters'*; vol. 3, by Master Sawan Singh, (1st ed.) Beas; 1996, p. 227.
21. *Bible* (RSV), James 5:4.
22. Ralph Waldo Emerson, cited in *'Wisdom of the Ages'*, (ed.) Mark Gilbert (New York, 1934), p. 42.
23. *The Cloud of Unknowing* (London: 1978), Chapter 66, p. 139.
24. *Adi Granth*, Guru Arjan Dev Ji, p. 1358.
25. *Adi Granth*, Guru Arjan Dev Ji, p. 391.
26. *Qur'an* 17:37.
27. *Bible* (RSV), Exodus 20:15,17.
28. *Dhammapada* IX:8 (123).
29. Master Sawan Singh, *Gurmat Sidhant* Beas.
30. Master Jagat Singh, *In the Footsteps of the Master* Beas, Letter dated 18 April, 1949, p.77.
31. *Dhammapada* XXIV:22 (355).
32. Marcus Aurelius, *Meditations* VII:33-34, tr. George Long, revised by Classics Club editors, in Marcus Aurelius and his Times, (New York: Walter J. Black, 1945), p. 85.
33. *Bible* (KJV), Mark 10:24-25.
34. Master Charan Singh, *Die to Live;* (Beas, 1995) answer to question 17.
35. *Rubaiyat-e-Sarmad.*
36. Thomas Paine, *The Age of Reason*, part 1, *"The Author's Profession of Faith"* (1794).
37. Kafian Bulleh Shah, Punjabi (ed.) (Beas, 1994) p. 39.
38. *Bible* (KJV), Matthew 23:25-26, 28.
39. *Sultan Bahu*, by J.R. Puri and K.S. Khak, English ed. (Beas, 1997) Bait 31.
40. *Kabir Sakhi Sangreh*, Part 1 (1980).

41. *Adi Granth*, Guru Nanak Dev Ji, p. 1245.
42. *Paltu Sahib ki Bani*, 1:240.
43. *Adi Granth*, Guru Nanak Dev Ji, p. 1245.
44. *Dhammapada* III:10 (42).
45. *Bible* (KJV), Luke 8:11-15.
46. *Kabir Granthavali.*
47. *Dhammapada* XXIV:9 (342).
48. *Dhammapada* XXIV:1 (334).
49. *Adi Granth*, Guru Nanak Dev Ji, Japji, p.1.
50. *Adi Granth*, Guru Arjan Dev Ji, p. 1019.
51. *Kafian Bulleh Shah*, p. 254.
52. *Bible* (KJV), Matthew 16:26.
53. *Benjamin Franklin*, letter dated 9 August 1768, in Complete Works, Vol. 4, ed. John Bigelow (1887-88).
54. *Meister Eckhart*, 2 vol. (ed.), tr. C. de B. Evans (Watkins) as cited in *A Year of Grace*, p.291.
55. Master Charan Singh, *The Master Answers*, answer to question 273.
56. *Rubaiyat-e-Sarmad.*
57. *Dhammapada* XII:7 (163).
58. *Thomas a Kempis, The Imitation of Christ*: Four Books, revised tr. (London), Book 3:XXX!:3.
59. *Ethics of the Fathers in The Prayer Book*, p. 252.
60. *Bible* (KJV), Matthew 16:24.
61. Master Charan Singh, *Divine Light*, letter 351.
62. Master Charan Singh, *Quest for Light* (Beas), letter 400.
63. Master Charan Singh, *Quest for Light*, letter 322.
64. Master Charan Singh, *Quest for Light*, letter 107.
65. Master Charan Singh, *Quest for Light*, letter 224.
66. Master Charan Singh, *Quest for Light*, letter 378.
67. *Ravidas Darshan*, (ed.) And tr. by Prithvi Singh Azad (Chandigarh: Sri Guru Ravidas Sansthan, 1973).
68. *Adi Granth*, Namdev, p. 718.
69. *Dhammapada* IX:3 (118).
70. *Ralph Waldo Emerson.*
71. *Aristotle, Nicomachean Ethics* II:1.
72. *Bible* (KJV), Mark 12:41-44.
73. *Philokalia*, vol. 1, p. 243.
74. *Martin Heidegger, "The Field Path", World Review*, Jan. 1950, as cited in A Year of Grace, p. 238.

75. *Mikhail Naimy, The Book of Mirdad* (New York, 1971), p. 17.
76. *Bible* (KJV), Matthew 6:2-4.
77. Kabir, *Kabir Sakhi Sangreh*, Part 1, p. 72.
78. Master Charan Singh, *Light on Sant Mat* (Beas, 1994), letter 331.
79. *Thomas a Kempis, The Imitation of Christ*, Book 3, XXV:5.
80. *Bible* (KJV), Matthew 6:25-30.
81. *Ethics of the Fathers in The Prayer Book*, p. 239. Also *Bible* (RSV), I Chronicles 29:14.
82. *Adi Granth*, Kabir Sahib, p. 1375.
83. *The Sufi Path of Love: The Spiritual Teachings of Maluna Rumi*, by William Chittick (New York, 1983), Discourse 3072, p. 344.
84. *The Mathnawi of Jalaluddin Rumi*, tr. by Reynold A. Nicholson, Vol. 2 (London: Messrs Luzac & Co., 1960) p. 251.
85. *Bible* (KJV), Matthew 6:19-21.
86. *Adi Granth*, Guru Nanak Dev Ji, p. 6.
87. *Dhammapada* VIII:4 (103).
88. *The Sufi Path of Love*, (F 130/140-141) p. 154.
89. *The Sufi Path of Love*, (*Masnavi* III:837), p. 174.
90. Master Sawan Singh, as cited in *Heaven on Earth*, by Dariyai Lal Kapur, (2d ed.) (Beas, 1986), p. 198.
91. Marcus Aurelius, *Meditations*, tr. by C.R. Haines (Heineman), cited in *Year of Grace*, p. 128.
92. *Marcus Aurelius, Meditations* VII:2 (New York 1964), p.105.
93. *Bible* (KJV), Matthew 18:3-4.
94. *The Wisdom of Baltasar Gracian*, p. 72.
95. *Confucius, Analects* XII:22 as cited in *Wisdom of the Ages*, p. 291.
96. *Bible* (KJV), Matthew 7:12.
97. Marcus Aurelius, *Meditations*, XLL:17 in Marcus Aurelius and His Times, p.129.
98. Susan Ratcliffe, (ed.) *Oxford Quotations and Proverbs*; Pt -II, New York, Reprint; 2006. p. 133. *Note:* Sociological tendency in education is the only way fo changing the psychology, and personal habits of the people to project themselves as *Hindus* and *Muslims* are superior, and else are degraded like *'Dalit Hindus'*, *'Dalit Muslims'* and *Dalit Christians* during the political system of India it has been observed by the *Chamar* author as his own insult in the hands of upper castes like Hindu-Brahmins and degraded the *Rajput* without knowing original concept of human history. They were also the part of *'Sudhra Race'* at one time as *'Surya Race'* of the *Ravidas* concept. But certain

idiots like modern politicians, they exploited the historical facts of human history on the concept of *'Vote Bank'* and now *Sudhra* are awares in the 21st century to crush them with the stroke of natural pen.

Conclusion

From the above discussion, it indicates that the exogenous factors of the Living Master with the prediction of the historical writings of the '*Nam*' in every age, the Lord of this Universe drew his bow before the God and man, and unleashed his arrows at the Triple City of the God, i.e., Third World, burning its demons without '*Nam-mantra*' and hurling them into western ocean, for the welfare of creation. Then the Three-Eyed God restrained the fire born of his own anger, saying to it: "Enough! Do not reduce' the world to ash", as mentioned in the *Mahabharata*. There is one vital point for the focus of the knowledge distinction which sets from all the ages of the life of this Universe completed with the study of '*Nam*' as a challenge to the negative forces of the Father, as trinity, Siva the Destroyer who worked in self style manner on this earth, they must have pay the prices of the same, i.e., death. In the study, it has also been learnt that spirituality is in fact played a vital role to teach a lesson to the active force of the man as a bad element of the society. One Reality treasured reside in the temple of man. He always tries to destroy the natural beauty of this earth which is meant for human being and living creatures. To conclude the various aspects of the life, i.e., plants, animals, and other natural resources of the man, i.e., air, water, earth, concept of the poverty and social justice, caste system, and religious propaganda against man to man to exploit the poor people of the lower strata of society, as it became their business to cheat them that we are more responsible person of the society else stands nowhere. This document is a threat for them we are going to establish our own history on the basis of Scientific Truth as the founding Father of the Spiritual Knowledge of this world as a Universal Truth resides in *India* as term *'India*; called *'Light'* within the man working as God on earth from the very ancient period of the history of the man and *Chamar* is responsible for this challenge. Every civilization is every age of the world, whether high or low, corresponds in exact ratio with beautiful natural environment, beautiful person of the Jammu and Kashmir State are endowed with beautiful craftsmanship, they have worked in the history of man with the powers of the *'Nam'*, as realized Truth of the Universal Knowledge having a very high artistic sense to run the administration of the world. As a Qualitative Control Act of the Universal Truth. There is a vast difference between two natural forces, i.e., positive and the negative, based on artificial sickens because the positive forces are conducted with *'Sound Current'* of the *'Nam'* a natural idea of natural force, and a challenge of the black mole politicians of the period, having corrupt background and corrupt-knowledge for the destruction of the man and its environments. The gains from the inflow of money of the natural diamond of the *Ravidas* period has generated a great boom on this earth in the internal market of the *Leh* or *Sindh* river for the demand of both agriculture and non-agriculture consumer's goods, eating the economy of the Father as a load on earth, therefore, it is necessary to strike the *'Nam'* as a Scientific Truth on this earth to decide the economic status of the man. It has definitely shown in the study as the old agricultural class of the *Sudhra Family* arrived on earth for the cultivation of harvesting and New Plants, and animals are going to create in natural form (see Plate IV & V). To answer this question, we have divided the history of mankind into four distinct classes or groups which Brahmins could not understand the idea of *'Sudhra'* and they discriminated on them without logic and reasoning. These species are divided into four groups meets with a different sort of experience after death in it.

1. The first class includes *all who have no Living Master*, or *Satguru* of the present period. This, of course, takes in the great bulk of mankind. All of these are obliged to meet the emergencies

of death unsupported, unescorted, Absolutely alone and helpless under the '*Law*' to attain his power of their own *Karma*, based on *Panch Karma*, or Five Therapies of detoxifying the body of the '*Indus Culture*' into modern '*Culture*' reflect the past both in India and abroad, deeds and actions. They are now to receive payment in full for what they have earned from this life, because life has been given by the Father. Of them the messengers of death ask not when they shall come, neither do they ready to listen to their cries of distress, they must be punished according to their action and deeds. They are relentless, merciless according to their behaviour and rational approach towards mankind. They will have to operate under the orders of their Masters, the negative force, i.e., 'Brahminical Ideology' whose duty is to administrae absolute justice without favourtism. As we all known this class of element include the vast majority of mankind. No matter to what religion they may belong, no difference between king or peasant, no living matter have good or how bad, all alike must face '*the dark angel*', and follow where he leads. They must go when the hour strikes in natural way, whether they are ready to go or not. Their individual wishes are not consulted, they will go for the survival of life as bad elements of the society man to animals. There is no remedy of the false propaganda, no scope of liberty. They will have to ready for the hell as problem created of the society including *ati Sudhra* having 'Brahminical Ideology' and corrupt background of the character assassination of the others as culprit man of the Father. They must have pay the prize as the accounts of the book reveal, their account will not be postpone, it must be settled on spot with the 'Judgement of the Father'. If a person has been very bad like modern politicians, living a selfish life, indulging his evil passions, a disciplinary punishment will be given as animals of the dogs family. As early as 3000 B.C. the prehistoric culture of the *Indus Valley Civilization* of the '*Sudhra Family*' of Akhnoor, its seals and plants were regarded less as holy as 'Nam' by converting into the Brahminical society of the various sects in themselves than as the home of Divine Spirit with powers beneficial to mankind on the base of their *Karmas* and based on *Sudhra thought*.

This sentence is not final, like that of the orthodox hells as an evil minded soul. When the period of his diciplines expires, which may be years, a century or a thousand years, he has another chance to make good as '*Nam*' on earth.

If one has lived a better life, he will have given a better environment, to sort of paradise where he/she may enjoy the good life as his forefather lead. He must finally return to earth by life after his earnings have been spent. Thus, each and every species must tread the wheel of birth and death, age after age, until his good deeds and actions eventually brings him to a Living Master of the period. Higher Enlightenment provided by plants, as shown in the 7th century A.D. novel, written by *Kadambari*: 'He gave his usual pleasures for the joys of the forest', and trees became now forest or jungle.

2. The second class of the life is that, *those who have received initiation from a Living Master*, but who have done, but little or nothing in the way of spiritual exercises. A few may have actually indulged their passion in negative way. As a result, they have made no progress on the path. Yet they have a Master. What happens to them after death? In what respect do their experiences differ from the common lot of mankind? There is a very important difference. The Master meets them to death or a little before, that is, he makes himself visible to them and he notifies them that their time is up. They must go ahead. They respond with joy and sorrow on the day of the tragedy. At least we have never known or heard of one who was not glad to go with the Master at the time of his or her departure, and that without hesitation across the moment. They fear nothing, have no regrets at having to leave their families or the world. He will come in his *radiant* form as his astral form. As soon as they leave the physical body, the Master himself takes them in a sort of training school where they made good progress under his directions. If they have done very wrong, the Master himself administers whatever punishment or discipline, he may deem necessary as Master is always Lord of the situation, and no one can obstruct his path.

3. The third groups of the species are those who have made good progress on the path of the Masters, but have not yet attained sainthood themselves. All of this class know the day and the hour when they are to go long before it comes. The entire process of death is under their control, and there is never a shadow of difficulty

or distress during the process of passing. Neither do they lose their consciousness for a single movement, they are the sufferer peoples of the '*Nam*'. They pass out of the body as easily as one has taken the dose of *Sutra* of the *Medicine of Buddha* of *Maha Baisya Guru*. In their daily practice, there should be a *satsang* of the Father, so the whole of the performance is quite familiar to them as God's rule is there on earth. It is just like going back to their real home. They will be free to go where they wish without bonds of *Gandhi's ruppe*, there will be a leather coin of the *Deepit Raj*. They will go directly to that region, under the escort of their Master, where they are to abide for the time until they are ready to go higher and higher on their original home of the Master that is '*Nam*'. Of course, the Master is with them during all of this change. They will also make it in great joy and of their own free will work in the heaven for the welfare of the State. There is no compulsion. Of Course, they will have absolutely nothing to do with the dark angel or with the King-Judge. Like the second class citizens of the world, they will taken care by the Master, as hero of the '*Nam*' like *Dr. Ram Dass* and others. It is an occasion of joyful home coming of the Master.

These two classes never return to earthly life again, unless it is so willed and ordered to the Living Master to generate the new things from bad to good. Generally, they are taken on up and up, grade by grade to form the fresh government of the '*Nam*' an old concept of democracy, until they reach the highest level of the Father, these souls are welcomed in the *Sach Khand*, before he leaves the physical body. The way to this, they worked in the society, they are welcomed by the Master. But in actual practice, not a very large percentage ever accomplished by the author so much, he has to work more for the societal development as Mastermind of the earth, and his dreary cycle of birth and death is finished. He is independent soul of the Lord.

4. The fourth and the last class of the society are the Masters themselves called *Chamar, Chura, Megha, Dum, Batwala, Barawala, Nai, Dhobi, Darzi* some clans of the Rajput society including the all working-class. When the time comes that a Master wishes to leave his body for all time for the conventional group, he simply lays it down of his own will and steps out of it as *Dr. B.R. Ambedkar* to *Baba Gurinder Singh ji Biaswale* and souls of previous life converted

into '*Reserve Quota*', as *Sant* of the period and some of them denied him, they must be punished on the basis of their mistrust on the 'Living Maser' of the period as an advancement idea of the man in human history to brought a social change in the society with Spiritual Knowledge, they get the new life of the man. If one breaks the cord and discords the body as an instrument for which he has no further biological use. He will go into the hell. The entire process of his passing, as well as all circumstances connected with it as a matter of fact to reveal the system of the entire world in circulation manners as picture demonstrates the life of the man and the different species. The transmigration of the soul from body to body as *B.R. Ambedkar* to *Baba Gurinder Singh ji Biaswale*, take the example of the previous life, that should worked for the betterment of life provide the knowledge of the 'Law', as a practical knowledge of the life, there is a great social change in the life of man from bad to good in materialistic growth, now question rises, we are trapped in the illusion of the knowledge only in the religious books and the money-matter, who will lead the world problem as an Imperialist Thought that three great Empire of the modern world, those of Great Britain, the United States and the former Soviet Union, all developed a form of world Archaeology used in History for the construction the past history of the man, usually from a single point of view that is authentic history of the world through the study of '*Nam*'. The British model was comparatively seeking lead in the Spiritual-Knowledge of the man as Insight-Study of the man which is equivalent to '*Infinite*'. Hence, Grahame Clark's description of technology in prehistoric approach a Scientific Truth of the man's life will again established in the history of man as a healing touch of the *Ambedkar's* policy of previous life to modern Brahmins. Unsurprisingly, given it super-power status after the World War II to World War III, the United States model has been mostly followed by the Indian's with theory of '*Nam*' as a 'Super Power of the World History'. Trigger regards, the '*New*' Archaeology of 1960s as an example of the Imperialistic approach of the scientific study of the man to lead the world for historical knowledge as Truth based society or as 'Crude and rather colourless spectrum when white light passes through bulk water', as a thought of the man for Humanism to Rationalism against the have-nots people of the society. We cannot imagine any life without it, on the base of historical study of the modern period, the people of *Devanagari* script, they have founded, there no mistake in the writing of the history of the modern man. Given the concept of the global village, the need of the hour is to understand the concept of the modern man, who wants to lead a happy and prosperous life in all areas of human activity is more pronounced today then ever before in the pre-historic, period to the *'Chamar Dynasty of Kashmir'* (From 6th century A.D. to 12th century A.D). In fact, this study can be even more demanding and challenging than original writings of the man, as it requires double efforts to find out the reality base data of the human history i.e., from destruction to reconstruction. Therefore, *Supreme Sat Purush* does not wish to have one of his beloved sons remained here in dark reign, the nature of which is more like a prison, he should keep inside the room, he must be come out in the society as a Universal Truth with prefect knowledge as God on earth and his great sacrifice toward Living Master that he surrounded everything unconditional only for the sake of Father, and a son of the present life.

Keeping in view, the above mentioned facts, *the world has never been without a 'Living Master'*, the concept of modern politician is totally wrong and corrupt in form, because if man never die in the universe till date, who it is possible that God died in the past, he remains with us, but it is the blind faith of our society, who never try to locate Him, because it is difficult task for them and they play on his tune. He is a great juggler of the man's theory, but without pious approach toward Him, we can not obtain His Bliss. Therefore, the concept of 'Honest Living' also play a very positive role towards His thought and to prove its identity we have to proceed ahead in search of Scientific Knowledge in sainthood theory, which is based on historical development as well as noble path of the Master of the period to realize the objective of life for the upliftment of moral and discipline theory of the man as an historical phenomena in the worldly life. *Sudhra* or modern *Dalit* concept is the same as Saint or *Sant*, but it is based on social justice and fraternity. On the other hand, concept of the scripture is the concept of idiot people, because scripture has no living Masterly idea as in the presentation, doctor need a patient to search out his disease according to that he provides the medicine. Due to the study of books of the doctor's description, patient cannot alive or survive as his nature need for the betterment of the health. Thus, the concept of Living Master, who came time and again on this earth, they have Universal Concept of Living Being and move the world from down grade to upgrade for a healthy society of man and spirituality is the primary cause of their life to promote the idea for the betterment of the society and a Welfare State in which man, animals and others can live comfortably as an idea of the Humanism of the "Life" as a '*Universal Truth*' of the man's 'History' on this earth as a progressive society of the modern man above the caste distinction.

Plate – IV

Fig. 4: Concept of the Egg During Global Warming – A Natural Phenomena. Artist: Victoria John, London, 20th Century A.D.

Plate - V

Fig. 5: The Play of "LIFE" is like a Great Circle. The Soul Actors Journey Round and Round, from body to body, Costume to Costume in Tanning Life, playing different Roles, for Millions and Millions of Lifetimes - A Spiritual Concept of the Insight - Knowledge of the Man. Artist: Victoria John, 20th Century A.D.

Appendix – I

Names of the Different Plants and their Families

Section I : Sacred Plants

No.	*English Name*	*Botanical Name*	*Family*	*Sanskrit Name*	*Hindi Name*
1.	Banyan	Ficus bengalensis	Moraceae	Nyagrodha	Bar
2.	Lotus	Nelumbo nucifera	Nelumbonaceae	Padma	Kamal
3.	Holy Basil	Ocimum sanctum	Labiatae	Tulasi	Tulasi
4.	Flame-of-the-Forest	Butea monosperma	Ppapilionaceae	Palasha	Dkah
5.	Coconut	Cocos nueifera	Palmaceae	Narikela	Nariyal
6.	Bel	Aegle marmelos	Rutaceae	Bilva	Bel
7.	Ustram Bead	Elaeocarpus ganitrus	Elaeocarpaceae	Rudraksha	Rudraksha
8.	Indian Hemp	Cannabis sativa	Cannabinaceae	Vijaya	Bhang

(Contd.)

(Table Contd.)

No.	*English Name*	*Botanical Name*	*Family*	*Sanskrit Name*	*Hindi Name*
9.	Sacred Fig	Ficus religiosa	Moraceae	Ashvattha	Pipal
10.	Jamun	Syzygium cumini	Myrtaceae	Jambu	Jamun
11.	Margosa	Azadirachta indica	Meliaceae	Nimba	Neem
		Section II: Medicinal Plants			
12.	Indian Pennywort	Centella asiatica	Umbelliferae	Brahmi	Brahmi
13.	Asparagus Racemosus	Asparagus Racemosus	Liliaceae	Satavari	Satavar
14.	Ashoka	Saraca asoca	Caesalpinaceae	Ashoka	Ashoka
15.	Castor	Ricinus communis	Euphorbiaceae	Eranda	Rendi
16.	Indian Gentian	Androgdiphis prinkulita	Aeanthaceae	Kalamegha	Kalmegh
17.	Liquorice	Glycyrrhiza glabra	Papilionaceae	Yastimadhu	Mulethu
18.	Vasaka	Adhatoda vasica	Acanthaceae	Vasaka	Adusa
19.	Chebulic Myrobalan	Terminalia chebula	Combretaceae	Haritaki	harad
20.	Emblic Myrobalan	Emblica offieinalis	Euphorbiaceae	Amlaki	Amla
21.	Bauhinia	Bauhinia variegate	Caesalpiniaceae	Kanchnara	Kachnar
22.	Swallowwort	Calotropis gigantea	Asclepiadaceae	Arka	Aak

(Contd.)

(Table Contd.)

No.	English Name	Botanical Name	Family	Sanskrit Name	Hindi Name
23.	Indian Laburnum	Cassia fistula	Caesalpiniaceae	Argvadha	Amaltas
24.	Plantain	Musa paradisiaca	Musaceae	Kadali-phala	Kela
25.	Eclipta Alba	Eclipta alba	Asteraceae	Bhringaraja	Bhangra
26.	Hogweed	Boerhaavia diffusa	Nyctaginaceae	Punarnava	Gadahpurna
27.	Indian Madder	Rubia cordifolia	Rubiaceae	Manjishtha	Manjith
28.	Arjun	Terminalia arjuna	Combretaceae	Arjuna	Arjun
29.	Indian Bedellium	Commiphora mukul	Burseraceae	Guggulu	Guggal
30.	Thorn Apple	Datura alba	Solanaceae	Dhatura	Dhatura
31.	Winter Cherry	Withania somnifera	Solanaceae	Ashvagandha	Asagandh
		Section III : Culinary Plants			
32.	Cumin	Cuminum cyminum	Umbelliferae	Jiraka	Jeera
33.	Black Pepper	Piper nigrum	Piperaceae	Marica	Kalimirch
34.	Coriander	Coriandrum sativum	Umbelliferae	Dhanyaka	Dhaniya
35.	Mango	Mangifera indica	Anacardiaceae	Amra	Aam
36.	Bitter Gourd	Momordica charantia	Cucurbitaceae	Karavela	Karela

(Contd.)

(Contd. Table)

No.	*English Name*	*Botanical Name*	*Family*	*Sanskrit Name*	*Hindi Name*
37.	Palmyra	Borassus flabellifer	Palmae	Tala	Tada
38.	Cardamom	Elettaria cardamomum	Zingiberaceae	Ela	Ilaichi
39.	Indian Cassia Lignea	Cinnamomum tamala	Lauraceae	Tamala Patra	Tejpatta
40.	Eggplant	Solanum melongena	Solanaceae	Vrintaka	Baigun
41.	Drumstick	Moringa oleifera	Moringaceae	Sigru	Sahajan
42.	Tamarind	Tamarindus Indica	Caesalpinaceae	Chincha	Imli
43.	Garlic	Allium sativum	Aliaceae	Rasona	Lasan
44.	Ginger	Zingiber officinale	Zingiberaceae	Shunthi	Adrak
45.	Cinnamon	Cinnamomum zeylanicum	Lauraceae	Tvak	Dalchini
46.	Mahua	Maduca longifolia	Sapotaceae	Madhuka	Mahuva
		Section IV : Cosmetic Plants			
47.	Henna	Lawsonia inermis	Lythraceae	Madayantika	Mehndi
48.	Sesame	Sesamum indicum	Pedaliaceae	Tila	Til
49.	Indian Sarsaparilla	Hemidesmus indicus	Asclepiadaceae	Sariva	Anantmul
50.	Hibiscus	Hisbiscus rosasinensis	Malvaceae	Japakusuma	Gurhal

(Contd.)

(Contd. Table)

No.	*English Name*	*Botanical Name*	*Family*	*Sanskrit Name*	*Hindi Name*
51.	Areca Nut Palm	Arcacatechu	Palmae	Puga	Supari
52.	Soap Nut	Sopindus	Sapindaceae	Aristaka	Ritha
53.	Turmeric	Curcuma longa	Zingiberaceae	Haridra	Haldi
54.	Indian Kamila	Mallotus philippensis	Euphorbiaceae	Kampillaka	Kampillaka
55.	Lime	Citrus medica	Rutaceae	Nimbuka	Nimbu
56.	Saffron	Crocus sativus	Iridaceae	Kumkuma	Kesar
57.	Betel Leaf	Piper betle	Piperaceae	Tambula	Pan
58.	True Indigo	Indigofera tinctoria	Fabaceae	Nili	Neel
		Section V : Aromatic Plants			
59.	Jasmine	Jasminum grandiflorum	Oleaeeae	Jati	Mogra
60.	Fragrant Screw Pine	Pandanus odoratissimus	Pandanaceae	Ketaki	Kevda
61.	Bakula	Mimusops elengi	Sapotaceae	Bakula	Bakula
62.	Nutmeg	Myristica fragrans	Myristicaceae	Jatiphala	Jaiphal
63.	Clove	Syzygium aromaticum	Myrtaceae	Lavanga	Long
64.	Camphor	Cinnamomum camphora	Lauraceae	Karpuram	Kapur

(Contd.)

(Contd. Table)

No.	*English Name*	*Botanical Name*	*Family*	*Sanskrit Name*	*Hindi Name*
65.	Golden Champa	Michelia champaca	Magnoliaceae	Champaka	Champa
66.	Aloeswood	Aquilaria agallocha	Thymelaeaceae	Agaru	Agar
67.	Kadamba	Anthocephalus cadamba	Rubiaceae	Kadamba	Kadam
68.	Vetiver	Vetiveria zizaniolides	Gramineae	Ushira	Khas
69.	Hundred Leaf Rose	Rosa centifolia	Rosaceae	Shatapatri	Gulab
70.	Sandalwood	Santalam album	Santalaceae	Chandana	Safed Chandan

Note: Generations pass while some trees and small plants stand, and old families never die. They still there in this Universe. Their woods are lovely, dark and deep in study as a discovery of the God and man in this Universe, a plant of the whole world. Greater are non beneath the Sun or Surya, but their self study to live than other things to do. It is 'Golden Journey' of the God and man itself on this earth as *Ravicanal.*

Appendix – II

Brief Notes on Certain Authors and Their Works

Adi Guru Granth Sahib. The scripture held sacred by the Sikhs of the *Ravidas Family*, containing writings by various saints of the Indian subcontinent, who lived between the twelfth and seventeenth centuries A.D. The 1430 page book was compiled by *Guru Arjun Dev Ji* at the end of the sixteenth century and includes the teachings of *Guru Nanak Dev Ji* and five of the nine *Gurus* who succeeded him. The common thread throughout the *Adi Guru Granth Sahib* is the importance of the *Word* or *Name* and the need for a Master on the spiritual path of the Living Master or *'Zindh Pir'*.

Aristotle. (384 B.C.-322 B.C.) Born in Northern *Greece*, he was a great philosopher of the scientific study, logician, and scientist whose works greatly influenced Western culture.

Aurelius, Marcus. (121 AS – 180 A.D.) Born in *Rome*, he was both Roman emperor and an exemplar of Stoic philosophy of the world history.

Bahu. (1629 – 1691) *Hazrat Sultan Bahu* was one of the best known poet saints of the Punjab. A contemporary of *Saa'* in *Bulleh Shah*, he wrote a great number of books in Arabic and Persian as well as one in *Punjabi* expounding mystic philosophy of the Living Saints called *Guru* in history.

Bhagvad Gita. Literally, *'The Song of the Lord'*, it embodies the teachings of Lord *Krishna*, given in the dialogue between *Krishna* and *Arjun* on the battlefield of *Mahabharata*, and is one of the most popular books of Hindu philosophy spoiled by the Hindu leaders in original form.

Bible. The sacred scripture of Judaism and Christianity, written over the period of c. 1000 B.C. to c.100 A.D. Consisting of the Old and *New Testaments* (according to the Christian designation), only the Old Testament is recognized by Judaism. The Roman *Catholic Bible* also contains the books of the 'official' *Apocrypha* (e.g. *Ecclesiasticus* and the *Wisdom of Solomon*) which are absent from the Protestant Bible and not included in the *Hebrew canon*, because there was the great conflict between the Old and New. New believes on creative Method and Old believes ready made methods.

Bu Ali Qalandar. (1202 – 1324) *Hazrat Bu Ali Qalandar* was born in Iraq. His family later settled in *Panipat*, India. He wrote mystical poetry in both *Persian* and *Punjabi*.

Bulle Shah. (1680 – 1758) *'Saa'* in *Bulleh Shah*, a disciple of *Inayat Shah*, lived and taught chiefly at *Lahore*. He composed numerous songs of mystical love and longing in Punjabi for historical development of the society from one generation to another.

Cloud of Unknowing. Devotional classic of the Protestant tradition, it sprang from an age when English mysticism was in full flower (1200-1300). The author is unknown but is thought to be an English priest who lived during the latter half of the fourteenth century as a man of the original history.

Charan Singh. (1916-1990) *Master Charan Singh* was the Master at *Dera, Beas*, from 1951 to 1990. A lawyer by profession, he traveled widely and carried the Universal Teachings of the saints, *Sant Mat*, through the world as a Sufi Saint of the modern world along with *Baba Rasila Ram* of *Saidpurwale*.

Confucisu. (551 B.C. – 479 B.C.) Born in *China*, he was *China's* most famous teacher, philosopher, and political theorist about the Taoism.

Dadu or Dadu Dayal. (1544 – 1603) *Dadu Sahib*, a saint of Rajasthan, was well known for his boldness in defying the orthodox priests and teaching the path of the Word. He was born in *Ahmedabad* in *Gujarat*, and taught chiefly in *Jaipur* and other centres in *Rajasthan*. It is said that Akbar, the *Mughal* emperor, invited him to *Fatehpur Sikri* in 1584 and listened to his discourses. He was often called *Dadu Dayal*, the compassionate one.

Dhammapada. The Primary book of Buddhist scripture, it includes 423 verses attributed to the *Buddha* regarding the "*way of Righteousness*" as 'Nam's study of Buddhist culture.

Einstein, Albert. (1879–1955) An *American* physicist born in Germany, he was awarded the Nobel Prize for Physics in 1921. He believed that religious experience is the driving force behind scientific research in the study of Living Master.

Emerson, Ralph Waldo. (1803 –1882) American essayist, poet and philosopher.

Ethics of the Fathers. part of the *Mishnah*, it was composed by *Rabbis* who lived during the first century B.C., through the second century A.D. It is a collection of comments about life, submitted in the name of the great teachers of *Judaism* as fatherly advice to the people they sought to educate the *Nam-mantra* theory in logic and reasoning of the Prefect Master.

Baba Farid. (1181 – 1265) *Sheikh Farid*, a Muslim saint whose verses are preserved in the *Adi Granth*, was the earliest-known poet of the *Punjabi* language. Born near *Multan* (now in Pakistan), Farid undertook rigorous self-discipline and physically punishing methods to achieve his goal of God-realization. Eventually, he was advised to go to *Qutub-ud-Din Bakhtiyar Kaki* of *Delhi*, who revealed to him the path of the Word. He spent the later part of his life in *Pakpattan*, *Punjab* (now *Pakistan*).

Franklin, Benjamin. (1706-1790) *American* statesman, writer and noteworthy inventor. He published many written works on the subjects of economics, religion, philosophy and science for the development of the historical approach in human history.

Gracian, Baltasar. (1601-1658) A Spanish mystic and clergyman, he authored many books, including *EL Comulgatario* (On Holy Communion), his only religious work to explore the logic and truth of the living beings..

Guru Arjun Dev Ji. (1553-1606) Fifth in the line of *Guru Nanak Dev*, his teachings are recorded in the *Adi Granth*. Through great effort *Guru Arjun Dev Ji* collected, classified and compiled the writings of the *Adi Granth*, including saints of like minds to emphasize the oneness of God, the equality of all people and the pursuit of truth,. He was supported by Emperor *Akbar* to help establish the unity of God and the brotherhood of men. Jahangir, *Akbar's* successor, thought *Arjan Dev* a heretic and had him tortured to death by the 'Brahminical Ideology' of the Living being society of the period.

Guru Nanak. (1469 – 1539) Born at *Talwandi*, near *Lahore*, *Guru Nanak Dev* spent a large part of his life travelling to spread the teachings of the Word or Name. He was the first in the line of the ten Gurus whose teachings are recorded in the *Adi Granth*, the sacred scripture of the Sikhs as a true follower of the '*Nam History*'.

Heidegger, Martin (1889-1976). Born at Mess *Kirch,* Black Forest, *Germany*, his works gave rise to the modern philosophical movement called *Existentialism* in class struggle theory.

Jagat Sigh (1884-1951). *Sardar Bahadur Jagat Singh* was a devoted disciple of *Master Sawan Singh*, who appointed him his successor in 1948. He was Master of the *Radha Soami Satsang Beas* from 1948 until his death in 1951. He served the society as a *Sufi* Saint of the period.

Jaimal Singh (1839-1903). *Baba Jaimal Singh* was the founder of the *Radha Soami* colony near *Beas* in the *Punjab*. He was a disciple of *Soami Ji Maharaj* of *Agra* and was appointed by him to propagate the *Sant Mat* teachings in the *Punjab*. He appointed *Master Sawan Singh* as his successor for the development of the '*New Society*' of the '*Nam*' or '*Chamar*'.

Kabir Sahib (1398-1518). Born in *Kashi* (*Banaras* or *Varanasi*), *Kabir Sahib* travelled throughout India, teaching the practice of the Word. In *Kashi*, one of the main centres of Hindu orthodoxy, he earned a meager living as a weaver and faced unrelenting opposition from the priestly class for teaching people of all castes how to worship God. He attracted a large following of disciples, Hindus as well as Muslims, and was outspoken in condemning ritualistic observances made by the idiot *Molavis* and *Pandits*. The versatility and power of his poetry is still widely acknowledged and enjoyed throughout the world.

Kempis, Thomas a (1379/8-1471). Born in *Germany*, he is renowned as the probable author of the Imitation of Christ, an important Christian inspirational work of the fifteenth century A.D.

Krishna. Much loved throughout India, he is believed by Hindus to be the incarnation of *Vishnu*, the preserver. The *Bhagvad Gita* (Song of the Lord) is a philosophical dialogue between Lord *Krishana* and *Arjun*, held on the battlefield of the *Mahabharata.*

Mathnavi/Masnavi. From of *Persian* and *Urdu* poetry consisting of couplets corresponding in measure, each rhyming independently, interspersed with explanatory headings in prose. A *Masnavi* is a narrative verse written in a specified metre running through the entire work, and would generally describe love stories or the deeds and exploits of kings and heroes. The *Masnavi* usually refers to the *Masnavi* written by *Jalaluddin Rumi*, known also as *Maulana Rum* (1207-1277). It was a landmark epic of mystical poetry regarded by his followers as a veritable treasure house of esoteric knowledge during the time of Slave Dynasty of India of the '*Sudhra Family*' along with other followers. .

Meister Eckhart (also Eckehart). (1260-1327/8) Born in *Germany*, he was a philosopher and mystic in writing and teachings.

Naimy, Mikhail. (1889-1970s) Born in Lebanon, he was educated as a professor of science in *Palestine*, a theologian in *Russina* and a lawyer in the United States. The Book of *Mirdad*, published in 1948, is a weave of legend, mysticism, philosophy and poetry, addressing the deep meaning of human existence based on Living Master of the period.

Namdev. (1270-1350) Born in *Maharashtra, Baba Namdev* was a tailor and calico printer by profession, and was initiated into the path of the word by *Visoba Khechar. Baba Namdev's* songs, known as *abhangs* or 'songs eternal' are preserved in the *Gatha.* He spent the later part of his life in Punjab and died in the village of *Ghuman*, the birthplace of *Baba Jaimal Singh* some five hundred years later as a *Sudhra* Saint.

Paltu *Sahib*, (1710-1780). A grocer by profession, was a saint who preached the path of the Word and lived most of his life in *Ayodhya, Uttar Pradesh*, the birthplace of *Lord Ramchandra* and a centre of Hindu orthodoxy. Disciple and successor of *Govind Sahib, Paltu Sahib* asserted that people of any caste can worship God and strongly denounced ritualistic observances; ultimately he was burnt alive by the local priests of the old society.

Paine, Thomas (1737 – 1809). English born *American* political philosopher and author best known for his pamphlet Common Sense in which he urged the *North American* colonies to declare their independence form *Britain* called 'First American War of Independence' in European History.

Philokalia. A collection of texts written between the fourth and fifteenth centuries by spiritual masters of the orthodox Christian tradition.

Qur'an (Koran). The *Islamic* sacred book, believed to be the word of God as revealed to the *Prophet Mohammad* who was born approximately 570 A.D. died in paradise of Kashmir history with his friend *Durlabh-Vardhana* – I of Kashmir of '*Karkota Dynasty*' or '*Chamar Dynasty*' of Kashmir a fellow founder of *Islam* in original form as '*Nam*' on earth at that period in the 7th century A.D. All memorized and written material that was available was gathered and compiled in the present authoritative version approximately twenty-five years after his death in 632 A.D. in Kashmir History of *Kalhana's Rajatarangini* only *Ruqaiyyah Maqsood's* work '*Islam*' teach yourself historical work of a lady writer who gives the authentic information.

Ravidas. *Guru Ravidas* was a well-known saint who lived in *Kashi* and traveled across Rajasthan and other parts of India. He was a contemporary of *Kabir* and is believed to be a disciple of *Swami Ramanand*. Born into a low-caste Hindu community called *Chamar* or '*Nam*', he supported himself by making and repairing shoes in spiritual manner. In spite of this social handicap, he had a great impact on the many people who came to him for spiritual guidance, including Princess *Mira Bai* and *Raja Pipa*. Some of his writings are preserved in the *Adi Granth* as a writer's and founder of the Mughal Kingdom in Kashmir.

Rumi (1207 – 1273). *Jalal al Din* (*Jalaluddin*) *Mohammad Rumi*, the most famous of the *Sufi saints*, known also as *Maulana Rum* ('our Lord from *Rum*'). He was born at *Balkh* (then *Persia*, now *Afghanistan*); from there the family migrated to *Konya* in *Turkey*, which was known as '*Little Rome*' (Rum) at tat time. *Rumi* was a renowned religious scholar. When he met his Master, *Shams Tabrizi*, he achieved mystic realization.

Sarmad (1618-1661). *Hazrat Sarmad* was born in a Jewish family in *Kashan, Persia*. He lived in North India and taught the practice of the Word. As his name indicates, he remained in a state of God-intoxication (*sarmad*). He *was* beheaded for heresy by Emperor *Aurangzeb*, and was thus known as *Sarmad Shaheed* (*Sarmad*, the martyr)

Sawan Singh (1858-1948). Known affectionately to his disciples as the 'Great Master', *Master Sawan Singh* was the successor of *Baba Jaimal Singh* and the Master of the *Radha Soami Satsang Beas* from 1903 to 1948, equivalent to the *'Chamar History'* of Modern period.

Glossary

Abhijjha – Covetousness.

Abhinna – Higher Knowledge or Supernatural Knowledge.

Adhimokkha – Determination.

Adhitthana – Resolution.

Adinnadana – Taking what is not given.

Adosa – Loving-kindness, absence of hatred.

Akasa – Ether.

Akasa – Space.

Akasanancayatana – The first immaterial absorption pertaining to the base of infinite space called '*Nam*' or *Chamar*.

Akiacannayatana – The third stage of immaterial absorption pertaining to the base of nothingness i.e., God and man.

Alaya Vijnana – Self Consciousness.

Aloka – Circle of light in infinite shape.

Amarvasya or *Bahulavasya* – New moon's idea as Qutab or Aibek.

Amitaha Buddha – 'Infinite Light' and 'Infinite Life' as mathematical prove.

Amussati – Recollection, reflection.

Anagami – Non-returner, third stage of sainthood or Third Eye.

Anagatamsa nana – Knowledge of future existences.

Anankara – Products of the ego, against the doctrine of Cosmic Evolution.

Anapanassati – Awareness of respiration.

Anavastha – 'Infinite regression' of the life as 'Nam's power.

Anjali – Joining one's hands in a gesture of respect.

Antagunam – Intestinal tract.

Antam – Intestines.

Antariksa - Between the middle air; the abode of birds, clouds and demigods. This picture of the world was much complicated by later religious thoughts of the Brahmins that God never lives above, it limited to ourselves as a 'blind faith' of the society.

Anu – Atoms.

Anuman – Inference or result of the problem which lies in man itself as an historical study of the Truth, i.e., Nam or God on earth.

Anupalabdhi – Non – perception of the natural force as bad element of the society.

Anusaya – Underlying, latent,

Anuttaro purisadammasarathi – The peerless charioteer of men to be tamed in the life of real saint.

Anyonyasraya – Dilemma of the 'Word' (*Sabda*) between the man and God as a unique power of the world.

Apana – Indigestible parts in the abdomen, and responsible for excretion.

Apo dhatu – Water element, the quality of cohesion or fluidity in the context of Nam's study.

Appamanna – Illimitable.

Appana – Absorption, attainment.

Araham – One who is free from defilements, the final stage of sainthood.

Ariya – Holy, Noble One.

Ariya magga – The Noble Path.

Arthapatti – Presumption of the intuition value through the study of '*Nam*' as a result of the historical Truth or realization of God.

Arthaprasanga – *Reductio ad absurdum*, classical logic of the life as the companion of the God in man form as *Dr. Raj Kumar, Baba Gurinder Singh Ji Biaswale Dr. Ram Dass, Master Deepit Raj and Baba Rasila Ram Saidpurwale* of the same concept.

Arupa – Immaterial, formless.

Assu – Tears.

Asubha – Foulness, impurity.

Atmasraya – *Ignoratio elenchi* of the life.

Attavada – Notion of self.

Atthi – Bones.

Atthiminjam – Marrow.

Avajjana – Reflection.

Avijja – Ignorance (Skt. *Avidya*).

Ayukkhaya – Expiration of the life span from one generation to another.

Ayurvedic – A system of practice, physician of the present day, *India* remains the same. Though Indian very early conceived of the existence of microscopic forms like as 'Nam' on earth. It was never realized by the *Brahmins* and the *Molvies* that *Sudhras* are meant for the cure of diseases, without their study, there might be cause diseases in India; but if Indian surgeons had no true idea of antisepsis or asepsis, they encouraged scrupulous cleanliness from the heart and mind, as they understood the disease, and recognized the therapeutic value of fresh 'Air' and 'Light' as 'Nam' is a generator of the Power through *Vayu* or winds of the life. The Pharmacopoeia of ancient India was very enlarge, and comprised animal, plants, vegetables and mineral products of the life to realize them without Truth one can not lead the life on this earth, because *Ravidas* is a Dictator of the world.

Bhagava – Blessed.

Bharatavarsa or *India* – The Land of the sons of *Bharata* to repeat the History of man itself.

Bhava tanha – Desire for existence or craving for becoming a Saint in future life, as a good of the History.

Bhava-ditthi – Belief in eternal existence.

Bhavana – Meditation, development.

Bodhi – Enlightenment.

Bodhisatta – Buddha-to-be (Skt. *Bodhisattva*) as true saint in the house of Lord.

Brahmanda – Egg of Brahma between man and God, Brahman exploited this term that our race belong to Brahma. Keeping in view the term Brahman, it shows that man was attached in their body to tell a lie to the *Sudhra* people in the absence of their illiterate race of the '*Nam*'. They exploit them on the basis of term politics, which lies in history to find out the '*Rajniti*' means the study of Vedic period, which have been based on scientific study with the practical of body process by absorbing the '*Nam*' in it, to find out the scientific knowledge of the 'Life' as its objective.

Brahmavihara – divine abiding, sublime states of mind called Nationalism.

Brhaspati – Jupiter.

Buddha – Mercury.

Buddhanussati – Recollection of the virtues of the Buddha in form of God or Nam.

Buddhi – Intelligence developed from *Prakrit* – Knowledge.

Buddho – Spiritually awakened theory.

Byapada – ill-will, dislike, aversion without *Nam-dan.*

Cakra – Circular argument of the life is called 'Infinite' power, used as for Civilizational growth from one period to another.

Candra or Soma – Moon and Sun is a force like *Siva* and *Parvati.*

Candra or Soma – Moon or Sun are used these words for them.

Carita – Temperament, characteristic.

Cetana – Volition.

Chanda – will.

Chaulmugra tree – Traditionally prescribed as a specific species for leprosy, and still the basis of the modern treatment of the disease i.e., '*Nam's* tree.

Dukkha – Suffering, the first Noble Truth.

Dana – Giving, generosity.

Danta – Teeth.

Deva-Duta – 'Divine Messengers'.

Dhamma – Teachings Truth, Reality, Things, Phenomenon, Spiritual Knowledge.

Dhammadesand – Teaching the doctrine of the Lord.

Dhammasavana – Hearing the doctrine of the Lord.

Dhatu – Element.

Dibbacakkhu – Divine eye, clairvoyance.

Dibbasota – Divine ear, clairaudience.

Dinara – The Golden coins of the Gupta period, who works in hides and cutters in hide, and defeated by the natural forces from the sexual '*organ*', whereas the Brahmins the believe on the sexual intercourses to increase the population on earth one or the other hand, as a burden on the earth, therefore, the law of controlling the population as used by Malthusian in economic study *'Nam'* is a such force who control it in natural way and rule over the world with logic value of the *'Nam'* to avoid the reasoning of the malpractices of the life, for example, assassination of character of the women and a subject of controlling the system of discipline in the society of a period.

Ditthi – Wrong view.

Dosa – Anger, ill-will.

Dosa – The basic concept of Indian Medicine *'Nam'*, *Sutra* used by both the *Mughals* and European particularly the Britishers for humours.

Dravyas – Non-atomic substances, i.e., soul is of the Father.

Dvavyarthika – Object itself as God on earth as realized soul of the Father.

Dvitiya – *Asadha* or *Svavana* called second system of the Lunar and Solar system.

Eight Auspicious Characteristics – (1) Youthful complexion, (2) a soft body, (3) lips coloured like red, (4) bright gourd, (5) face like a full, (6) clear moon, (7) emitting fragrance from pores and mouth, (8) department as awesome as that of a lion in graceful manners in walking and talking and 'Thirty-two *Marks* of Greatness' in Buddha form as Lord on earth.

Eight Types of Divinities'- (1) Gods (*deva*), (2) *Asuras*; (3) The *Gandharvas*, (4) The *Kinnaras*' local spirits known as (5) *Yakshas Yaksa*, mythical serpents of the death, (6) *Mahoragas*, (7) The *Nagas*, (8) The Celestial eagles known as the *Garudas*.

Ekaggata – Concentration, one-pointedness of mind during the process of meditation to see the Lord.

Gandha or *Gandhi Concept* – Odour, as the idea of *Mohan Dass Karam Chand Gandhi*.

Hadayam – Heart.

Hetu – Reasoning value of the life as term indicates, God is Great.

Hora – Hour, it was first used from the West to India by Gupta rulers, who works in hide and cutter in hide, called *Chamar* of the period; working in disguisly the history of *'Nam'* and reveal the Truth of life in fundamental system in God and man or Living Master's of the period; hatred by *Brahmins* and *Molavis*, they called *'Untouchables'* of the period as *Ravidas* of the period was degraded by them, but with the power of *'Nam'* he established *Mughal* Empire in India.

Iddhividha – Supernatural Powers destroyer of illegal race.

Jambu – A rose – apple as it is a distinctive trees of Father, which gives 'light' to world, and he always rises from the country of Jammu and Kashmir as His permanent seat in the Natural Assembly of the Father as an Enlightened man of the period. Thereafter, the title of this country has been given as *Jambudvipa*, a lightening force of Father, who repeat the history of man itself as *Ravidas* of the period in the form of *Dr. Raj Kumar*, an Enlightened man of the History.

Jhana – Meditative absorption, trance.

Jivitindriya – Life continuum.

Kama tanha – Sensuous desire of feeling.

Kamacchanda – Sensuous desire controller.

Kamesumicchacara – Misuse of the senses, often limited to sexual misconduct as used by Brahminical historians.

Kamma – Action, deed.

Kammakkhaya- Expiration of the productive *kammic* force.

Kammatthana – Work place meditation subject as Living Master of the period.

Karisam – Excrement.

Karuna – Compassion.

Kasina – Whole, complete, a meditation device of the '*Nam-History*'.

Kayagata sati – Mindfulness of the body.

Kesa – Hair of head.

Khanika – Moment.

Khanti – Patience.

Khelo – Saliva.

Kilesa – Defilement.

Kilomakam – Pleura.

Krsnapaksa – Dark half without Natural Though.

Krta – "Established man" in the form of a tribe.

Kusala – Wholesome theory of God or *Nam*.

Lasika – Fluid of the joints.

Lila – Sports of the period, as God and man.

Lobha – Greed.

Lohita – Red, blood.

Lokavidu – Knower of the worlds.

Loma – Hair of body.

Magga – The path, the fourth Noble Truth.

Magganana – Path Insight – Knowledge called *Nam* or *Indus*.

Maha Kala – Siva as Vedic God *Rudra, Ravidas, Kabir* etc. Having the elements of destruction against *Brahmins* and *Molvies*.

Mahabhuta – Through self-consciousness emerge the five elements (*tanmatra*), invisible matter like '*Nam*', it can only survey from his 'Labour' in this field and its most ethereal form is '*Nam*' on earth, they are five, "ether" (*Akasa*), air (*Vayu*), 'Light' (*Agni*), Water (*Jal*), and planet or (earth). From the subtle elements of the material life, every object have been emerged from the basic nine natural number and four are working above in this Universe for the establishment of '*New Society*' called '*Chamar*' or '*Radha Soami*', having the same basic concept of the '*Nam*' or *Chamar* on earth. Working in this material world, self-consciousness is important in the life to achieve the objective of life, it produces five organs of sense (*Jhanendriya*), (1) Hearing, (2) Touching or feeling, (3) Sight of the study, (4) Taste of the study, and (5) smell, which creates problems for the man's study, but without '*Nam's*, study, we can control these senses, because, they have been trapped by the material world as a destructive element of the life works in self-style manner as 'egocentric' by nature; and creates problems for the society. The other five action (*Karmendriya*) or the theory of working class i.e., (1) Speech, (2) Grasping, (3) Walking (4) Evacuation, and (5) procreation is the force of the Father, and they were called as *Dalit* of the period, and have been born from the previous 'Light' of the Father, during there was strong rigidity of the '*Brahminical Ideology*' against the working class in the absence of the Father, they were exploited by them, and the fresh birth of the Father, by keeping the force in 'Reserve Category' to launch in the society as his special interest for advancement of man, but they were exploited by the Brahmins as degraded force of the Father, having no history, no right, when history proves their status as existence force of the 'Natural Forces' i.e., '*Nam*' or *Chamar* of the period, *Brahmins* try to stand nowhere in the history of man as a destructive force of the Father as negative element; and Father do not like them as superior forces of the '*Nam*', because He belongs to the working class as a race of Humanism and Rational approach.

Mahat – The Great one.

Mamsam – Flesh.

Mana – Conceit.

Manas – Mind, weight of 40 kg.

Manasikara – Attention.

Mandala – Circle, a meditation object.

Mangala – Mars.

Mara – The evil one, a *Satan* figure who resists spiritual advancement in the life of human history.

Marana – Death.

Marananussati – Mindfulness of death.

Matthalumgam – Brain.

Mayon – 'The Black One' like Brahmins.

Medo – Fat

Metta – Loving-kindness.

Miccaditthi – Wrong view.

Moha – Delusion.

Mudita – Sympathetic joy.

Mula magga – Basic path.

Musavada – Lying, wrong speech.

Muttam – Urine.

Naga – Having Snake spirit as '*Nam*' has to eat the mind spirit.

Nakha – Nails.

Naraka – Below *Patala* there is *Naraka* or purgatory, divided the life of the universe zones to repeat the history, during there was misery on earth led by *Brahmins* and *Molvies* and to punish their souls, the birth of historical God takes place to defeat them in human form. Thus, the Universe hung in empty space, and was virtually isolated from other universe to regain the life of man as a top species.

Nataparinna – Full understanding, penetration of Reality.

Nekkhamma – Renunciation.

Nevasannanasannayatana – The fourth stage of immaterial absorption pertaining to the base of neither perception nor non-perception.

Nharu – Sinews.

Nibbida – Disgust.

Nila – Blue.

Nimitta – Sign, image.
Nirodha – Cessation.
Nivarana – Hindrance.
Nyaya – Logic-system of the life, i.e., *Nam-mantra* of the Living Master or called 'Science of the Soul'. Early saints of the *Sudhra Families*, they were also used to it for the revival of the history original concept, which lies in the Brahmins authority. They only study the scriptures not the Living Master of the '*Life*' who control the whole system of this Universe, a challenge for the '*Brahminical Ideology*'. According to the later *Nayaya* schools of thought lies in human history, particularly in the *Sudhra Family* of the period. It has been based on four school of thought of the same category of the '*Radha Soami Concept*' i.e., *Sirsa, Rajasthan, Saidpur, Beas* a big centre of the period.
Odata – White
Oja – Nutriment.
Ojas – Energy producer as '*Nam*' produce in the body as a realizing power of the earth.
Pacayana – Reverence.
Pacceka Buddha – A solitary or private Buddha.
Pahanaparinna – Full understanding as abandoning misconception
Paksa – Decide the good and bad as a third force.
Panatipata – Killing.
Pancakkhandha – Five aggregates as *Pandavas*.
Pancavayava – A correct inference of the *Pandava's* study is the study of Living Master, to defeat the Brahmins with the help of their study in Truth form.
Panna – Wisdom, insight knowledge.
Papphasam – Lungs.
Paracitta vijanana – Knowing the thoughts and feelings of others, telepathy.
Parikamma – Preparatory.
Parinna – Profound knowledge, full understanding of the '*Nam-History*'.
Parisuddhi-Sila – Morality consisting in Purity, by obtain the 'Nam' process.
Pariyutthana – Arising.

Paryayarthika – Four truth of the objective of the *'Living Master'* in the study of Science of the Soul, i.e., Guru, Father, Friend and Wife.

Patala – Below the seven stages of the earth as Truth of Father is lie there, and search out with power of the *'Nam'* as a True study.

Pathavi dhatu – Earth element, the quality of heaviness and lightness.

Pathavi-dhatu – 'Earth element', or 'Solid element'. It is cognizable through the sensations of pressure, touch, cold, heat, pain, etc., - About the 4 elements *S. Dhatu, Khandha* (1, a)

Patibhaga – Counter-sign or object for meditation as *'Nam'* on earth.

Patikulasanna – Perception of loathsomeness.

Pattanumodana – Rejoicing in the merit of others.

Patthana – Aspiration.

Pattidana – Dedication of merit.

Pharusavaca – Harsh speech.

Phassa – Contact.

Piakam – Spleen.

Pisunavaca – Slander.

Pita – Yellow, golden colour.

Piti – Joy, pleasure in the object.

Pittam – Bile.

Pratijna – Five members were known as the proposition of *Pandava's* study as *'Nam'* on earth as a special force of the Father as *Dr. Raj Kumar, Master Deepit Raj, Ramyian Bhardwaj, Amrit Bhardwaj, Amri Devi,* the mother of the writer.

Pratyaka – Perception of Life, where from it comes, it comes of the Living Master of the present period.

Preta or Bhuta – Haunted by *'Ghosts'*, *'Logos'* during the dark period of the man, and establish their rule in Heaven, and land to crush them for the repetition of history.

Pubbabhaga magga – Preliminary path.

Pubbenivasanussati – The ability to remember one's former lives.

Pubbo – Pus.

Purnimavasya – Beginning of the full moon.

Pvana – Heart feeling.

Rajas – Passion, to keep tolerance against the negative elements.

Rasa – Taste.

Rig- Veda – Universal – Knowledge as '*Nam*' has.

Rupa – Matter, material form as the life of God.

Rupaka – Silver coins of the Gupta period.

Sacca – Truth, truthfulness.

Saddarsana – Six Doctrines of *Sudhra Family*, Guru and *Pandavas*.

Samana – Absorbed in the body as '*Nam*' as a diet of the man to realize the God, which proceeded to the heart or liver for satisfaction or solace.

Samata – Calm tranquility of mind, peace-loving idea.

Samghata, Kalapa – Proportion in a molecule.

Samma – Right (cf. Lat, *summa,* the highest, the best).

Sammasambuddho – Fully self-enlightened absorbed in the '*Nam*' became '*Nam*' itself.

Sampajanna – Clear; perfectly or thoroughly understanding.

Samphapalapavaca – Gossip of the nature.

Samudaya – The origin of suffering, the second Noble Truth of craving.

Sangha – Holy community, realized disciples.

Sani – Saturn of life.

Sankhara – Mental formations, volitional activities.

Sanna – Perception of sense objects to listen the music of the '*Nam*'.

Saptabhangi – 'The seven fold division'. This system of seven aspects of prediction is known as '*Syadvada*' or *Sapta-Sindhu* or *Hapta-Hindu*, means study of '*Nam*' in metric sense as it is called in Arabic, Seven in English; *Satya* in Hindi. *Syadvada, Jainas* had another seven fold system of predication known as *Nayavada*, the theory of standpoints as '*Nam*' stands in History not in artificial Sciences like Geology, Geography, Botany, Chemistry, Physics, Zoology and in other branches of the same practicals like Biology and Psychology, etc., or the way of approaching any object of observation or study not in artificial architecture like *Mandir* and *Masjid*, it is right in the God made structure, i.e., the body of the man itself, a precious natural structure of the life to realize the Truth as God on earth.

Sarad – Cold season or a thing.

Satamana – Earliest silver specimens of the life like childhood as a true nature of the God as mirror of the society, corrupted by the man itself.

Satapanna – Stream winner, the initial stage of sainthood.

Sattha devamanussanam – Teacher of gods and men.

Sattva – Virtue.

Sedo – Sweat.

Semham – Phlegm.

Siddhanta – Five astronomical System or Five *Pandevas.*

Sila – Morality.

Silavata – Rites and ritual of the '*Nam*', signify through '*Air*'.

Singalika – Mucus.

Sisira – Cool season, December – February.

Sugato – One who has achieved the way, title of the Buddha through the process of '*Nam*'.

Sukha – Happiness, pleasant feeling.

Suklapaksa – New moon called bright half.

Sukra – Venus.

Sunnata – Emptiness.

Sunya – The mathematicians of zero (0) and infinity, never more than vaguely realized by classical authorities, were fully understood in medieval period during *Sudhra* rule in India like Akbar and others. Earlier mathematicians had taught that X/O = X, but *Bhaskara* proved that it was infinity, who was working at that time. He also established mathematically what had been recognized in Indian theology at least a millennium, that infinity, however, divided, remains infinite, represented by the equation 00/x = 00. Medieval Indian Mathematicians, such as *Brahmagupta* of the 7th century A.D., he proved the word seven of the Arabic language as Truth or *Satya. Mahavira* in the 9th century A.D., and *Bhaskara* in the 12th century A.D., made several discoveries which in Europe were not known until a Renaissance or later. They understood the import of positive and negative quantities, evolved sound systems of extracting square and cube roots, and could solve quadratics and certain types of indeterminate equations. For ð *Aryabhata* gave the usual modern approximate value of the Sun or *Surya*.

3.1416, expressed in the form of a fraction 62832 /20000.

This value of ð, much more accurate than that of the Greeks historical thought that God made the man, man made the Religion, which has no truth, Truth = T ð stands man to man. God never dies, he always lives in human form one or the other form, it is the 'blind faith' of the man, which cannot prove Him in the scripture, without realizing the Truth in the body which made of man's study itself, and was improved to nine places of decimals of the later Indian mathematicians they were 'Nine Nanda Rulers of the *Nam* or God' on earth, the very organs of the body which function in this Universe for thinking and feeling for the realization of the Scientific Knowledge, but the Linear Mathematic is a problem in the society to control the system without 'infinite' power of the God in terms of mathematical solution. Some steps were made in trigonometry, which lies in three persons of the God, that is *Dr. Raj Kumar, Baba Gurinder Singh Ji Biaswale, Master Deepit Raj*, a modern mathematicians of the society who controls the society with 'Infinite' power, it is exhibited in his study. He is a man of spherical power as geometry and calculus, chiefly in connexion with astronomy of the Father, he will knows in calculation to find out the Truth or T value into man and its existence people by realizing the historical fact of the Natural study that is '*Nam*' of the seven planets (*graha*) of the ancients India, Sun as *Surya, Ravi* as *Ravidas* system or Culture to work for the society, as we learnt by the Muslim world i.e., *Arabic Islam* means a '*Law of Nature*' either through merchants trading with the west coast of India derived from *Sindhi* Family of *Rai Dynasty* of *Sudhra Family*, and *Mohammad-Bin-Kasim*, study the 'infinite' and defeated the *Bhamanabad* of the *Sindh* area which Hindu could not understand the meanings of the language and power of 'infinite' which is invested in man's himself, or through this '*Nam-mantra*' language they conquered the *Sindh* and defeated them with power of 'Infinite'. In earlier Inscriptions of India dates and other numerals are written in a notation not unlike that of the Romans, Greek and Hebrews, with separate symbols for the tens, i.e., 10 in words and in English language it composes of 1+0, 'I' stands for 'ego' and 'O' stands for 'Infinite' and hundreds, in increasing numbers of the '*Sudhra Family*'. The earliest inscription recording the dates by a system of 'Nine' digits as 'Natural Numbers' of the man, when became in the power of a zero (O) or '*Infinite*', it gives the shape of God and man on earth as natural forces of the '*Nam*' element to defeat the '*egocentric*' approach of the man. God never dies, it is our '*blind faith*' that we hate to each other. If man is there, Why no God is there. He is into man to man but 'ego' is a problem to "*Bakshali Manuscript*", which is a copy of a text of the 4th century A.D., and the terse *Aryabhatiya* or *Aryabhata*, written in 499 A.D., it proves from the study that before the Linear Mathematic, there was a '*Matric System*' called basic study of the future course of life. For a long period of the study, it was thought that the decimal system of numerals was invented by the *Arabs*, that there was a 'One God', the term Arabs itself reveals its phonetics A+ra+b+s, 'A' stands for one 'God', *ra* stands for 'Way' or 'Thought', 'b' stand for 'Bliss' and that is '*Santhood*' or 'Sainthood, as a study of the man, but this is certainly not the case found in India itself, it has been found in elsewhere of the country that Jammu and *Kashmir* State, wherefrom the Spiritual Knowledge of the Earth to Starts to defeat the 'Brahminical Ideology' with the writing of true study of the '*Nam-History*; not with Linear Mathematic. The theory of Arabs calculation themselves called 'Mathematics' 'the Indian Art', called '*Ar*' or 'skill' in Latinized word is the solution of the problem of the *Ravidas Philosophy*, otherwise (*hindisat*) is not meant for the *Sudhra* force, but for negative force, called *Brahmins* or *Molvies* of the period, who degrade the societial based knowledge of the man in human form. There is, no doubt, from the study that now the decimal notation, is ready for mathematical lore to defeat by searching out Him, and it is a tough task, therefore *Brahmins* and *Molavis* always became shrewd to shirk the work and creates problems for the man itself, they always believe on copy, not investigation of the Truth or T form value as a practical training of the man's history and notation are placed in *Maya* to find out the 'infinite power'. In this Universe for realization of the Scientific Truth and Insight-Knowledge, where 'Infinite' stands in human History.

Through the necessity of accurately laying out the open-air site of a sacrificial man i.e., *Dr. Raj Kumar* very early of the life evolved a simple system of geometrical, but now in the sphere of Practical-Knowledge' he gives a challenge to the mathematicians to prove the 'Infinite' as a Truth as it resides in man's itself not in books. Books are meant for confirm the Truth through evidence, it is not in scripture, it lies in human body, with the practice of '*Nam*' or *God-mantra* called *Gurumantra* or *Madhumantra* of the Living Master. They were always there in every period in the past and present society, but He is a challenge for the Brahmins to explore 'Him' as 'Infinite Pow *Taco* – Skin, leather, *cham, khal*.

Tamas – Dullness in nature like Saint or *Sant* of the period, do their work in Silence or in Reserve nature.

Tanha – Lit. Thirst, craving idea of the '*Nam*' in life.

Tanka – Silver coins of the man called *tanner* in the early life of the man as *Chamar* existed in the study of this book as an old species of the '*Nam*' on earth. It was this drama with the Gods to repeat the history of man from the prehistoric to modern man as an old species of the animals called Primate of the period, originated from the Jammu and Kashmir State, as depicted from the South Asian study of the man, as they have deep rooted life of the man on earth in human form as Dictators of the world for the establishment of the 'New Society' of the forefathers by defeating the *Brahmins* and *Molavis* on the basis of Truth.

Tathagata – The Buddha, 'thus come' like previous *Buddhas* or '*Nams*'.

Tattva – *Sankhya* (the count) is the perhaps the oldest system of the six *Pandava* theory, Guru +Five *Pandavas* as mention in the *Bhagavad Gita*, according the primitive system of the *Upanisads*. *Kaplia* was the founder of this system called *Isvarakrsna* means our *mana* is of the God, referred twenty five basic principles (*tattva*), of which the first is *Prakrit*, 'Word' or *Chamar*, as term usually loosely translated as "Living Matter" of life for the development of the history, as *Ravidas*,

Babar, Kabir and Nanak developed this thought during the 15th and 16th centuries A.D., for the establishment of the 'New Society' a 'Peaceful Society' and in most of the universities and colleges, their ideas have been vanished by the Brahminical Thinkers to hold the power in their own hands. This is the challenge to the negative elements of the forces that the development idea invested in the theory of Saints or *Sants* of the period, have already mentioned in the text.

Tejo dhatu – Fire element, the quality of heat and cold.

Thina – middha – Sloth and torpor, drowsiness, sleepiness.

Tipitaka – Three baskets, the divisions of the *Pali* scriptures.

Tiranaparinna – Full understanding as overcoming concept of the life.

Tisarana – Triple gem.

Ubhayakkhaya – Expiration of both lifespan and *kammic* force.

Ucca – As per the achievements of the Indian astronomers in mathematics study made advances on the knowledge of the Greeks, explored from the Insight – Knowledge of the man's study, and passed in the folklore in *Arabic* system through European traders as early as 7th century A.D., through the *Calipa* of *Baghdad*, who was employed in Indian astronomy, as one ward of the terminology of the Medieval European astronomy 'aux', the highest point of a planet's orbit is certainly called *Ucca* in Sanskrit 'aux' in Arabic, as a terminology study of the standing units of the *'Nam'* already mention above in the study, i.e., *Dr. Raj Kumar, Master Deepit Raj, Dr Ram Dass and Baba Gurinder Singh Biaswale, and Baba Rasila Singh Saidpurwale.*

Udaharana – Example of the life concept.

Udariyam – Stomach.

Uddhacca-kukkuca – Restlessness and worry.

Uggaha – Acquired object of the Life i.e., *'Nam'* or *Chamar.*

Upacara – Access, neigbourhood.

Upadana – Attachment.

Upamana – Inference by analogy or comparison.

Upanaya – Application of the life to proceed the things in right direction.

Upasama – Peace, calmness.

Upeccheda–Kamma – Destructive *kamma,* untimely death.
Upekkha – Equanimity, undifferentiation.
Utpata – Interpretation of dreams and omens with the help of '*Nam mantra*', blind faith will remove.
Vakkam – Kidneys.
Vamana – The dwarf elements of the Vedic study.
Vanna – Colour, visible form.
Vasa – Grease.
Vasita – Ability.
Vavatthana – Analysis.
Vayo dhatu – Air element, the quality of motion and movement as '*Nam*'.
Vayu – Winds as '*Nam*'.
Vedana – Feeling or sensation of the '*Nam-theory*'.
Vedanga – Subsidiary study of the astronomy as a part of the Vedic folklore, not a reality.
Vedanta – End of the '*Nam*' rule, and to begins the *Brahmins* and *Molavis* concept of the Mind only, as a historical study of Father, emotional school of thought.
Velan – Medicine-man holding of a spear.
Vetala – Special class of demon, like *Amitabh Bachan, Sanjay Dutta, Shrukh Khan, Maduri Dixit,* and many more of the period.
Veyavacca – Service.
Vibhava tanha – Craving for annihilation of caste system into *Pure-system.*
Vicara – Sustained application of the life.
Vicikiccha – Skeptical doubt in different religions system to find out the Truth is the real study of the God and man.
Vijjacarana sampanno – Endowed with knowledge and good conduct.
Vinnana – Consciousness.
Vinnanancayatana – The second stage of immaterial absorption pertaining to the base of infinite consciousness.
Vipassana – Insight, seeing things as they really are in the human body.
Virility – Sant Bhava.
Viriya – Energy, effort, Energy, literally means 'Virility'.
Viseses – Individual characteristics as '*Nam*' has on earth, as an atomic power of the earth, with the 'Voice of God', he will

destroy the *Brahmins* and *Molavis* of the period and waiting for the chance as *Deepit Raj* of the period.

Visuddhi – Purity or Sudhra.

Vitakka – Initial application of the Lord.

Vitikkama – Transgression.

Vyana – Generally a diffused wind, causing the motion of the blood and the body.

Vyapti – The basis of the generalization of the Truth is found, there is smoke, there is fire or *Agni* on earth to defeat the political forces as a bad elements of the society or negative elements of the society like BSP, Indian National Congress, SP, BJP, etc.

Yakanam – Liver.

Yama – Guardian of the Southern quarter, the death-god of the Vedas like Brahmins of the period found in politics as well in the society as a negative element of the society.

Yana – Vehicle, the path.

Yathabhuta – As they really are iconoclastic people of '*Nam*'.

Yathakammupaga nana – knowing the *kamma* of others giving rise to their rebirths.

Bibliography

(A) Principal Works

1. Ain-i-Akbari : Tr. By Jerrett, H.S. & Blochmann H. New Delhi, Vol. 1-11, Reprint, 1978.
2. Alberuni's India : Tr. By Edward, C. Sachau, Vol. I – II, New Delhi, Reprint, 1989.
3. Ambedkar, Dr. B.R : *The Buddha and His Dhamma*; Nagpur, 1997.
4. Ambedkar, Dr. B.R.. : *Annihilation of Caste*, Aurangabad, 2003.
5. Ambedkar, Dr. B.R.. : *Who were the Shudhras*? Aurangabad, 2003.
6. Ajnat, Surendra : *Letters of Ambedkar*; Jalandhar; 1993.
7. Abraham, T.M. : *Handicrafts in India*; New Delhi, 1976.
8. Aggrawal, Ashvini : *In Search of Vedic – Harappan Relations*; New Delhi, 2005.
9. Ali, Athar M : Symposia Papers; Elements of Social Justice in *Medieval Islamic Thought*, IHC, Chennai, 1996.
10. Bernal, J.D. : *Science in History*; England, Vol. III, Reprint 1969.
11. Briggs, John : *History of the Rise of the Mahomedan Power* Tr. From the Original Persian of Mahomed Kasim Ferishta; Calcutta, Reprinted, 1966.
12. Benerji, Projesh : *Aesthetics of Indian Folk Dance*; Delhi, 1982.
13. Briggs, G.W. : *The Chamars*; Delhi, Reprinted, 2004.
14. Basham, A.L. : *Adbhut Bharat*; Agra, 1993.
15. Basham, A.L. : *The Wonder that was India*; Delhi, Reprint 1971.
16. Basham, A.L. : *A Culture History of India*, New Delhi, 1975.

17. Buddharakkhita, V.A : *The Buddha Law of Kamma and Rebirth*; Bangalore, 2001.
18. Born, M : *The Natural Philosophy of Cause and Change*, Oxford, 1949
19. Bhattachary, S.K : *The Story of Indian Art*, Delhi, 1966.
20. Bhattachary, S.K: *Indian Religious System*; Delhi, 1968.
21. Bhushan, J.B: *Indian Jewellary, Ornament and Decorative Designs*, Bombay, 1964.
22. Bondi, Hermann : *The Universe At Large*, London, 1961.
23. Burke, Edmund: *Thoughts and Details on Scarcity*, (1795), (1846), IV.
24. Carr, E.H: *The New Society*, London; 1960.
25. Carr, E.H: *What is History*? New York, Reprint, 1984.
26. Clayton, A.C: *The Rig-ved and Vedic Religion*, New Delhi, 1981.
27. Cole, W. Owen: *The Guru in Sikhism*, London, 1982.
28. Chattopadhyaya, K.D: *Handicrafts of India*, Delhi, 1975.
29. Chapdekar, N & Nalinee: *Ancient India and Greek*; New Delhi.
30. Dhawalikar, M.K: *Man and Environment in Prehistory*; Symposia paper IHC, Mysore, 1993.
31. Davids Rhys: *Buddhist India*; Delhi, 1903.
32. Dhamma Rewata: *Emptying the Rose-Apple Seat*, U.S.A. 2003.
33. Duba, S.C: *Tribal Heritage of India*, Vol. I, New Delhi, 1977.
34. Eccles, John C: *The Human Mystery*, Edinburg, 1977-78.
35. Ezekiel Isacc A : *Kabir the Great Mystic*, Beas, 2003
36. Ezekiel Isacc A: *Sarmad Martyr to Love Divine*, Beas, 2005.
37. Engels, Fredarick: *The Origin of the Family, Private Property and the State*, Lucknow, 2006.
38. Fabres, Charles : *Indian Dress*; New Delhi, 1977.
39. Gamble, Clive: *Archaeology*; *The Basic*, New York, 2002.
40. Grover, S & Grover, B.L: *A New Look at Modern Indian History (From 1707 to the Modern Times)*, New Delhi, Reprint, 2005.
41. Goodspeaker, Prince : *Buddhist Tales for Young and Old*, U.S.A., 1995.
42. Grolier: *Encyclopaedia of Knowledge*; Danbury, Connections, 1991.

43. Husain, Majid: *Geography of Jammu and Kashmir*, New Delhi, 1985.
44. Howell, F.C: *Life Nature, Early Man*; Nederland, 1970.
45. Horold, A Gonld: *The Hindu Caste System*; Delhi, 1987.
46. Hugel, Baron, C: *Kashmir and the Punjab*, Delhi, 1972.
47. Hutchison, J & Vogal, J.Ph: *History of the Punjab Hill States*, (H.P.), 1982.
48. Ghurye, G.S: *Caste and Race in India*; Bombay,1969.
49. Goswami, Karuna: *Kashmir Painting*, Delhi, 1998.
50. Ibbetson, Sir Denzil: *Punjab Castes*, Language Department Punjab, Reprint,1999.
51. *Jalaluddin Rumi*, cited in Philosophy of the Masters Vol. 3, by Master Sawan Singh, 1st ed. Beas, 1996.
52. Johnson, Julian P : *With Great Master in India*, Beas, 2002.
53. Johnson, Julian P: *The Path of the Masters*; Beas, Reprint, 1997.
54. Jonson: *History of Art*, New York, 1996.
55. Jones, Victoria: *The Journey of the Soul*, Beas, 2004.
56. Julian, James: *The Story of Great Invention*, London, 1967.
57. Jai Singh Hari: *Indian between Dream and Reality*, New Delhi, 1989.
58. Jauhari, Manorama: *Politics and Ethics in Ancient India*, Varanasi, 1968.
59. Jois, M. Rama : *Guruji and Social Harmony*, Karnataka, 2006.
60. Jagadeeshan, P: *Social Justice and Challenges in Contemporary India*, Lecture Series, Bangalore, 2006.
61. Jaiswal, O.P. : *Science and Society in Ancient India Some Reflection; Presidential Address; 66th Session*, Santiniketon, 2005-06, IHC.
62. Josi, M.S: *Guru Arjun Deva* (Hindi), Beas, 2000.
63. *Kafian Bulleh Shah*, Punjabi ed. Beas, 1994).
64. Khan, I. Alam: *History and Archaeology, Symposia Papers*, Amritsar, 2002, IHC.
65. Kindersley Dorling: *Ultimate Visual Dictionary 21st Century Supplement*, London.
66. Khobragade, Ram, Adv: *Dr. Ambedkar, A Symbol of Global Socio-Political Revolution*, New Delhi, 2005.
67. Kane, P.V.: *History of Dharmasastra*; Poona, 3 Vols. 1968.

68. Khan. Mohd, Ishaq: *History of Srinagar*, Srinagar, 1979.
69. Kalhana's Rajatarangini: Tr. By A.A. Stein,; Delhi, Vol. I-II, Reprint, 1989.
70. Kak, R.C: *Ancient Monument of Kashmir*, New Delhi.
71. Kak, R.C: *Anitquities of Basohi and Ramanagar*, New Delhi, 1972.
72. Kingsley, C: *The Limits of Exact Science as Applied to History*, London, 1860.
73. Kangle, R.P. (ed.): *The Kautily Arthasastra*; Bombay University, 1969.
74. Khurana, K.L: *Historiography*, Agra (India), 2003.
75. Khurana, K.L: *World History*, Agra (India), 2006-07.
76. Khurana, K.L: *Ancient India*, Agra (India), 2003.
77. Khurana, K.L: *The Twentieth Century World*, Agra (India), 2005.
78. Katoch, A.C.: *Discovery of Kangra*, Gurgaon, 2004.
79. Kumar, Raj: *Paintings and Lifestyles of the Jammu Region*, (17th to 19th Century A.D.) 2 Vols, Delhi, 2006.
80. Kumar, Raj: *History of the Brahmans*; Delhi, 2006.
81. Kumar, Raj: *History of the Chamar Dynasty* (From 6th Century A.D. to 12th Century A.D.) Delhi, 2 Vols. 2008.
82. Kumar, Raj: *Encyclopeadia of Untouchables, Ancient Medieval, and Modern*, Delhi, 2 Vols. 2008.
83. Kumar, Raj: *Ambedkar and His Writings, A Look for the New Generation,* Delhi, 2008.
84. Kalimat-i-Taiyibat *by Inayatulla Khan Kashmiri* (ed.) S.M. A Husain, Delhi, 1982.
85. Lawrence, Walter R: *Provincial Gazetteer of Kashmir*, New Delhi, 1985.
86. Labour of Love: *Medical Relief Society*, Beas, 1996.
87. Leening, Joseph: *Yoga and the Bible*, Beas, 2004.
88. Luniya, B.N: *Evolution of Indian Culture*, Agra (India), 2005.
89. Limbale, Shuran Kumar: *Towards an Aesthetic of Dalit Literature*, Tr. From Marathi to Eng. Alok Mukharjee, New Delhi, 2004.
90. Lessen, Christian: *Indische Alterthumskunde*, London, 1866-1874, Vol. I.
91. Lenin: *The State and Revolution*; Lucknow, 2006.

92. Master Jagat Singh, *Science of the Soul*, 9th ed. (Dera Baba Jaimal Singh, India: Radha Soami Satsang Beas, 1994), IV:8.
93. Master Charan Singh, *Die to Live* 1999).
94. Mikail Naimy, *The Book of Mirdad* (New York: 1971).
95. Master Charan Singh, *Light on Sant Mat* Beas, (1994), letter 331.
96. Mookerji, R.K: *Ancient India*, Allahabad (India), 1956.
97. Mookerji, R.K: *Ancient Indian Education*, London, 1989.
98. Maqsood, Ruqaiyyah: *Islam*, U.S.A, 1975.
99. Moosvi, Shireen: *Man and Nature in Mughal Era*, IHC, Symposia paper, Mysore, 1993.
100. Mathew, P. Johan; Samuel, V.C; Thomas and others: *Christianity*, Punjab University, Patiala, 2000.
101. Majumdar, R.C: *The Vedic Age*, Bombay, 1988.
102. Majumdar, R.C: *Age of the Imperial Unity*, Bombay, 1960.
103. Nayanatiloka: *Buddhist Dictionary*, Ceylon, 1970.
104. Patnaik, Naveen: *The Garden of Life, An Introduction to the Healing Plants of India*, New York, 1994.
105. Plamintr, Phra Sunthorn: *Basic Buddhism Course*, U.S.A, 1991.
106. Puri, J.R & Khak, K.S: *Sultan Bahu, Beas*, Reprint, 1999.
107. Prabhupada, A.C.B.S: *Life Comes From Life*, Bombay, 1979.
108. Puri, J.R: Guru Nanak Ka Ruhani Updesh; (Hindi Book) *Radha Swami Satsang Beas*; 2002.
109. Puri, J.R: *Guru Nanak This Mystic Teachings*, Beas, 1982.
110. Prabhavananda, Swami: *The Spiritualism Heritage of India*, London, 1962.
111. Puri, J.R. & Sethi V.K: *Sant Nam Dev*, Beas, Reprint, 2002.
112. Puri, J.R. & Shamgari, T.R: *Bulleh Shah*, Beas, 1997.
113. Paradhan, M.D: *Similes in Manusmriti*, Delhi, 1960.
114. *Proceedings of the Indian History Congress, 64th Session*; Mysore, 2003.
115. *Proceedings of the Indian History Congress, 65th Session*, Bareily, 2004.
116. *Proceedings of the Indian History Congress, 66th Santinikatan*, 2005-06.
117. *Proceedings of the Indian History Congress, 67th Calicut*, 2006-07.

118. *Punjab History Conference Proceedings,* Patiala, March 18-20, 2004.
119. *Punjab History Conference Proceedings,* Patiala, March 18-20, 2005.
120. *Punjab History Conference Proceedings,* Patiala, March 18-20, 2006.
121. Quest for Light: *Maharaja Charan Singh*; Beas, Reprint, 2002.
122. Raju, Dr. (Lt. Col.) P.A: *Gandhi and His Religion*, New Delhi, 2000.
123. Rao, B.V: *World History*; Delhi, Reprint, 2003.
124. Rose, H.A: *A Glossary of the Tribes and Castes of the Punjab and Northern-Western Frontier Provinces*; Language Department of Punjab, 3 Vols. Reprint, 1999.
125. Rajwade, Chanravati: *Tukaram, The Ceaseless Songs of Devotion*, Beas, Reprint, 2004.
126. Ray, S.C: *Early History and Culture of Kashmir*, Calcutta, 1957.
127. Ramesh, B.G: *Biography Series, Dr. B.R. Ambedkar*, Bangalore, 2005.
128. Rizvi, S.A.A: *Fatehpur Skari,* New Delhi, 2002.
129. Rajshekar, V.T: *Brahminism*, Bangalore, 2002.
130. Ramasami, T: *Education and Personality Development*, New Delhi, 1993.
131. Ratcliffe, Susan (ed.): *Oxford Quotation and Proverbs*; Pt II-III, Reprint, New York; 2006.
132. *Srimad Bhagavadgita*: Tr. By R.N. Koul & Aggarwal, Vol. II, Gorkhpur (India), 2006.
133. Sangari, T.R: *Sant Charandas* (Hindi), Beas, 2005.
134. Sangari, T.R: *Japuji Sahib* (Hindi) Beas, 2006.
135. Sethi, Virendar: *Mira Prem Dewani*, (Hindi) Beas, 2001.
136. Sangari, T.R. & Alam, P.S: *Sarmad Shaheed*, (Hindi) Beas, 2002.
137. Sethi, Shanti: *Message Divine*, Beas, Reprint, 1996.
138. Sethi, V.K: *Sant Nam Dev* (Hindi) Beas, 2004.
139. Sethi, Shanti: *Sant Kabir* (Hindi), Beas, 2003.
140. Sethi Rajinder: *Sant Paltu*, (Hindi), Beas, 2003.
141. Singh, Gopal: *Guru Granth Sahib* (Tr. Into. Eng.) New Delhi, 1969.

142. Singh, Maharaj Jagat: *Atam-Gyan*, (Hindi) Beas, 2000.
143. Singh, Baba Satinder: *The Jammu Fox*, New Delhi, 1988.
144. Su, Kinh Duoe: *Sutra of the Medicine Buddha*, U.S.A, 2001.
145. Satyanarayana, Adapa: *Nation, Caste, and the Past: Articulation of Dalit Bahujan Identity, Consciousness and Ideology*, 65th IHC, Bareily, 2004.
146. Singh, M.F: *Honest Living, A Means to and End*; Beas, Reprint, 2001.
147. Shangari, T.R. & J.R. Puri: *Bulleh Shah*; Beas, Reprint, 1995.
148. Salwi, Dilip, M: *Our Scientist*, New Delhi, 1987.
149. Sharma, Vasdev: *Cosmic View of Life in Guru Nanak Bnai*, Language Department Punjab, 1996.
150. Saxena, N.R. Swarup: *Principles of Educations*, Meerut, 2003.
151. Saxena, K.S: *Political History of Kashmir*, Lucknow, 1974.
152. Soanes, Catherine, Spooner, Alan & Hawker, Sara: *Compact Oxford, Dictionary, Thesaurus, and Ward power Guide*, Oxford Press, Reprint, 2004.
153. Singh, Khushwant: *The History of the Sikhs*, London, Vols. I-II, 1962.
154. Singh, Teja & Singh, Ganda: *A Short History of the Sikhs*; Patiala (Pb.) 1990.
155. Singh, Maharaj Charan: *Light on Saint John*, Amritsar (Pb.) Reprint, 1996.
156. Swarup, Shanti: *The Arts and Crafts of India and Pakistan*, Bombay, 1957.
157. Shukla, D.N: *Royal Art*, Ghaziabad (U.P.) 1969.
158. Sivarvamamurti, C: *'Chitrasutra of the Vishnudhar mothara'* New Delhi, 1948.
159. Sivarvamamurti, C: *The Painter in Ancient India,* New Delhi, 1978.
160. Sivarvamamurti, C: *Indian Painting*; New Delhi, 1970
161. Srivastava, R.P: *Arts and Archaeology of Punjab*, Delhi, 1990.
162. Srivastava, S.P: *Art and Culture of Patiala*, Delhi, 1991.
163. Sanders, C.W: *The Inner Voice,* Punjab (Amritsar), Reprint, 1991.
164. Sethi, V.K: Kabir, *The Weavers of God's Name*, Amritsar, (Punjab) Reprint, 1998.
165. Sethi, J.C: *Tale of the Mystic East* ; Beas, Reprint, 2006.

166. Sharma Neru (ed.): *Hamara Sahtiya*, (Hindi), 2007, Academy of Art, Culture and Language, Jammu.
167. Singh, Master Sawan, as cited in *Heaven on Earth,* by Dariyai Lal Kapur, (2d ed. Beas, 1986).
168. *The Sufi Path of Love: The Spiritual Teachings of Rumi*, by William Chittick (Albany, New York Press, 1983), Discourse 3072.
169. *The Mathnawi of Jalaluddin Rumi,* Trans. Reynold A. Nicholson, Vol. 2 (London: Messrs Luzac & Co., 1960).
The Sufi Path of Love, (F 130/140-141)
The Sufi Path of Love, (Masnavi III:837)
170. The Dawn of Light: *Huzur Maharaj Sawan Singh* ;Beas, Reprint, 1984.
171. The Science of the Soul: *Sardar Bahadur Maharaj Singh*; Beas, Reprint, 2002.
172. Tagore Rabindranath: *Boundless Sky*, Kolkata, 2006.
173. Tripathi, R.S: *History of Ancient India*, Delhi, 1960.
174. Tikoo, P.N: *Story of Kashmir*, New Delhi, 1979.
175. Thappar, Romila: *Ancient Indian Social History*, New Delhi, Reprint, 1998.
176. Thappar, Romila: *A History of India, India Volume One*, London, Reprint, 2002.
177. *The Life of the Buddha*, Part-II, Maha Bodhi Society, Bangalore, 1982.
178. Upadhyaya, K.N: *Guru Ravidas The Philosopher's Stone*; Beas, Reprint, 2005.
179. Upadhyaya, K.N: *Dtariya Sahib, Saint of Bihar*, Beas, Reprint, 2006.
180. Upadhyaya, K.N: *Dadu the Compassionate Mystic*, Beas, 1997.
181. Upadhyaya, K.N: *Param Paras, Guru Ravidas*, (Hindi), Beas, 2005.
182. Udall, D.H: *The Story of Life*, London, 1968.
183. Vaucouleurs, DE, Gerarel: *Discovery of the Universe*, London.
184. Vittie, G.C. Mc: *Cosmological Theory*, London, 1952.
185. Vidyadhar : *Jammu and Kashmir, Past and Present*, Jammu.
186. Whiterow, G.J: *The Structure and the Evolution of the Universe*, London, 1959.

187. Zakaria, Rafiq: *Muhammad and the Quran,* New Delhi, 1991.

188. Zanaide-A-Ragozin: *Vedic India*, New Delhi, 1961.

(B) Periodical, Papers and Magazine

189. Science *Reporter Magazine*: Dec. 2004.

190. *Science Newsletter*, Vol. III, Govt. College for Women, Parade, Jammu, 2008.

191. *A Discovery in Science*: An article published in Kashmir Times, 5.4.2008.

192. G.L. Khajuria: *Charming Chinar*, An article Published in Daily Exelsior, 21.11.2007.

193. Sonia's False Claim: State Times News 30.3.2008 *China has the largest Garden not of India.*

194. Usha Albuquerque: *Smart Skill*, A World of Opportunities for Biology Lovers; An article published 2.4.2008, The Tribune News Paper.

195. *Young India*, October 11, 1928.

196. Prof. Yash Pal: *This Universe*, An article publish the Tribune Magazine; 4.4.2008.

197. Stephen Wilson, *Study of Washington*; How nerve calls in the left and right sides of the brain are wired; the Tribune 4.2.2008.

198. Yoginder Sikand: *Islam and Science*: *Maulana Shihabuddin Nadwi's* 'Scientific' Approach to the Quran. Kashmir Times, 29.3.2008.

199. *Mughal Period Qurans Seized in Delhi*, News Delhi Agencies, 12.3.2008.

200. Dr. Vini Khurana,: *Specialist Neuro Surgeon Report*. Mobile Phones Could be more Cancerous than Smoking, the Tribune, 2.4.2008.

201. *Bible*, Revised Standard Version as on identify of the author job.

202. Albert Einstein as cited in Einstein, *A Life by Denis Brain* (John Wiley & Sons, 1996).

203. *Bible*, King James Version, Luke

204. *Ethics of the Fathers*, in The Prayer Book: Weekday, Sabbath and Festival, trans. And arranged Ben Zion Bokser (New York, 1957).

205. *Sri Daduvani*, (Jaipur: Sri Daduvani Prakashna Smiti).

206. *Dhammapada* V:3 (62)
207. Baba Jaimal Singh, Spiritual Letters, complete translation (Dera Baba Jaimal Singh, India: Beas), Letter 75.
208. *Philokalia*, trans and ed. G.E.H. Palmer, Phillip Sherrard and *Kallistos Ware*, Vol. ! (London: Faber and Faber, 1979).
209. Master Charan Singh, *Divine Light* (Dera Baba Jaimal Singh, *India*: Radha Soami Satsang Beas, 1996), letter 175.
210. *Adi Granth*.
211. *The Wisdom of Baltasar Gracian*, ed. And adap. J.L. Kaya (New York, 1992).
212. *Bible* (RSV), James 5:4.
213. *Ralph Waldo* Emerson, cited in Wisdom of the Ages, ed. Mark Gilbert (New York: 1934).
214. *The Cloud of Unknowing* (London: 1978), chapter 66.
215. Qur'an, 17:37
216. *Bible* (RSV), Exodus 20:15, 17
217. Maser Sawan Singh, *Gurmat Sidhant* (Dera Baba Jaimal Singh, India: Radha Soami Satsang, Beas).
218. Master Jagat Singh, in the Footsteps of the Master (Dera Baba Jaimal Singh, India: Radha Soami Satsang Beas), letter dated 18 April, 1949.
219. *Dhammapada* XXIV:22 (355).
220. Marcus Aurelius, *Meditations*, VII:33-34, trans. George Long, revised by Classics Club editors, in Marcus Aurelius and his Times, New York: Walter J. Black, 1945).
221. *Bible* (KJV), Mark 10:24-25.
222. *Rubaiyat-e-Sarmad*.
223. Thomas Paine, *The Age of Reason*, Part 1, "The Author's Profession of Faith" (1794).
224. *Bible* (KJV), Aatthew 23:25-26, 28.
225. *Kabir Sakhi Sangreh*, Part 1 (1980).
226. *Paltu Sahib ki Bani*, 1:240.
227. *Bible* (KJV), Luke 8:11-15.
228. *Kabir Granthavali*.
229. *Benjamin Franklin*, 'Letter dated 9 August 1768, in Complete Works, Vol. 4, ed. John Bigelow (1887-88).
230. *Meister Eckhart*, 2 Vol. ed. trans. C. de B. Evans (Watkins) as cited in *A Year of Grace*.
231. Master Charan Singh, *The Master Answers*.

232. Thomas a Kempis, *The Imitation of Christ: Four Books*, revised translation (London): Oxford university Press, n.d.), book 3:XXX!:3.
233. *Ethics of the Fathers in the Prayer Book.*
234. Bible (KJV), *Matthew* 16:24.
235. Master Charan Singh, *Divine Light*, letter 351.
236. Master Charan Singh, *Quest for Light* (Dera Baba Jaimal Singh, India, Radha Soami Satsang Beas), letter 400.
237. Master Charan Singh, *Quest for Light,* letter 322.
238. Master Charan Singh, *Quest for Light,* letter 107.
239. Master Charan Singh, *Quest for Light,* letter 224.
240. Master Charan Singh, *Quest for Light,* letter 378.
241. Ravidas Darsha, ed. And trans. Prithvi Singh Azad (Chandigarh: Sri Guru Ravidas Sansthan, 1973).
242. Ralph Waldo Emerso.
243. Aristotle, *Nicomachean Ethics* II:I.
244. *Philokalia*, vol. 1.
245. Martin Heidegger, "The Field Path", World Review, Jan. 1950, as cited in *A Year of Grace.*
246. Bible (KJV), *Matthew* 6:2-4.
247. Kabir, *Kabir Sakhi Sangreh*, Part I.
248. Thomas a Kempis, *The Imitation of Christ,* Book 3, XXV:5.
249. *Ethics of the Fathers in the Prayer Book,* Also *Biblo* (RSV), *I Chronicles* 29:14.
250. *Adi Granth*, Kabir.
251. Marcus Aurelius, *Meditations,* trans. C.R. Haines in Loeb Classical Library (Heineman), cited in *Year of Grace.*
252. Marcus Aurelius, *Meditations* VII:2 (New York:1964).
253. *The Wisdom of Baltasar Gracian.*
254. Confucius, Analects *XII:22 as cited in Wisdom of the Ages.*
255. *Marcus Aurelius, Meditations, XII: 17 in Marcus Aurelius and His Times.*

Index

Q

R

S

T